COME BUY, COME BUY

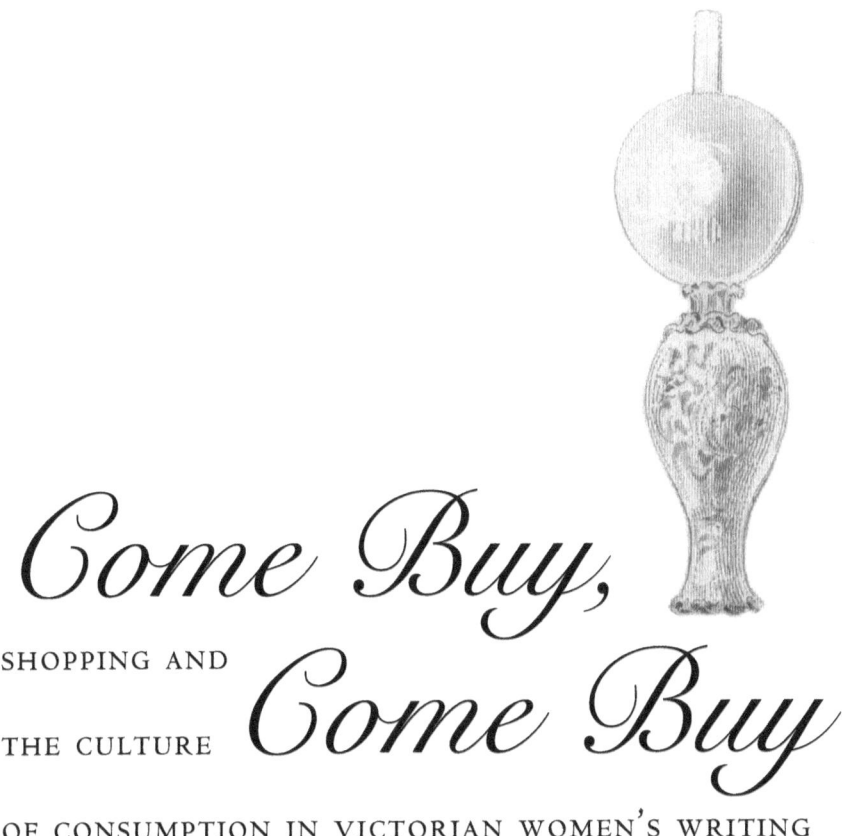

Come Buy, Come Buy

SHOPPING AND THE CULTURE OF CONSUMPTION IN VICTORIAN WOMEN'S WRITING

Krista Lysack

OHIO UNIVERSITY PRESS   ATHENS

Ohio University Press, Athens, Ohio 45701
www.ohioswallow.com
© 2008 by Ohio University Press
All rights reserved

To obtain permission to quote, reprint, or otherwise reproduce or distribute material from Ohio University Press publications, please contact our rights and permissions department at (740) 593-1154 or (740) 593-4536 (fax).

Printed in the United States of America
Ohio University Press books are printed on acid-free paper ∞ ™

15 14 13 12 11 10 09 08   5 4 3 2 1

Library of Congress Cataloging-in-Publication Data

Lysack, Krista.
 Come buy, come buy : shopping and the culture of consumption in Victorian women's writing / Krista Lysack.
   p. cm.
 Includes bibliographical references and index.
 ISBN-13: 978-0-8214-1810-9 (cl : alk. paper)
 ISBN-10: 0-8214-1810-6 (cl : alk. paper)
 ISBN-13: 978-0-8214-1811-6 (pbk. : alk. paper)
 ISBN-10: 0-8214-1811-4 (pbk. : alk. paper)
  1. Consumption (Economics) in literature. 2. English literature—19th century—History and criticism. 3. English literature—Women authors—History and criticism. 4. Women consumers in literature. 5. Shopping in literature. 6. Femininity in literature. 7. Identity (Psychology) in literature. 8. Women consumers—Great Britain—History—19th century. 9. Shopping—Great Britain—History—19th century. 10. Consumption (Economics)—Great Britain—History—19th century. I. Title.
  PR468.C68L97 2008
  820.9'3553—dc22
                                                                  2007052434

CONTENTS

List of Illustrations   vii
Acknowledgments   ix

Introduction
Danger, Delight, and Victorian Women's Shopping   1

One
Goblin Markets
Women Shoppers and the East in London's West End   15

Two
Lady Audley's Shopping Disorders   44

Three
Middlemarch and the Extravagant Domestic Spender
Managing an Epic Life   80

Four
To Those Who Love Them Best
The Erotics of Connoisseurship in Michael Field's Sight and Song   109

Five
Votes for Women and the Tactics of Consumption   136

Afterword
Becoming Elizabeth Dalloway
The Future of Shopping   171

Notes   179
Bibliography   217
Index   231

ILLUSTRATIONS

1.1	Liberty "Arab" Tea Room advertisement	25
1.2	Liberty advertisement	32
1.3	Front cover of Liberty's *Eastern Antiquities Catalogue*	39
3.1	"Table of Expenditure"	93
4.1	Aubrey Beardsley cover design	110
4.2	Title page of *Sight and Song*	118
4.3	Front cover of *Sight and Song*	120
5.1	"The Shrieking Sister"	143
5.2	"Always Make Room for a Lady"	143
5.3	Selfridge's advertisement	146
5.4	"Votes for Women" Directory	148
5.5	Derry and Toms advertisement	149
5.6	Pank-A-Squith advertisement	151
5.7	Panko advertisement	153
5.8	The N. W. London Union Shop in Kilburn	167

ACKNOWLEDGMENTS

I would like first to thank Mary Wilson Carpenter, my doctoral advisor at Queen's University, whose counsel I continue to cherish. I am also grateful to Linda H. Peterson for her advice and unstinting support over the last several years. To Maggie Berg, I express my gratitude for her encouragement, both past and present. In their different ways, all three of these mentors model the kind of feminist scholarship I aspire to, one that combines intellectual rigor with unflagging generosity.

I am also indebted to Lorraine Janzen Kooistra and the anonymous reader for Ohio University Press, who provided me with insightful assessment of the manuscript and useful strategies for revision.

At Ohio University Press, my thanks to David Sanders and Nancy Basmajian for their keen editorial direction and cordial correspondence. I also wish to acknowledge the important contributions of copyeditor Sally Bennett, of Beth Pratt for her cover design, and of Jean Cunningham for her marketing expertise.

To Mary Arseneau, D. M. R. Bentley, and Tilottama Rajan, I express my appreciation for practical assistance and advice. I thank Emma Jay for her friendship during our overlapping year of postdoctoral research in New Haven. And I would be remiss if I did not thank Oscar, whose own daily activities provide me with a whole new conception of the everyday.

Early research in London (UK) was made possible by a Dorothy Warne Chambers Travelling Fellowship from Queen's University. I am also grateful for the very significant support provided by the Social Sciences and Humanities Research Council of Canada in the form of a doctoral fellowship and, more recently, a postdoctoral fellowship, the latter of which was generously hosted by the Department of English at Yale University.

I am pleased to acknowledge people who have provided particular assistance with images and permissions, including Anna Buruma of Liberty plc, Owen Davies from the Victoria & Albert Museum, Valerie Howe of the British Library, Rory Lalwan of the City of Westminster Archives Centre, Lisa Tickner, and Mark Vivian of the Mary Evans Picture Library.

A version of chapter 1 appeared as "Goblin Markets: Victorian Women Shoppers at Liberty's Oriental Bazaar" in *Nineteenth-Century Contexts* 27, no. 2 (2005): 139–65. Chapters 3 and 4 are revised versions of articles published, respectively, as "Debt and Domestic Economy: *Middlemarch*'s Extravagant Women" in *Nineteenth-Century Feminisms* 6 (Fall/Winter 2002): 41–73, and as "Aesthetic Consumption and the Cultural Production of Michael Field's *Sight and Song*" in *Studies in English Literature* 45, no. 4 (Autumn 2005): 935–60.

I am honored to thank my parents, Margaret Manley Lysack and Michael Lysack, and my siblings three, Steven, Nathan, and Alissa. Perhaps they will find in these pages the traces of many family shopping trips to the Swan Valley Co-op.

Finally, I am grateful to my favorite Victorianist, Christopher Keep, who read and discussed so many drafts. Although I am in his debt, I know he is far too generous to have kept account. As much as his support in this endeavor has meant to me, his love means even more.

Introduction

DANGER, DELIGHT, AND VICTORIAN WOMEN'S SHOPPING

When Rochester takes Jane Eyre to a silk warehouse in Millcote and insists that she select six boldly colored dresses for her trousseau, his governess proves an unwilling and resistant shopper. Refusing the "brilliant amethyst dye, and a superb pink satin" he would foist upon her, Jane persuades Rochester to accept her choice of a more understated palette of "a sober black satin and pearl-grey silk."[1] The shopping excursion does not end here, however. It continues at the local jeweler's shop, where Rochester continues to ply Jane with purchases she does not want. "[H]arassing" rather than leisurely, this morning of shopping is also an affront to Jane's quest for autonomy. "It would, indeed, be a relief," she thinks, "if I had ever so small an independency; I never can bear being dressed like a doll by Mr. Rochester." When her protestations are met with Rochester's sultanlike smile, a smile like that of a master for his slave, Jane threatens to wear gingham for her wedding. His rejoinder—that he still would not exchange Jane "for the grand Turk's whole seraglio" (355)—provokes more defiant words from his fiancée. Refusing the implicit terms of possession that the harem signifies to her, Jane replies that she would "stir up mutiny" among any other "inmates" that Rochester might similarly buy and confine (355).[2]

The shopping expedition in Charlotte Brontë's *Jane Eyre* (1847) suggests that the struggle for female autonomy and independence, a motif in much Victorian domestic fiction, is a very economic matter. Shopping at Millcote is not merely an anecdotal moment in the novel, a momentary diversion from the main interests of the plot, but a significant scene wherein the material nature of sexual politics is staged. The dictates of fashion are in this instance male-authored, and marriage, cast here as another form of commercial and imperial exchange, conceals the ways in which men may come to regard women as commodities. In the face of Rochester's insistence, the novel's protofeminist heroine seems to garner her agency through forms of renunciation; his apparent generosity is that which Jane must refuse. Rochester's aggressive attentions cast shopping as a scene of temptation, as this dangerously enticing figure threatens to subsume Jane to his vision of what she should desire. While Rochester is the object of Jane's own libidinal interests, he is also a force that Jane must carefully manage precisely because he is so seductive.

Jane's cautious negotiation of the commercial sphere is emblematic of the vexed condition of the woman shopper who goes to market only to risk becoming an object of exchange herself. Set in a provincial town in the early decades of the nineteenth century, the episode anticipates the ways in which the dangers and delights of women's consumerism would become amplified through a new metropolitan experience that was to unfold in Britain by the 1860s, when shopping emerged as a fully articulated form of middle-class women's leisure. This midcentury historical moment, one that marked Britain's revolution in retailing, has often been formulated as one that also ushered in cultural anxieties about the woman shopper's relationship to the vicissitudes of consumer appetite. Increasingly figured as a particularly female pursuit, shopping could be associated with idleness on the one hand and compulsion on the other, forms of excess that were best managed through careful self-regulation. In *Unto This Last* (1860), for example, John Ruskin suggests that consumption has its proper place when he links the economic clout of Britain with the buying power of its citizens, a balance between supply and demand and between production and consumption. "[T]he wealth of a nation," he writes, "is only to be estimated by what it consumes"; such wealth "is finally measured by the mouth."³ While Ruskin thus acknowledges a legitimate role for a consumer class, he is troubled by what he sees as the excessive appetites of women and goes so far as to link women's consumer demands with the deteriorating industrial health of the nation and its laborers. In "The Nature of Gothic" (1851–53), Ruskin compares British workers to slaves whose monotonous toils in the manufacturing of glass beads can never fulfill women's desire for this trifling commodity: "Glass beads are utterly unnecessary, and there is no design or thought employed in their manufacture. . . . The men who chop up the rods sit at their work all day, their hands vibrating with a perpetual and exquisitely timed palsy. . . . [E]very young lady, therefore, who buys glass beads is engaged in the slave-trade."⁴ Women's insatiable appetite for mass-produced beads threatens to reduce factory labor to the economics of slavery. Apparently poised to deform the decorum of domestic middle-class femininity, which could in turn destabilize the manufactures of Britain, the woman shopper seemed a potential danger not only to herself but also to the nation as a whole.

Arguing that the new conditions of Victorian consumer culture linked the commercial interests of British imperialism to female appetite, Nancy Armstrong comments that "[i]t is difficult to imagine one of Jane Austen's heroines . . . endangered by shopping."⁵ Indeed, while Jane Eyre's shopping trip is underscored by the danger that she may be traded on an orientalized marriage market, a danger that cultural fears turned back onto the figure of the Victorian woman shopper, such a threat does not seem to exist in the world of Austen's novels. A visit to the provincial shops of Regency England in *Emma* (1816), for example, poses no apparent threat to that novel's women. Indeed, the shop in Highbury is a kind of haven for Harriet Smith, who takes "shelter at Ford's," the town's "principal woollen-draper, linen-draper, and haberdasher's shop united," when it suddenly begins to rain.⁶ Once inside, Harriet encounters Mr. Martin and his sister, Elizabeth, with whom she exchanges pleasantries. This shopping trip is a safe and innocuous precursor to the later courtship between Harriet and Martin and thus stands as another moment of the organic sense of community that typifies Austen's world. During the Victorian age, however, the consumer experience was fundamentally altered in scale and scope through the coming of the mass market and related developments such as the institutionalization of the department store and the wealth generated by imperial expansion. Armstrong's provocative claim about the dangers of

Victorian shopping is part of her contention that the female consumerist compulsions that emerged in Britain a few decades after *Emma* encode an anxiety "about a desire that earlier generations simply could not have felt."[7] Although Armstrong organizes her discussion of consumer appetite around *Alice's Adventures in Wonderland*, the argument about the formation of a new anxiety over desire also recalls Jane's impulse to refuse. The notion that Victorian femininity is characterized by the need for self-regulation suggests not only Alice's realization that she must curb her oral fixations over consumables such as orange marmalade—that "[a]ppetite gives way to an equally compulsive desire for self-control"—but also Jane's stoic refusal to purchase flamboyant clothing or to have it purchased for her.[8] That is to say, voraciousness is not the absence of discipline, but its correlative. Organized around poles of compulsion and restraint, Victorian middle-class femininity has often been characterized as such an economy, a system of oppositions that circulate and exchange in a regulatory fashion.

Literary studies of recent decades that address Victorian consumer culture (notably, those of Thomas Richards, Andrew H. Miller, Christoph Lindner, and Rachel Bowlby) have begun significant and illuminating work in discussing issues related to women's consumption and consumer appetite.[9] But in their various and intriguing approaches, they have tended to suggest a similarly regulated system of femininity, one in which Woman is subject to exchange because of her associations with the commodity. Women's symbolic role in the marketplace has historically relegated her to the status of being what Walter Benjamin described as "saleswoman and wares in one."[10] Karl Marx also suggestively genders the commodity as passively female when he writes that one can "use force" to "take possession of them."[11] Such descriptions, while usefully foregrounding the extent to which women were vulnerable under capital and the law, and also revealing that the nature of women's exploitation was often economic, do not fully account for women's historical condition. To emphasize only their affinity with the commodity is to risk leaving women mired as no more than objects of exchange. Similarly, literary critics have often seen only limited forms of agency and subjecthood in the act of consumption, ultimately reinscribing the predicament of women as vacillating, with women serving as both subjects and objects of consumption who seem unable to alter the economic constructions of femininity.[12]

Elizabeth Kowaleski-Wallace's work on eighteenth-century shopping, however, has both identified this predicament and considered the productive possibilities of women's consuming subjectivities.[13] In *Consuming Subjects: Women, Shopping, and Business in the Eighteenth Century*, she situates the rise of shopping as a women's activity in the eighteenth century, when the verb *to shop* first appeared and the noun *shop* came to refer increasingly to a discrete interior space in which trade is carried out.[14] During this century, she argues, discursive ideologies of the feminine were being constructed alongside the formation of commodities as consumable luxury imports of coffee, tea, tobacco, and sugar became more widely available throughout Britain in the relatively new and accessible venue of the shop, where women (not merely consumer goods) were subject to new kinds of surveillance. Kowaleski-Wallace considers how the notion of a gendered consumer appetite first appeared at this historical moment, as appetite "was diverted toward goods, . . . shopping became gendered as feminine, and . . . women's bodies became configured in relation to consumption."[15] In this, she not only identifies but also calls into question an essentialist conflation of women's bodies, appetite, and consumption to reveal how these connections were ideologically and historically constructed. By considering that women were not victims of their perceived excesses but acceded to the active status of "consuming subjects" in the context of the modern shop, she demonstrates how the discourse of commercial seduction that might construct women customers as compliant or vulnerable before male shopkeepers could also permit them to disrupt gendered codes of female propriety. Kowaleski-Wallace thus disturbs the tendency to align Woman with the commodity and reveals that normative femininity in the eighteenth century was produced as a natural fact through the operations of consumer exchange. In doing so, she extends Mary Poovey's contention that although culturally prescribed femininity is an effect of ideology, gender is not continuous but uneven and in its unevenness is "always open to revision, dispute, and the emergence of oppositional formulations."[16] The symbolic economies that sought to regulate and therefore conceal the intersections of femininity, appetite, and the commodity were therefore not discrete or homogenous.

The Victorian woman shopper was, in this sense, a continuation of the eighteenth-century shopper, who embodied early concerns over women's appetites. During the nineteenth century, these concerns came increasingly to be mapped onto larger anxieties over the integrity of middle-class women's bodies and the ways in which their shopping excursions outside of the bounds of domesticity might affect the solvency of the bourgeois household and the economic health of the nation. But the cultural meanings and tactical possibilities of women's shopping also began to proliferate following the eighteenth century, as a distinctive set of discourses and material practices significantly refracted and multiplied the forms of identity that were available to the Victorian middle-class consumer. If the agencies of the eighteenth-century shopper obtained through her subversion of existing gendered norms, the shopper of the next century is notable as a site for the production of forms of consumption that exceeded the norms of self-regulating femininity.

Although shopping does not seem to have been pleasurable to Jane Eyre, might we believe that this would be different if she were to go shopping on her own in the decades to follow, without the impositions and meddling company of a Rochester? Without his influence and his figuration as a version of the marketplace that dictated the terms of transaction and threatened to subsume women, what other modes of consumption would become possible for the reluctant shopper? Jane does declare that she would like to "furnish [her] own wardrobe" using her own capital after she marries, indicating a desire to consolidate a form of economic agency that would be inclusive of the sphere of consumption.[17] For in the latter half of the nineteenth century, it was becoming possible to formulate shopping as a form of urban leisure rather than something one did out of necessity or, as for Jane, under duress.

The material conditions of Victorian shopping were an effect of an expanded industrial and commercial age, including nineteenth-century developments in mass production and circulation, new practices in advertising, an increase in the flow of capital associated with imperial expansion, and the growth of the middle classes and their unprecedented access to expendable income. However, not only the profusion of goods but also the embodied and visual nature of the shopping experience were already changing by the 1830s, when such innovations as the wider availability of plate glass and the introduction of gas lighting were bringing shopwindows to life. By midcentury, the consumer experience in Britain's metropolitan centers, particularly in London, was eclipsing smaller-scale shopping such as that of the provincial silk warehouse of *Jane Eyre*. Lynda Nead has identified 1855–70 as the crucial period during which London "became part of a highly concentrated discourse on the modern" as it was "fashion[ed] . . . into a modern metropolis."[18] The middle decades of the century saw the conversion of many small draper's shops into larger, multifloor emporia. As Erika Rappaport has shown, London's West End in particular emerged during these decades as an urban consumer destination for middle-class women, becoming all the more accessible through the supporting infrastructure of women's tea shops, affordable mass transit, and public lavatories. Following the opening of Britain's first department store in 1863, the first of many purpose-built modern department stores, the notion of shopping as a leisure activity was becoming fully institutionalized. Featuring delightful displays of goods, department stores presented a carefully executed feast for the eye that offered customers an unprecedented encounter with consumer goods. Whereas goods in conventional shops remained largely behind the counters under the watchful eyes of an owner or assistant, shoppers in a department store could not only look at the wares but at times—and sometimes transgressively—handle them as well. This new proximity to commodities in the department store also created new identifications with commodity objects. If shopping had come to be defined more broadly with reference to a larger sphere of urban leisure, so too would the consuming subject, for her borders were no longer discrete, as her desires were formed in and through a world of goods.

Come Buy, Come Buy considers how middle-class women's shopping after midcentury enabled a variety of cultural and discursive constructions rather than the prescription, imposition, and regulation of a single identity. Underlying this contention is an approach that follows Michel de Certeau's discussion of consumerism as one of a range of everyday practices that, far from trivial, constitute the ways in which one can respond to one's inscription within capitalism. Along with other ordinary pursuits such as walking, playing games, speaking, and reading, de Certeau addresses shopping as a "tactic" by which subjects come to resist and reformulate their cultural condition. In *The Practice of Everyday Life*, de Certeau rejects the disciplinary emphasis of Michel Foucault's *Discipline and Punish*, which "privileges the productive apparatus (which produces the 'discipline')," and goes on to propose the often overlooked and underestimated activity of consumption as a potentially transformative form of cultural production.[19] This is not to say that consumerism is emancipatory, only that consumer practice makes visible the ways in which the subject may respond to and even resist her condition under capitalism.[20] In contrast to a Foucauldian scheme, wherein the state and institutions do not impose themselves directly but ensure power through subjects who have internalized the propensity to regulate themselves, de Certeau considers how shoppers formulate agency through what he calls the activity of "poaching," that is, through a variety of interventions, derailings, and disorders in the consumer marketplace.[21] Not to be confused with what is certainly the illusion of consumer choice, a fiction manufactured by capitalism, de Certeau's "ways of operating" or "*ways of using* the products imposed by a dominant economic order" are the tactical means by which subjects may leave their imprint on the dominant order "without leaving it."[22] Distinguished from what de Certeau terms a "strategy" that "postulates a *place* that can be delimited as its *own*," tactics do not assume an exteriority or stable locus from which one can launch attacks against the state; instead, one mines it from within.[23] "Pushed to their ideal limits," writes de Certeau, "these procedures and ruses of consumers compose the network of an antidiscipline."[24] Rather than being subjected to the prescriptions of consumer capitalism, women's uses of consumption (including such practices as window-shopping, shoplifting, or even setting up shop themselves) became the basis for their formation as active and resisting subjects within the Victorian marketplace.

De Certeau's notion of consumption as an engaged cultural practice—as a form of "antidiscipline" in which subjects fashion the world around them rather than regulate themselves according to it—is useful in an additional way, for it suggestively opens up a space for an alternative model of female identity beyond that of the self-regulating subject who keeps her appetites in check. Victorian women shoppers were fashioning forms of subjectivity predicated on the possibilities of pleasure in the marketplace rather than disavowal. Women's perceived vulnerabilities to both their own compulsions and the seductions of the marketplace, then, did not alone define the nature of Victorian women's consumer experience. For as other discourses of women's shopping—ones that revealed the proximity of the marketplace to such related scenes as the spectacle of empire, the bourgeois domestic sphere, aesthetic culture, and later the suffrage campaigns—had began to circulate by the 1860s, they inflected and complicated the idea that consumer appetite was a feminine impulse that could be managed only when it was mastered. Together, these alternative discourses of consumption open up and complicate notions of desire by emphasizing the agencies and mobilities that women obtained through their consumer practices and lived relationships to consumption, rather than their prescribed affinities with and purported vulnerability to the seductions of the commodity.

An article published in the *Saturday Review* in 1875 opens up one such discursive space by constructing shopping as a pleasurable pursuit rather than one to be regarded with caution. The likely author of "The Philosophy of Shopping," Eliza Lynn Linton, might seem an unexpected advocate of consumption, given Linton's condemnation of "the extravagance of fashion" in "The Girl of the Period" only a few years earlier.[25] Nevertheless, the article delights in formulating an understanding of shopping that distinguishes this activity from the ways in which one consumed out of necessity in the past. "Shopping," it begins, "is popularly supposed to belong to the useful and necessary occupations of life, and no doubt this was its character in its earlier stages. Going to a shop with a definite sense of want, and with a clear determination to purchase something, is of course quite correctly named doing business."[26] As the article explores the new ways in which the Victorians had come to regard shopping, we can clearly see that a peculiar value lies in the ways in which shopping falls outside of conceptions of what is thought to be necessary or useful:

> But this [setting out to buy with a particular want in mind] is not the common form of what is styled shopping. In its mystical feminine meaning, to shop is to pass so many hours in a shop on the mere chance of buying something. A lady every now and again makes up her mind to do a day's or an afternoon's shopping, just as she would decide to pass a similar period in driving through the Parks. Her resolve is not at all the result of a previous discovery of something wanting, but springs immediately from a taste for novel and various entertainment. . . . [I]f anyone should unkindly suggest that shopping is a prodigious waste of time, or that the greater number of articles purchased in the course of an afternoon's shopping are wholly unnecessary, or, finally, that women waste time and money in shopping just because they have no method in their domestic management . . . it would be enough to reply that, shopping being an amusement sought for its own sake, it is quite irrelevant to judge of it as part of ordinary business procedure.[27]

Shopping is no longer a chore that must be endured, the means by which to procure the necessities of life such as food, but an enjoyable diversion. Consuming for pleasure extends the sphere of middle-class women's activity beyond "the monotony of more strictly domestic pursuits" and therefore is distinguished from a form of labor to be conducted under the auspices of the daily running of the domestic household.[28] Rather, one can set out for a day of shopping with no particular end in mind other than the pursuit of enjoyment.

The article posits an almost aesthetic defense of shopping, in which a surplus of pleasure figures not as voracious appetite but as that which exceeds the norms of usefulness. In a gesture that recovers appetite and waste as "amusement sought for its own sake," pleasure is constituted as a value in itself. As shopping is conducted for its own sake, utility comes to be displaced by diversion or leisure, a seemingly limitless resource. Thus, the open-ended and itinerant pleasures of consumption, rather than its perceived risks, characterize the arrival of the Victorian woman consumer as an object of cultural interest.

Through their uses of consumerism for pleasure rather than utility, middle-class women shoppers inscribed forms of improvised, expansive identity premised on the unique material conditions of the Victorian shopping experience.[29] As we have seen, such a mode of being became possible as never before through the spaces and spectacles of urban consumption, through its plate-glass and gas-lit windows, and through the bountiful goods and amenities of its ever-expanding emporia. In locating where women consumers exceeded the cultural script of self-contained bodies whose compulsions must be kept in check, we uncover other possible ways of being that form through their supposed excesses. Rather than signaling victims of appetite, such surpluses may be revalued as forms of subjectivity that were commensurate with the roving opportunities of a consumer sphere that had come to include the commodity spectacle and tactile pleasures of the department store.

The forms of subjectivity that the Victorian shopper inscribed also enable a different understanding of desire, one that is constituted through the lived practices and materialities of consumption. As the condition of exorbitant selving, pleasure is of no small political importance. Following Regenia Gagnier, one can argue that desire is as important a category as labor, for example, has been in materialist critiques of capital. Gagnier writes that the "defense of desire is as justified as the earlier marxist defense of the value of labor.... Surely people are *both* producers and consumers, workers and wanters."[30] The politics of a materially constituted desire, then, must be brought to bear on an analysis of women's shopping. Consumer desire has the potential to disrupt the limits placed on women by gendered norms and to reformulate the ideologies of gender that were manufactured by the machinery of capitalism.

Figured not as voracious appetite but as tactical practice and discourse, women's desire is central to the making of subjectivities that are written through the acts of consumption. Evading her cultural inscription as object of exchange with an appetite that must be curtailed, the Victorian women shopper contested a traditional understanding of the self as distinct from objects. Rather than eliding the female subject, however, the breakdown of the boundaries between subject and object enabled a radical reformulation of the constitution of identity. Challenging the equation of feminine virtue with self-renunciation and the regulation of appetite, this consuming, desiring subject formed through her fluid, tactical operations in and through a new world of consumerism.

This mode of excessive subjectivity constitutes a useful departure from normative models of Victorian femininity, which depend on a careful observance of boundaries and appetites. De Certeau's practitioners of the everyday resist the rationalist logic of institutions and fashion their own ways of operating within the state. Consumers trace their own movements or "'indeterminate trajectories' that . . . do not cohere with the constructed, written, and prefabricated space through which they move."[31] Consumer tactics not only reimagine space and how to negotiate it but also collapse the usual distinctions between space and time. As both spatial and temporal tacticians, shoppers are always oriented toward the possibilities of "future expansions."[32] Without fixed destinations or goals in mind, they operate only according to leisure time, an excess that resists measure. "[C]irculating, com[ing] and go[ing] . . . over an imposed terrain," the shopper does not obey the authorized cultural script dictating the norms of femininity under capitalism.[33] The itinerant, even errant behaviors that were coming to be associated with the mid-Victorian shopping excursion, in which the shopper could go about browsing for pleasure without having necessarily to purchase anything, are both a cause and an effect of this new expansive consumer subjectivity.

The woman shopper, in this sense, can be understood according to what Gilles Deleuze and Félix Guattari have termed "becoming," a way of being in the world that Elizabeth Grosz has extended to mean a form of feminine identity that is not predicated on the absence of desire but is always in the process of being made.[34] Within the Deleuzian/Guattarian conception, one can begin to imagine forms of identity that are predicated on fluidity and discontinuity, ones, as Grosz notes, "without a psychical or secret interior, without internal cohesion" that reinscribes universalizing myths of self.[35] This form of subjectivity as becoming, which exceeds the limits historically placed on women's desires and spheres of activity, is thus an alternative to a Lacanian formulation in which women constitute a lack.[36] Without possession of the phallus as signifier—in this case, without historical representation in the masculine sphere of production—Woman stands as Other, an empty cipher in her historical identification with the commodity in relation to man in order to guarantee both his masculine subjecthood and economic mastery. Forming a self through the improvisations of consumption, and apart from the usual calculus of time and space, the shopper's consuming credits her with a futurity and inaugurates a new economy of plenitude and expenditure toward which this self-in-making is always directed.

The consumer practices that produce this mode of subjectivity are engagingly represented in literature written by Victorian and Edwardian women: poetry, fiction, and political journalism of the period imagine the possibilities of women's becoming through consumption. Focusing on the discursive construction of the shopper in British women's writing from 1862 until 1914, a period that saw the rise of the department store and the institutionalization of a women's urban sphere of consumption, this book examines the ways in which literary and popular writing represented the woman shopper as going to market on her own, not as an object of exchange but as a subject, and the expansive forms of identity that became possible when she took her desire with her. Recovering discourses of shopping that emphasize delight rather than dangers, it argues that these decades saw the formation of what de Certeau calls "*lignes d'erre*," or "sentences that remain unpredictable within the space ordered by the organizing techniques of systems."[37] Rather than a moment of rupture that inaugurated gendered forms of self-discipline, the emergence of modern shopping culture in the 1860s is better characterized as the proliferation of discourses of shopping and the female shopper. Challenging self-renunciation as the dominant mode of femininity within systems of exchange, women writers of this period often construct female shoppers as active, even transgressive agents in the marketplace. Together, these discourses reveal the constructed nature of prescribed domesticity and, in exceeding it, often enable the formation of transgressive and dissident identities.

The five chapters of this study trace a genealogy of the woman shopper from transgressive domestic spender to aesthetic connoisseur, from curious shopgazer to political radical. Consistent with the idea of genealogy—and Michel

Foucault's concern that any approach to history must always invite "discontinuity into our very being"—the chapters do not offer a decade-by-decade, progressive narrative of the shopper in literature; rather, the structure of the book is designed to resist the tendency to reproduce history as continuous and totalizable.[38] Chapters 1 through 3 focus on literary texts and cultural practices that emerge and recur from the 1860s through the 1880s, as a female sphere of urban consumption is institutionalized. Chapters 4 and 5 consider a women's consumer culture (established from the 1890s until just before World War I) while showing how the shopper at the end of the nineteenth century is often an iteration of the mid-Victorian consumer.

Together, these chapters demonstrate how women's lived relationships to consumption are materialized as discourse, as forms of narrative and poetic inscription that intervene in cultural representations of shopping to emphasize consumerism as productive of pleasure rather than seduction or loss. Addressing literary texts that represent a range of generic interests—from the sensuousness of Pre-Raphaelite and aesthetic poetry to the realism of the domestic novel, from the arresting scenes of sensation fiction to the urgent cries of suffrage journalism—these chapters attest to the extent to which literature contended with the figure of the woman consumer. By moving, moreover, between literary texts and cultural documents, including women's fashion periodicals, advertisements, shopping guides, and suffragette parlor games, this volume illustrates that the discourses of middle-class women's consumption make visible the porous boundary between so-called high and low culture and often traffic freely between them.

In one turn-of-the-century shopping guide, *Olivia's Shopping and How She Does It*, a persona named Olivia notes the absence of a guide that goes beyond merely listing the shops of London and distinguishes her book as one that will properly evaluate shops for a readership of discerning, middle-class women shoppers. Claiming that women are not being well served by "the vapid flatteries of shops to be seen in ladies' papers," she seeks to fill this gap in the market with a serious and sustained critique of shops that will document the merits and shortcomings of their various goods and services.[39] When she remarks that "[s]hops should be criticized like pictures or plays," Olivia does not reiterate the suspicion of the consumer marketplace that characterizes *Jane Eyre*.[40] Instead, she begins to anticipate a critical practice that neither dismisses women's shopping as trivial nor valorizes it as simply emancipatory. Similarly,

Come Buy, Come Buy maintains that the shops surely must be read and the discourses of consumption examined. By doing so, we may come to understand the degree to which gendered, historical subjects are inscribed within the operations of a marketplace that beckons them to "Come buy, come buy" and how, through acts of consumption, women might exceed their cultural prescriptions and make visible the many meanings of their spending and desiring.

One

GOBLIN MARKETS

Women Shoppers and the East in London's West End

In a Max Beerbohm caricature, a fashionably dressed Dante Gabriel Rossetti implores his plain sister, Christina, to choose something more fetching to wear. The Rossettis are apparently home-shopping in Dante's studio, surrounded by a display of softly arranged dress materials. The caption reads, "Rossetti, having just had a fresh consignment of 'stunning' fabrics from that new shop in Regent Street, tries hard to prevail on his younger sister to accept at any rate one of these and have a dress made. . . . 'What *is* the use, Christina,'" says an exasperated Dante, making recourse to his sister's poetry, "'of having a heart like a singing bird . . . , if you insist on getting yourself up like a pew-opener?'"[1]

"[T]hat new shop in Regent Street" may well be a reference to Liberty's East India House, which opened in 1875 as an oriental bazaar to sell silks from the East in London's fashionable West End. For it was at East India House, a half shop that would later expand to become Liberty's department store, that Dante Gabriel

Rossetti and other members of the Pre-Raphaelite Brethren, including William Morris and Edward Burne-Jones, often bought the shawls they used to drape models for their paintings.[2] In 1881, for example, Dante Gabriel inspected a number of silk shawls at Liberty's in an attempt to secure one for the model of *Found* to wear. He later laments in a letter to Frederic James Shields that he cannot find a suitable one for this painting.[3] Although Liberty's shawls were appropriate for some of his other paintings, the fallen woman represented in his more austere *Found* evidently called for a less opulent shawl.

The Beerbohm caricature does more than provide a possible source for the fabrics used in Pre-Raphaelite paintings, however. It also does something other than recall the scene of Rochester and Jane's shopping trip to the Millcote silk warehouse, in which another imposing male figure similarly instructs a hesitant woman shopper to select from among notably luxurious goods. For the illustration also participates in the construction of Christina Rossetti as a renunciate who is indifferent to material pleasures and female preoccupations with dress. Whereas early considerations of Christina Rossetti tended, much like the caricature, to contribute to a view of her life and writings as somehow detached from the materialities of Victorian culture, recent critics have attempted to correct this image of her as a poet of self-denial by addressing the cultural and historical relevance of her writings.[4]

Despite a wealth of illuminating criticism on *Goblin Market*, there remains more to explore of the cultural work of consumption in the poem. Several critics have effectively and carefully addressed the poem's economic themes; however, most of these analyses have tended not to ensure a space for the production of female desire *within* market economies.[5] But by shifting the focus to a consideration of shopping as a form of leisure at a time in Britain when the West End was associated with the pleasures of consumption, we begin to see the marketplace of Rossetti's poem not simply as a place of danger and temptation for women but also as a significant site for the formation of their identities and desires.

If the question of consumer appetite as it becomes constituted within the marketplace remains to be explored more fully, so also are the ways in which pleasure came to be produced through imperialism, or how empire, capitalism, and the gendering of consumption were historically concomitant projects. That is to say, *Goblin Market* concerns the production of consumer desire at a time when issues of imperialism and race complicated the relationship of women to the marketplace in Victorian Britain, a marketplace that was being bolstered by British commercial interests abroad.[6] Consumption during this century, then, was not simply a result of the century's broad industrialization, retailing revolution, or consolidation of the middle class. This imperial marketplace inscribed women as imperial subjects and created the conditions for specifically gendered desires for exotic goods. Mary Wilson Carpenter makes a suggestive link between imperialism, consumerism, pleasure, and Rossetti's poem when she remarks that *Goblin Market* "suggests its location in the . . . intersection of imperialist culture and consumer capitalism" that Nancy Armstrong has identified in "The Occidental Alice."[7] Carpenter goes on to examine the female body as commodity to reveal how *Goblin Market* affirms female desire by proposing a sisterhood that "permits the female gaze to feast on the female form."[8] Extending these intersections between consumer desire, imperialism, and visuality to an emphasis on the production of pleasure in Victorian consumer culture, this chapter considers not a renunciative Rossetti but a Rossetti who locates strategic desires for women in the consumer marketplace of Britain's empire at home.

On at least one occasion, the author of such apparently self-negating poems as "Song" ("When I am dead, my dearest") and "Remember" ("Remember me when I am gone away") revealed that she was not indifferent to the material delights of commodities and consumption. In a letter to Amelia Barnard Heimann in August 1853, Rossetti betrays a shopper's interest in "certain water proof cloaks (at least they profess to be water proof) apparently made of a sort of grey alpaca, which one can procure at Swan and Edgar's . . . [for] 26/s or 27/s."[9] Her description of the cloaks is carefully qualified; they only "profess" to be waterproof and are "apparently" made of alpaca. Thus, she is careful to interrogate for herself the claims of Swan and Edgar (the stylish draper's shop, established at No. 10 Piccadilly in 1812) while indulging in a description of dressmaker details. A few lines later in the same letter, Rossetti relates that her landlord has just "sent us a liberal present of gooseberries and black currants," which she, her mother, and sister Maria "have [had] made into jam"—a delightful, if not coincidental, conflation of shopping with the consumption of fruit and a departure from the dour, resistant consumer that Beerbohm depicts.

If Rossetti's letter hints that she was not opposed to the pleasures of consumption, *Goblin Market* constitutes her most sustained exploration of consumer desire, particularly the specific kinds of desires that formed through an imperial marketplace. The poem suggests that she was aware of the appeal of imperial goods that were becoming increasingly available in Britain to consumers in the mid-to-late nineteenth century. There is little doubt that, by the 1880s, Rossetti's poem title had taken on imperial and commercial resonances. Writing in 1887–89 in Hong Kong, Rudyard Kipling narrates his experience in a crowded and chaotic Canton market, "Show[ing] how I came to Goblin Market and . . . Cursed the Chinese People."[10] In one "ancient curio shop, . . . nameless devils of the Chinese creed make mouths at you from back-shelves, . . . brazen dragons . . . all catch your feet as you stumble across the floor— hear the tramp of the feet on the granite blocks of the road and the breaking wave of human speech, that is not human! Watch the yellow faces that glare at you between the bars, and you will be afraid, as I was afraid!"[11] The term *goblin market* clearly carried a racialized meaning full of suggestive dangers, including xenophobic fears of losing the integrity of the British body politic within a notably commercial space and of the susceptibility of the consumer's body in such a space. Such goblin markets were encountered not only abroad but also within Britain. As a flood of exotic goods were imported, they were often marketed to women in oriental bazaars such as Liberty's East India House and in specialized departments of Whiteley's, Debenham and Freebody, and Swan and Edgar; by 1895, Harrods' catalogue also included an advertisement for an Eastern goods department in its Knightsbridge store.[12] The empire abroad was up for sale in the empire at home, in the shops and department stores of London's fashionable shopping districts, where women consumers encountered new delights.

In what is perhaps the best-known poem about a shopping expedition in English literature, we locate an unlikely but compelling engagement of an apparently reclusive Victorian woman poet who confronts the vicissitudes of a public, racialized marketplace. By situating *Goblin Market* within Britain's emergent imperial consumer culture, one can locate the poem's radicalness in the ways in which it affirms female desire within such a marketplace. The poem addresses the vexed relationship between women and the Eastern aesthetic they consumed within the economies of imperial capitalism. This chapter considers how the reception of Rossetti's poem is enhanced by an understanding of the ways in which capital mobilized to incite women's participation in empire, as it attempted to inscribe women within its imperial project through the construction of women as consumers of oriental goods. The instrument of this incitement was the imperial exhibitionary complex of luxury shops that sought to decontextualize oriental goods and thus prohibit women's identification with the forces of exploited labor by which these goods were produced.[13] Women occupied a contradictory place within this imperial-commercial program, an instability that capital attempted to manage by constructing women as the consumers rather than the consumed. Women shoppers, however, could subvert this condition and disrupt capital, not through a retreat from its signifying economics but through alternative forms of desire within these economies. The commodity, like a fetish, is a contradiction that allows for alternative modes of desire that threaten the illusion of the continuity of empire.

Thus, Goblin Market does not so much pose the question of whether women can go to market (or how they might escape the market) as consider how women can desire without cost. To this end, Rossetti does not posit the marketplace as separate from a diametrically opposed domestic space. Instead, the poem contends with the ways in which women are inscribed within capitalism and how capitalism underscores women's desire—and the desire to look—within the imperial exhibitionary complex of this marketplace. One form of this affirmative desire, in which women consume but are not consumed, look but do not buy, can be seen in Goblin Market in the ways in which the sisters, Laura and Lizzie, learn to look at and to steal what they desire in the midst of the dazzling machinery of an exotic commodity display. The poem suggests that Rossetti anticipated and understood the appeal of imperial consumer goods, a market that was already in place midcentury in the form of such luxury emporia as Liberty's East India House and was poised to explode in the decades following the publication of the poem. As such, the poem stages desires that the Beerbohm caricature dismisses, showing Rossetti's awareness of not only the dangers but also the delights of a burgeoning, imperial consumer spectacle for women shoppers, a spectacle that formed the cultural conditions that gave rise to the modern department store and the visual forms of pleasure it produced.

West End Shopping and the Imperial Marketplace

Even as Rossetti was publishing Goblin Market in 1862, middle-class "shopping ladies" were becoming increasingly visible as urban figures in London.[14] Having become "ideologically separated" from the trade and commercial activities of the more easterly City of London by the 1860s, the West End was both a geographical and an imagined place.[15] As a district, it included not only the more affordable draper's shops of Oxford Street, many of which were expanding into larger emporia at this time, but also the luxury shops of Regent Street and Bond Street. Although the latter two had been the domain of aristocratic shopping during the eighteenth century, the shops of even these exclusive streets were available for the democratic activity of window-shopping, a relatively new pastime for unchaperoned middle-class women.[16] The West End also included such regions as nearby Piccadilly, Burlington Arcade, Leicester Square, Tottenham Court Road, and the Strand.[17] Although farther afield, shopping in more-suburban areas of London such as Kensington was also part of the city's consumer landscape. Indeed, developments in transportation were key to the increased mobility of shoppers. Omnibuses and, by 1863, the underground railway were affordable means by which women traveled from the suburbs to the West End, while the railways gave those outside London the opportunity for day-shopping trips. In 1886, the *Lady's World* observed, "Now that the train service is so perfect between London and Bath, it is quite possible to spend a day in town and return to Bath in the same evening. This is no small advantage when you have a day's shopping to get through."[18] In the 1880s, several other conveniences were introduced to the West End that enabled a woman to remain away from home for many hours at a time; these conveniences included the Ladies' Lavatory Company, which opened its first public restrooms at Oxford Circus in 1884, and eating establishments for women such as A.B.C. restaurants, the first of which opened in 1880. Amenities such as these helped to make London a viable destination for middle-class women, enabling them to venture away from home for the entire day.

As women were charged with the role of domestic consumers for a Victorian bourgeois class with new and greater access to capital, shopping became increasingly gendered as a female activity. Disposable income and the capacity to spend it became a way to signify through the consumer marketplace the material success of the bourgeois household.[19] But, as seen earlier in Eliza Lynn Linton's musings on the pleasures of shopping, women's consumption could exceed the bounds of utilitarian definition. As women consumed for pleasure, shopping came to exceed the mere buying of necessities. Less and less did shopping involve the strict spatialization of the shop and its codified exchanges with shopkeepers who traditionally supervised the proceedings from behind the counter. During these decades, consumption was no longer a discrete activity but had become part of an urban leisure network for women. As Erika Rappaport explains, shopping was not limited "merely [to] purchasing goods in a shop. . . . Shopping meant a day 'in Town,' consuming space and time *outside* of the private home. A shopper might have lunch out, take a break for tea, and visit a club, museum, or the theatre. Shopping also involved discussing, looking at, touching, buying, and rejecting commodities, especially luxury items such as fashions, furnishings, and other fancy goods."[20] The Angel in the House thus could buy out of want rather than need or simply go about looking and enjoying the pursuit of shopping as an expansive public pleasure.

Perhaps more than any other Victorian institution, the department store was a women's destination that encoded the multiple pleasures of an urban sphere of consumption and suggested the ways in which the practice of shopping mediated between women's traditional domestic sphere and a public one. If the domestic sphere previously marked the proper limit of middle-class women's place, the department store mapped the continuity between home and marketplace in a space specifically designed to recall the comforts of home. Department stores often catered to their female clientele by supplying such amenities as cloak rooms, tea rooms, rest areas, lavatories, and writing rooms—in short, providing the sense of a home away from home. Britain's first department store, Whiteley's, opened in Westbourne Grove in 1863. Billed as the "Universal Provider," it boasted a wide range of goods under one roof and set competitive prices to attract a wide clientele.[21] But most London department stores were the result of more-organic and gradual processes. Among those establishments that had begun as smaller shops but were then expanded into department stores was Swan and Edgar, for example, which started its transition from draper's shop to a department store in 1866. Marshall and Snelgrove replaced its original shop, a series of houses, with a five-story building on Oxford Street by 1876. Harrods, originally founded as a grocer's shop in 1835, was expanded in 1874 and rebuilt into a five-floor structure in 1884. By 1902 it had become London's biggest store, boasting ninety-one different departments, and in 1911 it went on to cover four and a half acres. Inspired by the commercial success of the American department store Marshall and Field, former employee Gordon Selfridge opened Selfridge's on Oxford Street in 1909. Going beyond supplying domestic comforts, the store took shopping to new heights from the time it opened its doors, delighting shoppers with window displays that remained lit until midnight, perfume counters located on the main floor, an ice-cream fountain, and a roof garden.

The shopper's paradise that would come to be synonymous with such names as Liberty's, Harrods, and Selfridge's also introduced ways of looking, touching, roving, and desiring that were specific to department stores. Unlike the smaller space of a shop, where there was a greater expectation to visit with an expressed purpose of buying (or at least the ability to buy), the department store was predicated on wider access and enabled shoppers to enter and spend their time, as Rachel Bowlby has playfully termed it, "just looking." Even with the presence of shop assistants and floorwalkers in the Victorian department store, shoppers had unprecedented access to goods through the spectacle of the commodity. The prototype for this access, as Thomas Richards has argued, was the Great Exhibition of 1851, which he deems "the first department store."[22] The visual pleasures of the department store owed much to the display techniques employed during the 1851 event, which engaged an excited audience. The Crystal Palace helped secure the relationship between display and commodity: "the Exhibition elevated the commodity above the mundane act of exchange . . . [so that] things now spoke for themselves. . . . It was the first world's fair, . . . the first shopping mall."[23] Henry Cole believed that the exhibition would teach "not the manufactures only how to make, but the public how to buy."[24] Indeed, the exhibition displayed products rather than means of production, so that the goods resembled commodities that one could imagine owning. In doing so, it produced a new class of consumers who were appealed to through the eye on a scale never seen before.

The exhibitions of 1851 and 1862 also prompted the popularity of specifically exotic commodities within a visual field. More than a space in which the industry of Britain could be showcased, the exhibitions encouraged visitors to imagine a consumable East *within* Britain. The Crystal Palace struck Charlotte Brontë as a "Verdopolitan" spectacle that seemed to invite one to browse like a shopper: "It is a wonderful place—vast, strange, new, and impossible to describe. Its grandeur does not consist in *one* thing, but in the unique assembling of *all* things. Whatever human industry has created, you find there. . . . It may be called a bazaar or fair, but it is such a bazaar or fair as Eastern genii might have created."[25] Oriental commodities were also popular after the Exhibition of 1862, at which, after two hundred and fifty years of cultural isolation, Japan included a display. The Great Exhibitions, then, helped commodify an Eastern aesthetic, creating in the British public a consciousness of their status as potential shoppers in relation to the exotic goods they surveyed there. It is telling that after the second exhibition closed, part of the Japanese exhibit was bought up by a West End emporium, Farmer and Rogers Oriental Warehouse (where Arthur Liberty apprenticed while making plans to open his shop), to be sold to eager consumers.

When Liberty went on to open East India House, he created the West End's preeminent exotic consumer destination. Established on Regent Street, the shop seemed ideally situated. In 1858, just four years prior to Rossetti's publication of "Goblin Market," this street was being characterized by George Sala as "the most fashionable street in the world" and as an Eastern-themed location.[26] Recalling that Regent Street had been unexceptional in the goods it was offering in the 1830s, Sala proclaims its emergence as "an avenue of superfluities—a great trunk-road in Vanity Fair. . . . [T]hese are the merchants whose wares are exhibited in this Bezesteen of the world."[27]

When it opened in 1875, East India House was billed as an oriental bazaar devoted to a commodified vision of the East. At first it sold only imported silks and shawls, but by 1880 the original shop had grown to include seven departments: silks, embroideries, furniture, carpets, porcelain, curios, and miscellaneous.[28] The year 1885 marked the acquisition of another Liberty property on Regent Street, Chesham House, whose basement was dubbed an "Eastern Bazaar." With more expansion in the decades that followed, Liberty eventually consolidated the shops to feature a full-scale department store, adopting its famous Tudor facade in the 1920s.

Sala identifies shawl shops as a notable aspect of the luxury trade of Regent Street "Bezesteen," and indeed the popularity of Liberty's silk shawls is what granted East India House much of its initial success. Liberty took the taste for imported shawls and made them the cornerstone of his trade. This fashion for Kashmir shawls began in the eighteenth century, when the items first arrived in Britain with men returning from India. In the 1810s, these shawls cost from seventy to one hundred pounds each, a large sum that only affluent women could typically afford.[29] The trend for the shawls (those sold by Liberty in particular) continued well into the century. In 1879, the *Ladies Gazette of Fashion* was still raving about these textiles: "[T]he India mania daily increases, notwithstanding the opportunity from manufacturers of plain fabrics who declare themselves ruined."[30] The same paper recommended Liberty's silks and touted their authenticity: "Nothing can be more advantageous . . . than the Oriental silks. They are very serviceable. . . . [T]his is the case with the good qualities such as may be procured of Messrs. Lasenby Liberty, of 218, Regent Street. . . . [T]heir white 'Runchender' silks are evidently lineal descendants of those mentioned in the Arabian nights."[31] The *Ladies Gazette of Fashion* also showed Japanese-style house jackets, included advertisements placed by Liberty, and insisted that "[t]o own a pretty house full of pretty things is generally every woman's ambition" before going on to promote a recent fad for oriental screens.[32] The *Ladies Gazette of Fashion* also admitted that "[t]o be dressed in the robes of an Eastern odalisque on a chilly or foggy day is a discrepancy to be avoided, and yet how are we so to avoid it [in] our climate . . . ? Fashion has provided such things very plentifully, and to refuse to indulge in them [is] an amount of self-sacrifice hardly to be expected of feminine stoicism."[33]

Liberty's shop also offered indulgence and respite for shoppers in the form of its Eastern-themed tea room. An 1887 advertisement in the Liberty catalogue (fig. 1.1) advertises the "Arab Tea Room," a place of very literal consumption of the East, where women could hang up their coats in a cloakroom and then choose between the "Indian," "Lotus," or "Yang-Yin" blend. *Olivia's Shopping and How She Does It* describes this tea room as an authentic Eastern destination: "[It is] a little room for tea and biscuits (quite cheap). It is really the Far East, with more of the genuine atmosphere than is generally dispersed in such places."[34] This guidebook also mentions other similarly exotic tea rooms on nearby Bond Street that pop up and then seem to dematerialize: "Tea rooms here spring up like muffled mushrooms in a night. . . . There is sometimes a Lady Palmist on the premises. Then whiff, in a night, little Aladdin's miniature palace disappears, and in its stead, behold a blouse shop or somebody selling prints and rarities."[35] Olivia's comments on the fashion for Eastern tea rooms underscore the perceived vagaries of an imperial marketplace that continued until the turn of the century, one imbued with exotic pleasures that must be consumed immediately lest they disappear in a whiff of perfumed smoke.

Like the Beerbohm caricature of Dante Gabriel Rossetti, promotionals from the women's fashion papers and shopping guides appealed to a woman's sense of comfort and subtly informed her that to resist such pleasures would amount to unnecessary and excessive self-denial. The spectacle of imported

1.1. "Arab" Tea Room advertisement. Liberty Carpet Catalogue (London: Liberty & Co., 1887, 48). V&A Images/Victoria and Albert Museum, London

goods at shops and in advertisements signified an irresistible destination to its shoppers, suggesting an East against which "European culture" might define itself as an "underground self," a place of pure fantasy and delight that might be reasonably indulged in.[36] In the imperial marketplace, shoppers became tourists to their own desires within an empire at home that marketed a complete consumerist vision of an exoticized East.

Imperial Exhibition and the Shopper's Gaze

As ancillary services such as women's tea rooms contributed to the gendering of shopping and as shops and advertisements created new trends for a vast array of goods, luxury shopping emporia such as Liberty's East India House became the site of new kinds of gendered consumer behaviors. While the fashion papers often discussed the pleasures of imported goods, some reports of women's shopping betrayed the concern that the shopping experience could devolve into a kind of mania. When the goods were Eastern ones, women's behaviors seemed particularly remarkable. One year after the opening of East India House, Edward Godwin, who would go on to become Liberty's costume department director, reported that an excited group of shoppers had gathered at Liberty's to view a new shipment of fans from Japan. The crowd included several distinguished male guests whom Godwin identified, in addition to an unindividuated "bevy of ladies" who "filled up the rest of the floor space."[37] Cast in this light, these shopping ladies stand as an amorphous gathering, a volatile presence as they gaze upon highly desirable goods.

Nancy Armstrong has noted that the British female body, as "the object of objects," was susceptible to contagion within imperial consumer culture because "the quality of the objects was apparently transferred onto the consumer" so that "no desire for the goods of the Empire was ever free of danger because that desire was located in women [where] it took the form of an appetite capable of effacing gender, race, and class."[38] As though to quell this danger, the taxonomies of display in department stores carried with them a regulating function. Such "techniques of defamiliarization and montage" served to contain and domesticate the delectable items on display.[39] As the plunder of empire, imported goods were offered simultaneously as a feast for the eyes and as evidence of British success and prosperity abroad for those women who consumed this bounty. Free of context and with the labors of original manufacture concealed, the objects appeared not simply as booty but as commodities, as something magical, transcendent, and eminently consumable. Store arrangements also seemed to suggest specific desires for the women who came to look and buy. Tony Bennett points out that, like Michel Foucault's "exhibitionary complex" in which objects and bodies are regulated according to principles of display, the "architectural forms" of store departments and arrangements, like those of museums and exhibitions, concealed relations between power and knowledge even as they ensured self-discipline for those crowds of consumers who came to view.[40] The East, with its supposed attendant dangers, unruliness, and esoteric sexuality, was managed by neat displays, stalls, and mirrors. Even as the display technologies of the West End oriental bazaar served to contain delectable imports, they also spoke of a prosperous empire in which goods were domesticated and neutralized, rendering them safe, as it were, for British women's consumption.[41] "[T]he motif of the Orient as insinuating danger[,] [in which] [r]ationality is undermined by Eastern excesses," was apparently tamed in department store displays.[42] With goods thus flattened into signifying surfaces, disarmed of their supposed Eastern dangers, the oriental bazaars were a place in which women were authorized to explore a desire that was carefully prescribed for them, one that supposedly trimmed and contained more-volatile female compulsions.

Yet women shoppers were not without agency within the oriental bazaars and Eastern goods departments of London's shopping districts. As stores constructed a consumerist empire at home and the imperial metropolis became a destination for shoppers, women negotiated desire through the materialities of consumerism and the consumer gaze. It was not only goods that women pursued but also the opportunity to look at store displays that produced spectacle as something to be consumed. As Bennett suggests, display must be considered a kind of currency, as it signifies a shift from the *processes* of production to *products* or commodities, a move that depends on the fetishizing of seriality rather than the singularity of objects and is realized in the ways in which department store displays garner the eye through repetition.[43]

The nature of display meant that the imperial exhibitionary complex could not consistently secure, enforce, and regulate consumerist behaviors and desires. The organization of Liberty's into orderly departments did not safeguard against the potential for confusion. One woman's experience, recorded in the *Liberty Lamp*, points to the limited success of display technologies in regulating women shoppers, suggesting the tenuous nature of imperial representation. The employees' store publication recalls that "the mirrored walls [of the Chesham House] deceived staff and customers alike. How many humorous situations arose at seeing oneself reflected in so many ways! I remember an elderly dame apologising to her own mirror reflection, and craving pardon for her intrusion."[44] The dimensions of the departments that housed metalworks, furniture, vases, and more were multiplied by the presence of mirrored walls that could confuse customers, who might mistake their image for someone else's, while providing the illusion of a limitless space. Amid the mirrored displays of Liberty's and the manufactured look of an oriental bazaar, the fractures of this consumer spectacle were readily visible.

The mirror incident in Liberty's points to the degree to which the imperial marketplace was a space organized around ways of seeing. It also suggests that this spectacle was one in which consumer desire was secured through the work of commodification, which mirrors or negotiates use and exchange value. The ways in which consumer objects were naturalized as authentic goods from the

East within the decontextualizing spaces of department stores—within the "misrecognitions" that produced these orientalized goods—point to the extent to which commodification, representation, and ways of looking are inherent in the power structures of imperialism. Moreover, they make visible the degree to which imperialism relied on the mystification of commodities to ensure an apparently seamless visual field.[45]

Women shoppers, then, were not merely lost in the funhouse of an imperial display produced through the contiguous work of commodification and empire. Rather, this house of mirrors was also the condition under which new desires might be obtained and others refused. This exotic marketplace could not guarantee that its exhibitionary forms could secure women's ongoing consumerist desires or sell them a fantastic view of empire. For within this manufactured spectacle, women shoppers could aspire to become spectating subjects, producing knowledge by gazing. That is to say, the oriental bazaar does not resemble Foucault's regulatory panopticon, in which surveillance ensures civility consistent with institutional aims. Instead, an entire apparatus of exhibitionary forms produced spectators—women shoppers—as subjects rather than objects of knowledge.[46] As misrecognitions and fracturings pointed to imperial capitalism's manufacture, desire might become possible through the prerogative of the shopper's gaze. Women's presence in oriental bazaars such as Liberty's, as a version of commodities who have themselves gone to market, constituted a disruption to the imperial market's claim to uniformity and exposed the extent to which imperial institutions depended on commodification to ensure the visibility and continuous representation of empire. Thus, women's agency coalesced in the prerogative of gaze as women crossed between domestic and commercial spheres, looking but not necessarily buying. In traversing this marketplace, the shopper's gaze might disrupt the imperial market, revealing the extent of its surfaces, its spectacle, and its manufacture.

Popular accounts of shopping reveal that women's propensity to look rather than buy was a much-discussed phenomenon. An 1865 article in the *Leisure Hour*, "Shopping without Money," proposes a shopping trip that will cost the reader nothing. "This fine morning," the article begins, "we intend going out among the shops, in the hope of reaping a kind of profit which demands no previous outlay, and which can be gathered at will by all who have eyes to see. In a word, we are going on a shopping expedition without money to spend."[47] This expedition is made possible by the spectacle of the West End, for "the shops of London . . . constitute a museum which puts all other to scorn, and exhibit a thousand things of general interest which are not to be found in the index of the cyclopedia."[48] Similarly, a contributor to an American magazine, *Living Age*, sings the praises of West End shop displays: "The shops of London . . . display their thousand works of art in the most splendid frames, and the gayest colors; each shop is a *picture*."[49] In the latter part of the century, Lady M. Jeune implies that the practice of just looking is well established when she reports in the *Fortnightly Review* that "[m]any women go to shops for no reason beyond the desire of looking round, and generally surveying things."[50] Addressing department stores in particular, *Olivia's Shopping and How She Does It* concludes that Harrods "is surely built on just that large and generous plan which permits of wares being exhibited without fear of being purchased."[51] But women's propensity simply to look was not always welcomed by shop owners. In a satire of shopping entitled "A Woman in a Shoe Shop," a woman asks to see shoes even though, as she says, "I think in the end I shall take the boots."[52] After seeing several pairs of shoes, she leaves without making a purchase, pretending that she has accidentally been visiting the wrong shop. It was this sort of shopper that the *Warehouseman and Draper's Trade Journal* had in mind in 1863 when it railed against "ladies who go into shops to look and not buy."[53] Such shoppers were satisfied to look without purchasing, frustrating the retailing system in the process. In the context of Eastern goods, the shopper's gaze is similarly one of proximity; one could enjoy a display of exotic commodities but not necessarily buy.[54] Such a gaze, moreover, is embodied, mobile, and related to the other senses. The goods can be sampled, touched, tried on. It is not a voyeuristic gaze in which pleasure derives from distance. Far from one of mastery, this mobile form of seeing does not replicate the power relations inherent in masculine visual economies, in which there is a clear demarcation between subject and object. Rather, as Rossetti's poem shows, gazing in an exotic goblin marketplace becomes the basis for women to formulate desires of their own.

Poached Fruit: Shopping in Goblin Market

In considering Armstrong's argument that new conditions for female desire were produced during the nineteenth century specifically through the intersections of consumer culture and British imperialism, Carpenter revisits Armstrong's model of desire in which "*all possibility for pleasure splits off from appetite and attaches itself to self-control.*"[55] Carpenter, by contrast, suggests that in Goblin Market, desire is not restrained but "re-directed toward another female figure, where it is provoked, encouraged, and satiated."[56] In other words, the female body is not simply a commodity but is "'consumable' as a regenerative and self-propagating 'fruit.'"[57] Desire, appetite, is not something to be controlled and quelled but should be recirculated through a female bodily economy. In turning to the homoerotic relationship of sisterhood, Carpenter underscores the importance of "looking" in Goblin Market, where a female gaze, central to desiring, contributes to the formation of new female subjectivities. Goblin Market problematizes women's consumption not only within the body that ingests the fruits of empire but also within the marketplace, where the specular economies of the imperial exhibitionary complex are at work. The marketplace in Goblin Market is constructed along visual lines, and taste and desire are made and unmade through looking. This visual economy is structured in particular around the commercialization and fetishization of an imagined East and its forbidden fruits.

The goblins' call, "Come buy, come buy," near the beginning of the poem is clearly a call to market. As Herbert F. Tucker observes, the cry "betokens not hospitality but trade," and Laura and Lizzie "are conscious denizens of a market economy."[58] This invitation is, moreover, an advertisement that effectively packages the goods as commodities, as something more than everyday fruit, as highly tempting exotic comestibles. The sisters (Laura in particular) begin to buy "into the terms on which goblins do business: the terms not of real-goods presence but of representation, framing, and display."[59] For the fruits to be presented as larger than life, as more than English garden-variety produce, they must be packaged and sold as such through the discourse of advertising. The collection of exotic fruits hawked at the beginning of the poem is offered up as a kind of shopping list to engage the sisters' consumerist desires. The goblins' advertisement begins as a promotion of domestically available fruits such as apples, cherries, raspberries, and cranberries (lines 5–14) but quickly moves to rarer ones, including ones not native to Britain:

> "Our grapes fresh from the vine,
> Pomegranates full and fine,
> Dates and sharp bullaces,

> Rare pears and greengages,
> Damsons and bilberries,
> Taste them and try:
> Currants and gooseberries,
> Bright-fire-like barberries,
> Figs to fill your mouth,
> Citrons from the South
> Sweet to tongue and sound to eye;
> Come buy, come buy."
>
> (lines 20–31)[60]

Laura speculates about the origins of these consumables: "Who knows upon what soil they fed / Their hungry thirsty roots?" (lines 44–45). Later, the poem brackets off its own observation that these fruits are not the sort of wares that are typically available: "(Men sell not such in any town)" (line 101). The source of the fruit is never known, perhaps because the goblins' persistent cry comes to overwhelm Laura's question. They continue "their shrill repeated cry" (line 89), their "iterated jingle" (line 233), so often that Laura's sensible consumer inquiry is drowned out by the goblins' endless commercial. Having gained Laura's eye through their advertising blitz, these eager salesmen "bade her taste / In tones as smooth as honey" (lines 107–8) and invite her to sample wares that they earlier claimed are both "[s]weet to tongue and sound to eye" (line 30). The goblins' "iterated jingle" anticipates an 1880 Liberty advertisement for East India House that boasts of offerings of "Cabinets, Tables, Chairs, Rugs, Carpets, Mattings, Curtains, Materials, Jewellery, Embroideries, Shawls, Cashmeres, Silks, Brocades, Porcelains, Bronses, Bric-a-Brac, and Toys" from "Persia, India, China, & Japan." "Quaint!—Artistic!—Original!—Beautiful!—and Useful!" (fig. 1.2). Like the list of fruits, a whole catalogue of goods is offered up, and like the goblin fruit, the goods' origins are collapsed as nonspecifically Eastern (that is, from Persia as much as from Japan). Both the Liberty and goblin advertisements incite the desire to look, and in both instances, advertising exploits the commodities' uncertain origins to offer them as rare and desirable.

If the goblins' fruit is all the more tempting because of its vague origins, the goblins themselves are indeterminate creatures. Their representation in the poem recalls nineteenth-century racial iconography in the ways in which they

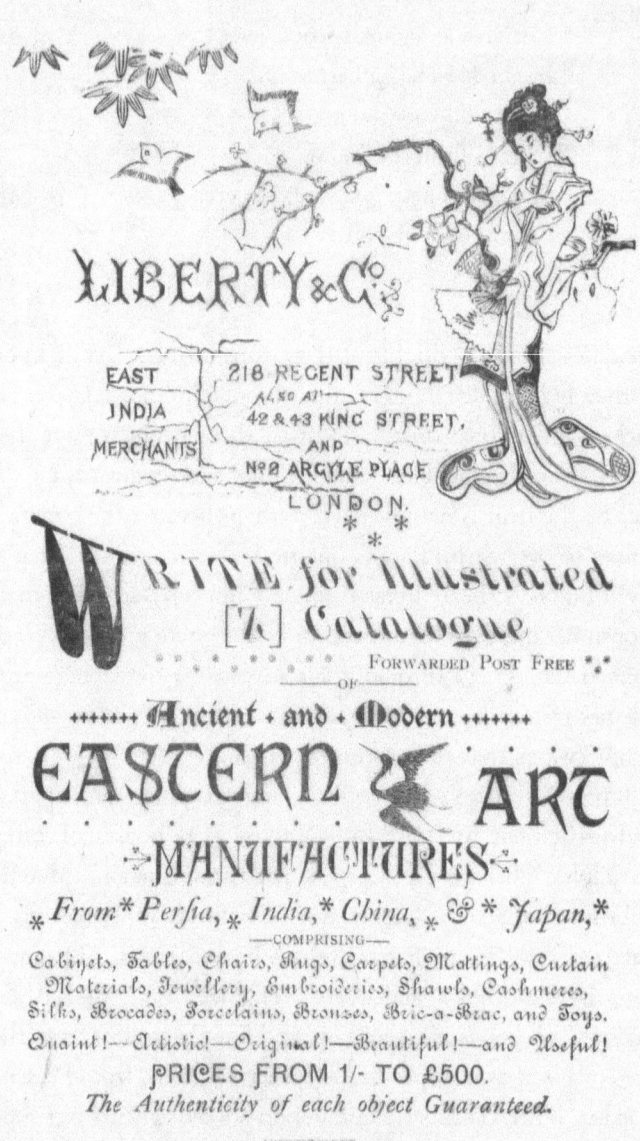

1.2. Liberty advertisement (loose item printed on tissue paper) (London: Liberty & Co., ca. 1880) *Courtesy of the City of Westminster Archives Centre and Liberty plc.*

are notably racialized. The qualification of the goblin "merchant m[e]n" (line 70) as nonhuman ("One like a wombat prowled obtuse and furry / One like a ratel tumbled hurry skurry" [lines 75–76]) is similar to a racist characterization of non-Europeans as animals or as subhuman, lesser in the evolutionary schema. The *Oxford English Dictionary* identifies the ratel as an African and southern Asian badger, suggesting connections between the goblins and a species from an exotic locale. Anne McClintock's discussion of the monkey figure used in nineteenth-century advertising for Monkey Brand Soap also deserves mention here: "In every respect the soap monkey is a hybrid: not entirely ape, not entirely human; part street beggar, part gentleman; part artist, part advertiser. The creature inhabits the ambivalent border of jungle and city, private and public, the domestic and the commercial, and offers as its handiwork a fetish that is both art and commodity."[61] McClintock suggests that primatology in Victorian visual culture stands for "a crisis in value and hence anxiety at possible boundary breakdown."[62] Thus, primates—or goblins—can signal the shifting nature of gender and of gendered space in the poem within the imagined space of the marketplace, a racialized marketplace like that of Liberty's oriental bazaar in which women and goods of uncertain origin mingled. The work of the commodity as fetish, as *racialized* fetish, is thus central to the manufacture of goblin marketplaces, where goods appear magically apart from the conditions of their manufacture, their vague origin making them all the more exotic.

As rather suspect salesmen, the goblins also recall "Street-Sellers of Cakes, Tarts, &c.," who are among the marginal urban figures that Henry Mayhew includes in *London Labour and the London Poor* (1861–62). Indeed, the goblins' menu of fruits resembles the kinds of pie and tart fillings available from these London "piemen": "The pastry and confectionary which tempt the street eaters" include tarts and pies of "apples, currants, gooseberries, plums, damsons, cherries, raspberries, or rhubarb."[63] Mayhew's catalogue of fruit fillings strikingly resembles the varieties of fruit that the goblins announce in Rossetti's poem. The similarities between piemen and goblins do not end here. These piemen, who would regularly ply their trade on the street and at public parks, fairs, and exhibitions, were "seldom stationary." Moving about, they "seldom begin business until six o'clock [in the evening], and some remain out all night. The best time for the sale of pies is generally from ten at night to one in the morning."[64] Perhaps it was in part the fact that pie-selling was largely an evening trade that contributed to the gendering of the customers; most were young boys, and Mayhew notes that "women, seldom, if ever, buy pies in the streets."⁶⁵ At a time when women were discouraged from engaging in transactions that would take place on the streets, such as buying from street sellers, middle-class women's access to late-night shopping in regular shops was also curtailed by the efforts of the Early Closing Movement. Founded in 1842, the movement's aims included the establishment of earlier closing hours for shops (which often remained open until at least eight o'clock in the evening in the West End) out of a concern for shopworkers' well-being as well as a corrective to the frivolous activities of night shoppers who, as the *Daily Telegraph* put it in 1858, go "gallivanting about the streets after nightfall, . . . making purchases which there is no earthly reason for them not to have made hours before."⁶⁶ Laura, however, does not observe daylight shopping hours, and she listens to these goblin street-sellers' regular cries each evening to come out and buy, despite her sister's urging to ignore them and their suspect wares: "Evening by evening / Among the brookside rushes, / Laura bowed her head to hear" (lines 32–34). Her lingering outside to listen to the goblins' call is transgressive of codes of femininity that situate appropriate shopping for women indoors and during daylight hours, rather than with goblin men on the streets at night.

Like a woman shopper tempted by the latest wares of Liberty's oriental bazaar or by the late-night cries of a fruit tart street-seller, Laura must have some of the goblin fruit, which seems safe enough to her. But her sister, Lizzie, is wary of the origins of "Citrons from the South" and of the goblins, and she cautions against any attempt to gaze upon the spectacle:

> "Oh," cried Lizzie, "Laura, Laura,
> You should not peer at goblin men."
> Lizzie covered up her eyes,
> Covered close lest they should look;
>
> (lines 48–51)

but while Lizzie resists all temptation to look, Laura does the opposite:

> "Look, Lizzie, look, Lizzie,
> Down the glen tramp little men.
> One hauls a basket,

> One bears a plate,
> One lugs a golden dish
> Of many pounds weight."
>
> (lines 54–59)

While Lizzie warns that goblins' "offers should not charm us, / Their evil gifts would harm us" (lines 65–66) and then stops her ears, closes her eyes, and finally flees, "Curious Laura chose to linger / Wondering at each merchant man" (lines 69–70). This market tempts through the eyes, revealing the extent to which it is a domain of the spectacle in which desires are made through the act of looking. This imperial marketplace, as the Liberty's advertisement underscores, is a visual field in which desire is structured around the gaze.

Enticed by the goblins' persistent "Come buy, come buy," Laura longs to taste the fruit. But without proper currency, she cannot gain access to the goblin market. For a penniless and hungry Laura, this is a shopping trip she cannot afford and must pay for in some other way: "Laura stared but did not stir, / Longed but had no money" (lines 105–6). She explains to the goblins,

> "Good folk, I have no coin;
> To take were to purloin:
> I have no copper in my purse,
> I have no silver either,
> And all my gold is on the furze
> That shakes in windy weather
> Above the rusty heather."
>
> (lines 116–22)

The goblins, however, see another source of currency in Laura, and they demand one of her golden curls, which she parts with with a tear. Selling a curl of her own, Laura can taste the fruit only if she mortgages a part of herself to a marketplace that dictates the terms of consumption. It is the manufactured delights of this marketplace that Laura can taste at last:

> She never tasted such before,
> How should it cloy with length of use?
> She sucked and sucked and sucked the more

> Fruits which that unknown orchard bore;
> She sucked until her lips were sore;
>
> (lines 132–36)

but Laura continues to pay for her visit to the market long after she consumes the fruit. First, she must endure her sister's upbraidings, as Lizzie scolds Laura for shopping after hours:

> "Dear, you should not stay out so late,
> Twilight is not good for maidens;
> Should not loiter in the glen
> In the haunts of goblin men."
>
> (lines 143–46)

Lizzie reminds her loitering sister of the fate of another woman shopper, Jeanie, "who should have been a bride" (line 313) but ate the goblin fruits, then "dwindled and grew grey" (line 156) and finally died. Lizzie's cautionary tale, in which Jeanie's symptoms resemble syphilis, recalls cultural anxieties over evening shopping and suggests that such anxieties extended from a logic that equated loitering with prostitution, and women in the market with women on the market.

Like a shopper who has forgotten to read the fine print of her credit agreement, Laura also continues to pay for her visit to the market in the sense that her desire for the fruits becomes addictive and insatiable. She plans to visit the market again the following day to address her mounting hunger. But after a day of milking cows, kneading cakes, and churning butter—domestic concerns that leave bored Laura "longing for the night" (line 214) and for the public sphere of the goblin market—she discovers to her horror that her previous night's consumption has had an unexpected effect: she can longer hear the goblins' routine cry. Her fear of having "[g]one deaf and blind" (line 259) suggests that the marketplace has victimized her by overloading her senses while ensuring that her appetites are never entirely satisfied.

Unable to locate the market anymore yet wracked with "passionate yearning" and "baulked desire" (lines 266 and 267), Laura attempts to grow her own fruit. She has kept a souvenir from her visit: a kernel that she plants one day "by a wall that faced the south" (line 282), hoping to replicate her experience of an exotic East. But when nothing grows—for the fantastic fruits exist only within the exhibitionary complex of the marketplace—she can only dream at night a notably orientalized fantasy

> . . . of melons, as a traveller sees
> False waves in desert drouth
> With shade of leaf-crowned trees,
> And burns the thirstier in the sandful breeze.
> (lines 289–92)

Laura finds that the delights of the goblin market cannot be obtained outside of the terms under which imperial commodities become exoticized; beyond these bounds, the advertisements of goblin men cannot be heard and their fruits cannot be seductively displayed.

With Laura near death, Lizzie resolves to make the trip to the goblin market on her sister's behalf. Cognizant of the costs of the goblin market, Lizzie learns how to gain access to it without sacrificing her autonomy. Whereas Laura came to market unprepared to spend, Lizzie "put[s] a silver penny in her purse" (line 324) and sets out. Despite Laura's earlier worries about stealing from the goblins (line 117), the goblins are not ultimately interested in the sisters' money. As with Laura, the goblins insist that Lizzie consume as they demand: "Nay, take a seat with us, / Honour and eat with us" (lines 368–69). The goods seem to have been designed with planned obsolescence in mind, and the goblins claim that the fruits would not survive cash-and-carry:

> "Such fruits as these
> No man can carry;
> Half their bloom would fly,
> Half their dew would dry,
> Half their flavour would pass by."
> (lines 375–79)

But Lizzie refuses to stay: "'Thank you,' said Lizzie: 'But one waits / At home alone for me'" (lines 383–84). Lizzie prefers takeout, while the goblins would like her to dine in. In the face of this refusal, the goblins attack:

> Barking, mewing, hissing, mocking,
> Tore her gown and soiled her stocking,

> Twitched her hair out by the roots,
> Stamped upon her tender feet,
> Held her hands and squeezed their fruits
> Against her mouth to make her eat.
> ....
> Lizzie uttered not a word;
> Would not open lip from lip
> Lest they should cram a mouthful in:
> But laughed in heart to feel the drip
> Of juice that syruped all her face[.]
>
> (lines 402–7, 430–34)

The goblins' violence is not only shocking, as Lizzie is assaulted, but also confusing. The goblin men, that is, are the antithesis of typically indulgent, obliging shopkeepers, and Lizzie's initial suspicions of them seem confirmed. Nevertheless, their vehemence seems a departure from their earlier craftiness. The cover of the 1897 Liberty catalogue presents a similarly unexpected image of violence. It depicts two individuals: one worker who is caricatured as foreign and another who is a creature of uncertain species. The latter is part human, part primate; "goblin" seems not an inappropriate designation. The goblin workers are pictured in the act of hammering metals; presumably, they are the foreign metalworkers who produce the goods that Liberty imports for its British consumers (fig. 1.3). The exaggeration of the goblin metalworkers is startling when compared to other Liberty catalogue covers, which offer serene, domesticated displays of goods, minus the suggestion of labor or production. The image is also an assaulting one when read in the context of the pages and pages of goods in the Liberty catalogues that are detached from their origins and displayed as commodities: the implication is that the labor and origins of imported goods, in the rare instance that these are depicted, cannot be imaged by the imperial imagination apart from a racialized violence. Another telling aspect of this atypical Liberty catalogue cover is that it lays bare the processes by which the imperial marketplace would come to be naturalized by the 1890s. The catalogue image reveals that the mechanism by which commodification and orientalism work is a violent one, since both depend on a wrested and concealed othering in which objects are assigned representational value as exotic commodities under imperial capitalism.

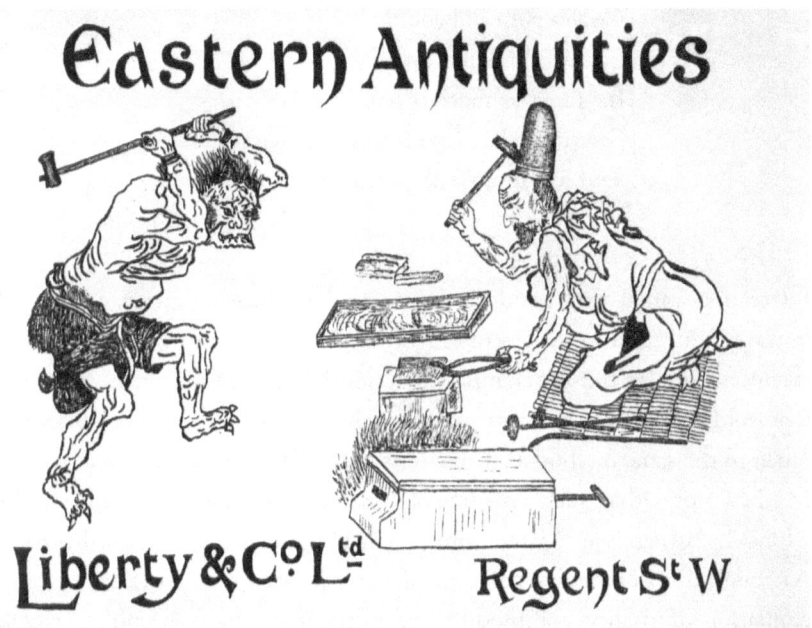

1.3. Front cover of Liberty's *Eastern Antiquities Catalogue* (London: Liberty & Co., 1897–1900). *V&A Images/Victoria and Albert Museum, London*

Lizzie encounters this violent marketplace with open eyes and on her own terms, refusing the goblins' forced consumption and ultimately triumphing as the goblins tire of this difficult customer. "Worn out by her resistance," they "[f]l[i]ng back her penny" (lines 438–39); she returns home with her own penny "[b]ouncing in her purse" (line 453), a bounce that is "music to her ear" (line 454), along with the goblins' fruit juices "lodged in dimples of her chin" (line 435). When Lizzie transgresses the marketplace and will not partake as the goblins prescribe, she encounters the violence of representation through which the imperial marketplace manufactures its vision of an exotic East. When she will not voluntarily yield up her desire, they force themselves on her. But like a shoplifter, she has not submitted to the rules of the marketplace, for she has stolen her own version of desire. As a personal shopper for her sister, she has found a way to look without having to buy, and transact without consuming. Her unplaceability in the imperial marketplace enables her to manufacture a very affordable desire, which she then invites her sister to partake of as antidote:

> "Hug me, kiss me, suck my juices
> Squeezed from goblin fruits for you,

> Goblin pulp and goblin dew.
> Eat me, drink me, love me;
> Laura, make much of me:
> For your sake I have braved the glen
> And had to do with goblin merchant men."
>
> (lines 468–74)

Interestingly, this "fiery antidote" (line 559) that Lizzie procures and then administers to Laura in the poem's highly charged moment of homoerotic exchange resembles the apparently throat-soothing, candied cough drops that were sold by mid-Victorian street sellers who would "prepare their sticks, &c., much in the same method as the manufacturers of the ordinary sweet-stuff."[67] Mayhew notes that such "medicinal confection[s]" were sometimes called "'lohochs,' which is an Arabic word . . . [that] signifies 'a thing to be licked.'"[68] As cough drop or candy-coated medicine, the poem's antidote emerges as a conflation of orality, commodity, and purportedly Eastern cure. Certainly, the antidote is both a sensuous, oral exchange and a bitter pill. After Lizzie has administered this cure, Laura's "lips began to scorch" (line 493) and "[s]wift fire spreads thro' her veins" (line 507).

While the imperial marketplace thus might appear to have supplied the sisters with both the cause of Laura's illness and the exotic cure, the way in which Lizzie uses the fruit as antidote is what enables her sister's recovery. Laura's shopping practices recall Michel de Certeau's emphasis on the importance of "what the cultural consumer 'makes' or 'does'" with commodities.[69] Laura's translation of the fruit into antidote is a productive "*poaching* . . . on the property of others" that makes visible both her inscription and transgressive mobility within consumer capitalism.[70]

Although Laura's cure is marked by "anguish" as much as "[p]leasure" (line 522), the ultimate enactment of desire in the poem—the sisters' oral exchange—is made possible only through a trip to the goblin market rather than a retreat from it. Laura's ability to take anything away from her experience with goblin men results from her bringing her willing gaze and desire to the market and going on to poach from it. Thus, the poem is not merely about whether women can wrest themselves from male signifying economies, in which their bodies are bound up with other forms of exchange, long enough to spend their coin. Indeed, the middle-class women shoppers who frequented London's oriental bazaars had access to enough currency to spend there. The goblins' violence indicates that they are not ultimately concerned with whether the sisters have money or whether they spend it in the market, and the poem is not primarily concerned with women's vexed relationship to capital. More significantly, as buyers conscripted to sell the empire, whether they use guile or force to do so, the goblins seem more intent on securing the sisters' compulsive and continued consumer desires, as evidenced by Laura's withdrawal symptoms once removed from the market. The goblins are consummate ad-men for imperial capitalism whose job it is to hawk and even impose tempting delights. Furbished by the ability of the imperial exhibitionary complex to showcase ever-new and exotic produce and to display the fruit in as tempting a manner as possible, the goblins hope that the sisters will ultimately, like any good shoppers, configure their ideas of desire and nationhood alike to those of the goblin market to be secured as loyal shoppers of the empire. *Goblin Market*, like the slippage of the Liberty catalogue cover, reveals the insidiousness of such a marketplace without downplaying the reality of its seductions. Endless consumer desire instead of curls or coins is what the goblins hope to gain.

If the violence of this marketplace is rendered transparent through the goblins' violent reactions, it is resisted through the actively desiring gazes of women shoppers. At the poem's climax, the moment at which the sisters deploy a shared bodily economics within which desire is produced, we must remember that the visual aspect of this exchange is enacted in the marketplace before it becomes a function of the sisters' exchange. Desire is first produced within the marketplace through technologies of looking, through window-shopping and the consumption of advertisements, not in an alternative female economy of the sisters' daily, domestic cake making and butter churning (lines 203–8) that grows up apart from the marketplace and routinely fails to satisfy Laura. Lizzie goes to market on her sister's behalf in such a way as to acknowledge the legitimacy of women's scopic desire in the marketplace. With her new determination to "[b]eg[i]n to listen and look" (line 328) at the very marketplace she had previously fled and warned Laura not to loiter in, Lizzie makes a well-calculated incursion into the goblin market that factors in the costs of doing so without sacrificing the pleasures of looking and tasting. Together, Lizzie and Laura carve out forms of resistance within an imperial space and, in the process, trouble forms of imposed consumerist desires manufactured by new technologies of spectacle, those technologies that were consistent with the aims of empire to fashion willing consumers of its symbolic economies.

As the exhibitionary spaces of British department stores sought to elicit women's desires through the orientalizing of commodities, women could locate possibilities for the deployment of desires within imperial capitalism. In imagining that women's pleasures need not be determined by consumer culture, *Goblin Market* suggests how women who shopped for exotic goods in early department stores such as Liberty's East India House staged through their unpredictable presence the tenuousness of the dream of empire. Women formed desires in the midst of a contested terrain, deploying a shopper's gaze that included the transgressive prerogative of looking without having to buy and, in the case of *Goblin Market*, of seeing through the constructed nature of imperial capitalism. The gendered consumer gaze reveals the extent to which empire's commercial mission relied on the naturalizing effects of commodification. Women's presence as lookers and shoppers in the Victorian oriental bazaars of the West End, as in Rossetti's goblin market, disrupted the apparently seamless imperial visual field that produced empire as something up for sale.

True to its fairy-tale form, *Goblin Market* imagines how women might figure within male economies, how they might subvert such economies, and how together they may bring their desires into a goblin market that has been created by the machinery of imperial spectacle. But not simply a fairy tale, the poem also functions as an (appropriately) orally transmitted shopping manual containing rather anarchic advice that the sisters pass on to their children:

> Laura would call the little ones
> And tell them of her early prime,
> Those pleasant days long gone
> Of not-returning time:
> Would talk about the haunted glen,
> The wicked, quaint fruit-merchant men[.]
> (lines 548–53)

As subversive shopping guide, it not only asserts the value of a shopping companion ("'For there is no friend like a sister'" [line 562]) but also advises that even women who would seem to occupy the peripheries of the marketplace will find that encounters with "wicked, quaint fruit-merchant men" (line 553) are inevitable. In other words, the poem resists any notion of origins, challenging the fiction that subjects are situated prior to or outside of capitalism and showing how women's pleasures form within the marketplace rather than outside of it. Judith Butler is similarly skeptical of critical projects that locate "specifically feminine pleasure 'outside' of culture as its prehistory or as its utopian future."[71] *Goblin Market* does not mark the typical retreat from the material facts of modernity, including its marketplaces and economies, but reveals the extent to which consumerism was produced as an imperial fantasy for women even as it explores how pleasure occurs in the midst of markets and materialities rather than apart from them. Rossetti's poetics of reserve elsewhere do not preclude the possibilities of a poetics of expenditure in *Goblin Market* that imagines such a marketplace. Despite the dangers of goblin commerce, Rossetti suggests that women need not sacrifice their desires in order to go to market.

Two

LADY AUDLEY'S SHOPPING DISORDERS

The year after Mary Elizabeth Braddon's *Lady Audley's Secret* (1862) appeared in volume form, Henry Mansel published "Sensation Novels," a *Quarterly Review* essay in which he accused sensation writers of "supply[ing] the cravings of a diseased appetite."[1] Mansel feared that sensation fiction was producing an undiscriminating class who read solely for "the pleasure of a nervous shock."[2] No better were the writers of sensation novels, he maintained, for they aimed for "[e]xcitement, and excitement alone" at the expense of promoting morality and good taste.[3] Many other reviewers seemed to agree with Mansel. A critic in the *Christian Remembrancer*, for example, charged that "[s]ensation writing is an appeal to the nerves rather than to the heart" and that its ultimate purpose was to "induce[ ] . . . a sort of thrill."[4] Clearly, the word *sensation* was beginning to acquire a new valence that emphasized affect as an uncontrollable somatic response. However, it was the "commercial atmosphere" of sensation fiction—an atmosphere "redolent of . . . the shop"—and the ways in which this genre's affective properties resembled the vagaries of consumer desire that also troubled Mansel.[5]

Sensation fiction owed much of its mass appeal to the commercial success of the periodical and circulating library, phenomena that for Mansel were not neutral modes of distribution but the means by which these somatic disturbances were perpetuated. In her assessment of sensation fiction in *Blackwoods* a year earlier, Margaret Oliphant had objected to "[t]he violent stimulant of serial publication—of *weekly* publication, with its necessity for frequent and rapid recurrence of piquant situation and startling incident."[6] By electing to publish in serial form, many sensation writers were ensuring a ready supply of consumable print that offered readers the serial pleasures of the shock of the new. *Lady Audley's Secret* appeared in installments, first in July 1861 in *Robin Goodfellow* and then, when that publication folded, in *Sixpenny Magazine* between January 1862 and December 1862. When the installments were collected together in volume form and deposited in circulating libraries, there was little to distinguish a sensation reader's "ephemeral interest" in the latest subscriptions and booklists from that of an aimless shopper's browsing: "the subscriber is often content to take the goods the gods provide him, glancing lazily down the library catalogue, and picking out some title which promises amusement or excitement."[7] Indeed, for Mansel, the circulating library "is to literature what a *magasin de modes* is to dress, giving us the latest fashion, and little more."[8]

The *grands magasins* or department stores, as seen in the previous chapter, were part of a new urban sphere of consumption that was being institutionalized in London's West End during the retail revolution of the 1860s. Sensation fiction and the new shopping emporia were thus historically coincident at a time when the domains of both sensation fiction and consumerism were increasingly becoming feminized in the cultural imagination.[9] The woman reader of sensation, as Susan David Bernstein puts it, was "the madame monster of the marketplace, the woman dazzled by her desires for material acquisitions and sensual pleasures."[10] In his objections to sensation fiction, Mansel thus suggestively links the affects of consuming sensation fiction—this "electrifying [of] the nerves"—to the feminizing affects of middle-class shopping, that is, a compulsion for ever-new consumerist diversions.[11]

As many critics were decrying the commodified mass appeal of sensation fiction and its reputed influence—its shocking tendency to evoke forms of mania in readers—an ancillary debate was erupting in that other commercial sphere, middle-class women's shopping, over the purported affects of consumerism on women. By midcentury, the popular, periodical, and medical press had begun identifying, classifying, and pathologizing new shopping disorders that ranged from idle browsing in the shops with no particular end or object in mind, to ransacking the goods but refusing to buy them, to outright shoplifting or kleptomania. Together, these discussions of women's frenzied behavior at sales, compulsive buying, and even stealing sensationalized a new breed of shopper who seemed particularly enabled by the democratic spaces and roving opportunities of the emergent department store.

Middle-class women's close proximity to commodities raised concerns that were not restricted to the public places where they shopped but extended to the homes that they were to maintain and decorate. Suspicion over the whims of commercially driven fashion and over a marketplace flooded with objects for the home led such interior decorating advocates as Julia McNair Wright, the author of *The Complete Home* (1879), to urge proper boundaries between people and objects: "Arranging the objects in the midst of which we live is establishing between us and them bonds of appropriateness or convenience: it is fixing habits without which man tends toward the savage state."[12] By the 1860s, the disorders of shopping associated with women's behavior in public had begun coming home, such that the bourgeois interior was not a space that guaranteed a discrete domestic subject but one in which the compulsive desires of the disorderly shopper and her serial relationship to commodities were reorganizing social relations and the relation of objects to the self. Just as sensation fiction was vilified by some for its disturbing influence on readers, so was shopping often criticized for its potential to incite women to forms of excess.

More than being historically coincident, however, the cultural logic that yoked the affects of consuming sensation fiction with compulsive consumer desire points to Victorian uncertainties about how to maintain normative femininity when this category was being deformed through the commercial marketplace. In keeping with what Ann Cvetkovich has termed the "affective economies" of sensation and an emphasis on "the forms of pleasure that capitalism produces"—that is, the contention that the political sphere does not exclude the affective domain and the everyday—this chapter considers how *Lady Audley's Secret* inscribes the disorderly woman shopper and her compulsive acquisition as a site of mid-Victorian anxiety, anxiety over the ways in which consumer practice and commodities were altering the bourgeois domestic subject's relationship to a world of consumer goods.[13]

Comprising an oppositional discourse to contemporary accounts of women's disruptions in the consumer marketplace—which emphasized such behavior as instances of deviance or pathology—*Lady Audley's Secret* shows how women's excessive spending and unruly conduct as consumers might be understood as transgressive practices that point to the constructed nature of femininity and class. The novel represents the unsettling affect of shopping through Lucy Audley's proximity to goods and her compulsive consumption, a spectacle that the text obsessively serializes through the practices associated with her self-fashioning, her exaggerated Pre-Raphaelite portrait, and the commodity objects displayed in her boudoir. Together, these come to figure as a kind of accumulation, a textual kleptomania that attests to the artificial nature of femininity. Lucy's secret is not madness, nor does it concern the revelation of any true or fundamental identity as Helen Talboys that might seem to exist apart from consumption. Rather, the fictive self produced through consumer disorders points to the constructedness of gender and class and how neither is formed prior to the operations of commodity exchange. Lucy performs and perpetrates a version of identity theft by producing "Lady Audley" through a world of commodities that is central to her economic negotiations and social mobility. When the novel's sole male consumer-turned-detective, Robert Audley, comes both to read Lucy's artifice as an index of her consumer-driven identity fraud and to renounce the feminizing affects of consumption in favor of male bourgeois identity, Lady Audley cannot be expelled from the text. Even when she is exiled to a continental asylum, the narrative of Robert's vocational and familial consolidation remains unstable. For the persistence of Lucy's boudoir as a scene of commodity display at the end of the novel attests to how the affects of consumption are reproduced as a remainder of capitalist exchange.

Rather than participating in a critique of consumerism and its capacity to disorder middle-class domestic subjectivity, *Lady Audley's Secret* explores possibilities for the self that formed in and through a world of consumer goods and practices to the extent that the subject is no longer seen to master them. Contrary to the Marxist conception of commodity fetishism, which argues that a relationship between things has been substituted for a relationship between people, *Lady Audley's Secret* reveals that there is no original or authentic relationship between people that has been displaced or lost by the fact of market exchange. Instead, the subject is shaped and formed through the performative act of exchange.[14] Jean-Christophe Agnew has argued for just such a "commodity aesthetic," one that "celebrates those moments when the very boundaries between the self and the commodity world collapse."[15] *Lady Audley's Secret* is deeply invested in a form of collapse, in the affecting proximity of commodities. This proximity does not threaten the integrity of any originary self but is the condition for the formation of bourgeois identity. Another form of de Certeau's cultural poaching—and a tactile practice, in contrast to Lizzie's visual tactics in *Goblin Market*—the disorders of consumption inscribe a mobile, commodified form of identity, one that alters the relations between people and objects and between the domestic and commercial spheres.

The bourgeois home, as a contiguous space of the department store, did not constitute and consolidate domestic subjectivity as a form of interiority. Rather, it revealed the ways in which identity was, by midcentury, being fabricated through the disorders of a world of consumer objects and practices.[16] *Lady Audley's Secret* acknowledges the proximity of commodity objects for the Victorians and the ways in which women's consumption in particular had the capacity to disrupt stable notions of gender, class, and subjectivity. Moreover, in documenting how the rogue desires of the compulsive shopper proliferate in excess of fixed notions of identity, the novel also imagines how the affect of serial consumption holds out the possibility for the production of new forms of mobile identities and pleasures.

"Formless Desires" and the Disorderly Shopper

By the 1860s, Britain's urban shopping districts seemed to have increasingly come to be populated by a new species of woman consumer, the disorderly shopper. Even as critics suspected that sensation novels were inciting compulsive appetite, particularly in female readers, so too did contemporary accounts document—even sensationalize—middle-class women's overwhelming desire to consume and the startling effects that commodity display was having on them. The world of commodities, like the world of sensation fiction, seemed to be provoking consumers in new ways and introducing unruly conduct into Britain's urban shopping districts. With the introduction of the department store and the general expansion of many established draper's shops into larger, multilevel emporia arose new practices of shopping. While shop assistants might still wait on customers, as they had in previous decades, there were new opportunities for customers to browse on their own. In the department store, the diminishing role of the shopkeeper or assistant as mediator between buyer and merchandise meant a greater access to goods, as these were more openly displayed or more available to the touch. In the department store, which often included waiting rooms and other services meant to recall the comforts of home, many women were not only getting comfortable while they shopped but also getting closer to the goods. The department store, then, offered not only a new visual spectacle but also a tactile experience, as women were handling the stock in unprecedented ways; this proximity to commodities was altering shopping practices and producing new identifications with merchandise.

Being surrounded by consumer goods was part of the pleasure of consuming, by which the very practice of shopping was being redefined. "[T]he delicious aroma which appears to attach to this amusement," mused Eliza Lynn Linton, "is somehow connected with the endless possibilities of indulgence which belong to it. The true delight of shopping seems to be realized when the potential purchaser is surrounded . . . with a whole region of material luxuries, in view of which she falls into a kind of reverie filled with deliciously absorbing fancies."[17] But with these new opportunities and access came the possibility for distraction, seduction, and temptation. In "The Ethics of Shopping," a plea for better working conditions for shopgirls, Lady M. Jeune addresses the ways in which shopping had become by the end of the century a "struggle against overwhelming temptations."[18] She recalls a time, decades earlier, when "[t]here was little or no display in the windows. Each shop had its own speciality. . . . We bought our goods at these various shops, and dutifully followed in the steps of our forefathers, paying for the things we had at the end of the year. . . . A bonnet or a cloak for winter, or a silk gown, was chosen, after due consideration as to colour, price, and material, and the placidity of life remained undisturbed by the intervention of any temptation to wander beyond the legitimate wants of the moment. . . . An afternoon's shopping was a solemn and dreary affair."[19] But with the proliferation of goods and the expansion of retail spaces, Lady Jeune notes, the days of quiet, measured, and deliberate shopping have ended. Instead, "when we get to our shop, there are so many more things that we never thought of till they presented their obtrusive fascinations on every side."[20] She goes on to account for the new "seductions of shopping" by enumerating the conditions of the affective domain of the department store, conditions that recall the "electrifying [of] the nerves" that Mansel associated with sensation fiction: "There are many shops in London into which one cannot safely trust oneself. There are the drawbacks of noise, heat, and overcrowding, but they are more than counterbalanced by the brightness of the electric light and the brilliancy of colour, and the endless variety on every side." By "gathering together under one roof all kinds of goods—clothing, millinery, groceries, furniture," the department store ensured greater convenience but also "contributed to the temptation of spending money."[21]

If the shopper was often constructed as a potential victim in the marketplace who might spend excessively when subjected to the sensory overload of the department store, the temptation to buy was linked to other possible forms of seduction in public. Judith Walkowitz has noted that shopping "exposed [women] to new dangers. For many Victorian observers, immersion in the sensuous world of consumption rendered women suspect—subject to the seduction of men and sales promotion and to their own uncontrollable impulses."[22] Although Linton elsewhere admits to the pleasures of shopping, in an 1862 article entitled "Out Walking" she sets out strict parameters for women's appearance in public, advising against excessive window-shopping and recommending that women adopt a neutral demeanor when they appear in public spaces of consumption: "If she knows how to walk in the streets, self-possessed and quietly, with not too lagging and not too swift a step; if she avoids lounging about the shop-windows, and resolutely forgoes even the most tempting displays of finery; if she can attain to that enviable street-talent, and pass men without looking at them, yet all the while seeing them; if she knows how to dress as only a lady can, avoiding loud colours . . . if she has nothing of the gaper in her ways," she need not "fear harassment. But if she lingers at shop-windows, counting the flowers in the bonnets . . . if, in a word, she does any thing to attract observation, she will most likely get more of it than she wants, and be made the object of attentions not altogether to her mind."[23] The threat of being "spoken to" was recognized enough that magazines such as *Girl's Own Paper* identified window-shopping and loitering in the streets as potential dangers that could invite harassment.[24] It was indeed possible to mistake the most well-meaning shopper for another sort of public woman; well-dressed prostitutes sporting the latest finery did frequent fashionable shopping districts, where they mingled with legitimate shoppers in similar dress.[25]

But as Rossetti makes evident in *Goblin Market*, the Victorian woman shopper could not be construed simply as a victim; by no means did she always respond with submission and compliance to the cries of the marketplace to "come buy." Lynda Nead points out that even "[t]he figure of the daydreaming window shopper . . . allows us to think [that] . . . [t]he intermingling and proximity presented by . . . the . . . shop window demanded a continual process of redefinition and renegotiation of identity . . . ; gendered identities could be adopted or assumed for a time and then relinquished."[26] While the marketplace may have called out for women to come and buy, they did not respond to this invitation uniformly; indeed, a woman shopper's operations in the marketplace could prove disruptive or less than legitimate. In the 1890s, the *Drapers' Record* (a periodical for retailers) classified versions of the most common disorderly shoppers: the "tab" looked over all kinds of goods and put unreasonable demands on shop assistants, while the "rover" "ransack[ed] an entire stock without making a single purchase."[27] Such shoppers recall Lizzie of *Goblin Market*, forming their own transgressive pleasure in the shopping districts of the West End by spending the day in the shops looking at goods, even ransacking them, but leaving without buying. An Edwardian musical satire of Harrods entitled *Our Miss Gibbs* included a joke that exploited what had become a well-known stereotype of shoppers:

> We'll take a look at all the lot,
> All the lot, all the lot,
> But we will not
> Attempt to buy,
> We'll look and try,
> But never buy![28]

Britain's retailing revolution had produced not only new temptations and dangers for women but also the grounds for a new, aimless version of shopping and for new gendered forms of public disorder associated with idleness. Idleness was not merely associated with women's victimization, for it was also being identified as the condition for women's potentially disruptive behaviors in the marketplace, and these shopping disorders came to be enumerated and even spoofed in popular form.

While the women's fashion papers often served to promote shopping as a pleasurable enterprise for women, they also seemed concerned with making sure that women directed their consumer attentions appropriately. In this other capacity as conduct or etiquette manuals, they constructed women's undirected desires as idleness that could lead not only to temptation or victimization but also to disruptive forms of conduct in public. The women's periodical *Queen* decried the shopping practices of women who wandered the shops aimlessly, full of appetite but possessing no ostensible purpose, only to "deposit the burden of their formless desire."[29] Women's behavior during sales is often figured as a particularly grotesque variant of women's shopping disorder, in which the individual shopper's obsessions become magnified into a form of group hysteria, with women's "formless desires"—in this case the vague desire for a bargain without a particular object in mind—leading to traffic jams in the aisles of shops and in the streets: "The crush at such sales is as bad as that of a fashionable entertainment, and the carriages which fill up the street during the sales are a serious impediment to locomotion."[30] The trade publication *Draper* published a popular joke concerning such shoppers that circulated among retail workers. "When is a lady not a lady? Answer: When she attends a sale."[31] The riddle cut to the heart of the matter by highlighting the ways in which a woman's disorderly shopping cast doubt on her respectability and class.

Some fashion papers sought to correct women's potentially unregulated consumer appetites by offering a model of the normative, self-regulating shopper that responded to and redressed disorder. The magazines advised women to ensure that their shopping excursions were always disciplined and purposeful. "By constructing women as rational consumers," Walkowitz writes, "magazines emulated the male ideal of the consumer," a masculine subject whom Rachel Bowlby characterizes as "calculating, and efficient, aware of his aims and wants."[32] *Queen* advised women to shop in such a way as to be beyond reproach in their public visibility. The proper shopper was one who did not wander without purpose or handle the goods too much but applied purpose or sensible "business habits" to the enterprise of shopping.[33] Just as women were to remain orderly while shopping, so were they to manage their consumer desires at home. To address this potential problem, women's domestic economy manuals (as the next chapter will show) inscribed the ideal of the female household manager in contrast to the extravagant woman, who spent beyond her means and put the solvency of her household at risk or wore clothes that were not commensurate with her social station.

Perhaps the most deviant permutation of the disorderly shopper was the "prowler," or shoplifter, who entered shops "not to inspect but to 'lift' these productions."[34] As Elaine S. Abelson explains, the shoplifter "represented something entirely different: its context was the department store, it was a pervasive phenomenon, and it demonstrated, quite dramatically, a form of deviant behavior by a new group, the middle class."[35] Although there had certainly been shop-thieves in centuries past, the Victorian shoplifter was a product of the midcentury retailing revolution, including the department store, where democratic spaces and displays invited middle-class women to roam relatively freely and to get closer to the goods, conditions that also lent themselves to avoiding detection.[36] The operations of the shoplifter, the disorderly shopper par excellence, best illuminate the seriality or aimless desire of Lady Audley's relationship to commodities, as well as the self-fashioned possibilities of commodified identity. As the exemplar of the disorderly shopper, the shoplifter was transgressive in the ways in which she amplified the problem of "formless desire" through the apparently random and serial nature of her conquests, stealing not out of need but apparently out of compulsive desire.

Posing as a legitimate shopper, and thus difficult to detect, the shoplifter introduced uncertainty about what it meant to appear as a middle-class woman in public. She presented an interpretive difficulty: how to read a woman as both thief and middle class, how to account for her exploits as random and even pleasurable. Attempts such as those made by the ladies' papers to discipline women's shopping could not account fully for respectable women who were committing acts that would ordinarily be deemed criminal. Whereas in previous centuries the working-class shop-thief had often taken her place alongside other common thieves, it was more difficult to criminalize middle-class women who stole in mid-Victorian times, since to do so would place pressure on stable meanings of gender and class. A popular street ballad, "Ladies Don't Go Thieving" (ca. 1867), delights in the topsy-turvy world of lady shoplifters and illustrates the difficulty of reading the activities of the middle-class shoplifter. Presenting herself in public as a lady, the ballad's shoplifter seems at first to conform to expectations of a proper feminine subject:

> Oh, don't we live in curious times,
> You scarce could be believing,
> When Frenchmen fight and Emperors die
> And ladies go a-thieving.
>
> A beauty of the West End went,
> Around a shop she lingers,
> And there upon some handkerchiefs
> She clapped her pretty fingers.
>
> Into the shop she gently popped;
> The world is quite deceiving
> When ladies have a notion got
> To ramble out a-thieving.[37]

As a popular form—anonymously authored and oft-repeated—the ballad seems appropriate to this roving shopper, who regularly transgresses the boundaries of proper ownership and the expected working of capitalist exchange where, to get that close to the goods, you are meant to have already paid for them. This ballad features a shopper who enjoys a closer proximity than usual to the goods. No obedient consumer, the shoplifter is represented in the midst of an elegant heist; she "lingers" nonchalantly in a West End shop before she "clap[s] her pretty fingers" upon some handkerchiefs. Unraveling the cultural logic that links woman as object to material goods exchanged in the marketplace, the shoplifter circumvents the logic of the market. Her caprice not only leads her to steal some handkerchiefs, but ultimately blurs the meaning of "ladies." "The world is quite deceiving," the ballad concludes wryly, "When ladies have a notion got / To ramble out a-thieving." Ending thus, it highlights this lady's pleasure as forming not only through the act of stealing but also from her transgression of what is considered acceptable behavior.

The lingering anxiety that becomes attached to this shoplifter is not self-consciousness on her part but the speaker's declared uncertainty about how to read what has just taken place. The ballad encodes not the difficulty of catching a shoplifter in the act but the question of how to read the woman who is involved, and how expectations about her class become disordered when she enters the marketplace and disturbs its operations. The shoplifter exploits this uncertainty about how to interpret middle-class women's normative behaviors in the consumer marketplace, about who is appearing there legitimately as a lady and who is exploiting her status there. Her transgression is not so much the crime of stealing but the pleasure she takes in perpetrating a fraud or kind of identity theft that permits her to appear in public as a respectable woman even as her conduct, her indulgence of a whim to lift some goods, undermines expectations about proper femininity.

The difficulty of reading ladies gone a-thieving is apparent not only in popular accounts but also in the psycho-medical discourse that sought to account for shoplifting as a female nervous disorder.[38] The medical community debated the extent to which kleptomania might constitute a legitimate form of disease. Although a diagnosis of kleptomania originally could apply to men and women equally, "kleptomania quickly attached itself to women, specifically to the female reproductive economy" by midcentury.[39] Much like hysteria, kleptomania was thought to be caused by menstrual disorders and by the disruptions of puberty, pregnancy, and menopause in the female life cycle.[40] When the compulsion to steal was not incidental but was accompanied by other physical disorders, often gynecological in nature, the diagnosis of kleptomania could carry medical validity.

Not only a subject of interest in medical communities, kleptomania emerged as a possible defense in criminal matters. As an increasingly recognized psycho-medical disorder, kleptomania could potentially become a way to account for—and sometimes even legally excuse—middle-class women's shopping crimes. While it is true that the eighteenth-century genteel shoplifter who was caught in the act might use her social position to secure a quiet end to the matter so that she and her family would not be publicly humiliated, the Victorian shoplifter could, unlike earlier shop-thieves, offer the defense that she could be shown medically to be a kleptomaniac, that, for all intents and purposes, she did not know what had come over her.[41]

While proving that a woman suffered from kleptomania might release her from criminal prosecution, the logic that produced her behaviors as "normative" also potentially confined her.[42] Whenever a woman was absolved of criminal responsibility for her shoplifting crimes because it could be shown that she suffered from a diagnosable case of the "stealing insanity," medical and legal discourse effectively reinscribed biological essentialist notions of femininity. "Letting cultural attitudes shape their diagnoses," Abelson writes, "physicians connected woman's mind and body in an analytical framework that, in its dependence on the organic absolutes of sexual difference and human nature, excluded other possible interpretations."[43] A diagnosis of kleptomania thus reproduced associations between femininity, irrationality, somatic disruption, and illness—conditions that recall popular descriptions of the reputed effects of commodity display on women shoppers.

Much like critiques of sensation fiction, then, which linked the supposed somatic disturbances of popular novels to the feminization of fiction, medical discourses of kleptomania tended to reaffirm feminine sexuality as pathological. However, in an article entitled "Kleptomania," published in the *Journal of Mental Science* in 1863, physician John Bucknill issued something of a departure from the usual conflation of women, disease, and consumption. Bucknill's medical opinion of shoplifting provides an interesting reformulation, one that problematizes women's shopping disorders with reference to the affective domain of consumer culture and the material realities of class. Bucknill does not limit his account of why women shoplift to a purely medical assessment; rather, his cultural diagnosis demonstrates how medical discourses about women's consumer compulsion, much like popular ones, were never purely clinical or objective but instead tied to prevailing notions of femininity.

Departing from a strict psycho-medical explanation, Bucknill also goes beyond Lady Jeune's observations about shopping as a temptation. Instead, he offers what amounts to a class-based analysis of how consumer culture has manufactured new objects of desire for bourgeois women and temptations that they find difficult to resist:

> But there is another aspect to this matter. The struggle for existence in the middle, and even in the upper classes of our complex social system, combined with the prevailing fashion of an emulative and showy expenditure, make the sense of want felt keenly in many an English home, where no traces of vulgar poverty are discernable. The really poor steal because they want bread; the relatively poor are tempted to steal because they desire the possession of that which seems, to a mind trained in a bad school, as essential as bread itself. And how are they tempted? . . . Are they not stimulated to covet its possession by every ingenious device which the mind of man or of woman can devise, by streets of gorgeous shops, touted in every possible manner by the most pertinacious inducements,

> and almost persecutions to buy, buy, buy; so that it has at last become the custom of the town-bred Englishwoman of the present day to spend no inconsiderable portion of her time in passing from shop to emporium, from haberdashery store to magazin de mode, in the discharge of that new and peculiar duty of life called "shopping." Can we be surprised that when the means fail to gratify the desires thus stimulated and thus tempted, that in some few instances the desire of the eye should prove too strong for the moral sense?[44]

Bucknill's analysis is that this new shopping compulsion is an affliction peculiar to middle-class women, whose moral resolve is to his mind understandably weakened in a new goblin market where luxuries have become necessities. While Bucknill refuses to apply a diagnosis of kleptomania where there is no medically sound reason to do so, he concedes that "we can find more pity for the poor woman who purloins a piece of lace . . . than for the smirking fellow who has caught her in his haberdashery trap by lying advertisements."[45] Although Bucknill insists on maintaining strict medical definitions regarding "stealing insanity," his assessment of shoplifting departs in this instance from the biological essentialism of many other medical theorists, in that he identifies shoplifting as a compulsion that is produced through consumer culture rather than being somehow endemic to women's bodily constitution and sees it as perpetuated by material desire, a desire for class mobility. In doing so, Bucknill rejects the terms of both medical and popular discussions of women's shopping disorders, both of which tended to cast consumer culture as a site in which women's preexisting, even biological tendency to disorder becomes detectible. Bucknill instead seems to intuit how women were formulating new desires that were not physiologically inherent but emerged through the lure of class mobility and the material conditions of Britain's new shopping environment.

Bucknill's diagnosis of the class implications of shopping disorder thus departs from those medical and legal discourses that attempted to account for women's shopping disorders and reinscribed essentialist notions of femininity. By attending to Adela Pinch's recommendation that, as cultural critics, we must "rehabilitate 'perversions' as symptoms of culture rather than of pathology," Victorian women's shoplifting can be seen not as an expression of pathology or aberrance but as a cultural index.[46] What is most interesting about the shoplifter is not so much her deviance from disciplined and normative middle-class femininity as what cultural work her shoplifting performs. Shoplifting, as a mode of disorderly consumption, depends on women's proximity to goods and their serial and even random acquisition. In an analysis extending de Certeau's tactics of the everyday, shoplifting may be considered as a performative tactic that makes visible the ways in which femininity is always a construction or a masquerade. The typical plunder of the shoplifter—often items such as handkerchiefs or gloves—serves as the props or supplements through which the guise of femininity is both fashioned and naturalized. With reference to shoplifting, Leslie Camhi points out that "[f]emininity is always already stolen, a dissimulated mask, veil, or fiction of difference."[47] Camhi here recalls the well-known essay "Womanliness as Masquerade," in which Joan Rivière refuses to distinguish "between 'natural' and artificial femininity."[48] "Womanliness," Rivière writes, "therefore could be assumed and worn as a mask, to hide the possession of masculinity and to avert the reprisals expected if she was found to possess it—much as a thief will turn out his pockets and ask to be searched to prove that he has not stolen the goods."[49] By ransacking commodity displays, the disorderly-shopper-turned-shoplifter rehearses a fundamental condition of gender: that femininity is always premised on a theft of masculinity. That she is middle class also casts doubt on stable notions of class. Moreover, through her anarchic behaviors in the marketplace, the shoplifter disrupts the usual terms of capitalism, which, like sexual exchange, depends on "the substitutional logic of the same."[50]

To regard stolen plunder as fetish objects and the disorderly shopper as fetishistic, however, is to risk reinscribing the concept of phallic substitution that stands in for women's cultural inscription as lack.[51] As a disorderly consumer, Lucy Audley is not such an embodiment of lack or of narcissistic self-division. In revealing how femininity is a fiction or construct, her masquerade is not merely compensatory but actively exploits the fictions of gender and class and in doing so actively fashions other forms of excessive identity. A version of the disorderly shopper, Lucy formulates a contingent self through the roving opportunities and "formless desires" of compulsive consumption. Rather than casting her confrontation with a world of objects as a dangerous loss of ego boundaries, we might better understand Lucy's proximity to goods as that which ensures the production of her classed and gendered performance as Lady Audley. This desire for mobility and for the appearance of affluence enacts a new relationship to objects. Confounding the usual terms of Victorian women's self-regulated relationships to objects, in which objects must be mastered so that one can "represent the self as an object in the world," Lucy's commodity goods do not serve to produce an autonomous form of subjectivity that is characterized by the desire "to keep objects in their place."[52] Rather, Lucy manufactures her identity as Lady Audley rather sensationally at the moment of projecting herself in and through a world of goods. In *Lady Audley's Secret*, the disorderly shopper rehearses the ways in which identity was increasingly tied to the operations of capital exchange, with subjectivity as the site of radical rearrangement. In the age of consumerism, identity had no existence prior to the marketplace but was generated through one's proximity to commodities, objects that were to be encountered in the department store and bourgeois home alike.

"Elegant Disorder": Home-Shopping with Lady Audley

Sensation novels were notorious for their disorderly domestic heroines, featuring disruptive, impulsive, criminal women who are not socially marginal but reside at the heart of legitimate places in British society. "The genre," Cvetkovich observes, "creates sensationalism by locating crime where one would least expect it—not only in the home but in the actions of a woman—and in the process violates the separation of the private and public spheres crucial to Victorian culture."[53] "What do we know," asks the narrator of *Lady Audley's Secret*, "of the mysteries that may hang about the houses we enter? . . . Foul deeds have been done under the most hospitable roofs, terrible crimes have been committed amid the fairest scenes, and have left no trace upon the spot where they were done."[54]

The crimes of bigamy, attempted murder, and arson in the novel seem rather expected, however, when we consider a less visible but arguably even more disruptive scandal. For perhaps the most disorderly impulses and mysteries of the novel are consumerist in nature. Lucy's relationship to objects, then, does more than rehearse the long-standing Western association of women with excessive ornament and voracious desire.[55] If, as Katherine Montwieler argues, the novel is a "subversive domestic manual" that reveals the secret "to becoming [a] lady," it is a truly radical form of conduct literature with advice that departs from the recommendations of ladies' magazines of the period to shop with composure.[56] Lucy's compulsive consumption in the novel—visible in her self-adornment and the decorated interior spaces that are associated with her—is not evidence of a lack of control but instead is central to her economic manipulations and her ambitions of class mobility, and thus it constitutes a threat to the status quo. The fact of Lucy's spending is not as scandalous as what this spending achieves and what ideologies it makes visible. Jill L. Matus points out that "what seems primarily to be the matter with Lady Audley is that she threatens to violate class boundaries and exclusions, and to get away with appropriating social power beyond her entitlement."[57] While mid-Victorian constructions of the disorderly woman shopper tended to attach the affective disorders of consumer desire to the supposed vagaries of the female bodily constitution, *Lady Audley's Secret* shows the operations of a materially produced desire for class mobility at work and reveals the gender and class implications of Lucy's acts of consumption. On the one hand, Lucy seems to manifest the symptoms that contemporary medicine typically ascribed to women kleptomaniacs. We are told that she suffers from nervous disorders for which she has been provided with several medicinal remedies (281) and that she is said to possess a "latent insanity" (385), a condition Lucy fears she has inherited from her mother. But while Lucy's profile recalls that of the kleptomaniac's, the novel's medical representative, Dr. Mosgrave, does not finally commit to diagnosing Lucy as medically insane: "The lady is not mad.... She has the cunning of madness, with the prudence of intelligence. I will tell you what she is, Mr. Audley. She is dangerous!" (385). Dr. Mosgrave senses that Lucy is all too aware of what she is doing through her excesses. She is no monomaniac but a canny manipulator of her economic and social situation.

The representation of Lucy in the novel, as compulsive consumer, an "Anglicized version" of Emma Bovary, thus constitutes an active intervention in mid-Victorian discourses of the disorderly shopper.[58] Although Lucy does not steal from shops as a more conventional shoplifter might, she perpetuates another form of disorder, deception, or heist: fashioning herself as an upper-class woman amounts to a form of consumer-enabled fraud. The clothing, accessories, and commodity goods with which she surrounds herself and with which she is repeatedly associated not only conceal her identities as middle-class Helen Maldon (and after she marries her first husband, George, as Helen Talboys) and later as governess Lucy Graham but also, and more important, secure her class performance as Lady Audley. While she aspires to an aristocratic station, her consumer project is a decidedly bourgeois one. Rudi Laermans points out that the bourgeois shopper emerged in the context of department stores and advertising, a field that "link[ed] status and 'good taste' to shopping and consumerism."[59] A compulsive consumer who is self-manufactured to a high gloss and is most herself when she is associated with her overstuffed boudoir, Lucy is a lady gone a-thieving who is guilty of transgressing and disordering class lines. She is poised to bring the scandal of her disorders into the home, even as she projects the image of an aristocratic version of the Angel in the House.

Fashioning herself as a lady, Lucy perpetuates a version of identity theft that reveals the mobile possibilities of an identity forged through commodities and consumer practices. Being a lady is a matter of performance; it can "potentially be faked."[60] Not the childish doll she appears to be, Lucy manipulates her appearance, then places this imprint of "femininity exaggerated" on the decorated domestic spaces associated with her.[61] As the text highlights the artifice of her class masquerade, it also reveals how gender, too, is a cultural construction. "By foregrounding Lady Audley's impersonation of proper femininity," Lyn Pykett observes, "the novel does more than simply focus attention on the feminine duplicity in which the entire narrative operates. It also explores and exploits fears that the respectable ideal, or proper feminine, may simply be a form of acting, just one role among other possible roles."[62] This hyperfemininity, moreover, is a commodified form of femininity that trades on stock images of women and, in doing so, reveals the constructed nature of gender.

Not only making visible the ideological production of class and gender, Lucy's consumerism also inscribes an alternative model of identity. Pykett has suggested that Braddon's heroines are marked by a slippery, discursive doubleness: "[F]requent changes in point of view involve the reader in constantly shifting power relations with the heroine. . . . These constant shifts tend to keep the heroine's meaning and significance in a state of flux."[63] Lucy's consumption is the specific condition through which she formulates her contingent form of identity. She is always in the process of making herself. An identity thief with an appetite for goods, Lucy suggests the transgressive possibilities of commodified identity, for the mobile, performative self that may be formed through an affecting proximity to consumer goods.

"The mask that [Lucy] wears" (290) is not obvious to Robert until much later, but from the beginning of the novel Lady Audley is a carefully arranged and mannered production. One of the first descriptions of Lucy emphasizes the manufactured nature of her appearance. She has perfected the image of the innocent angel:

> Lucy was better loved and more admired than the baronet's daughter. That very childishness had a charm which few could resist. The innocence and candour of an infant beamed in Lady Audley's fair face, and shone out of her large and liquid blue eyes. The rosy lips, the delicate nose, the profusion of fair ringlets, all contributed to preserve to her beauty the character of extreme youth and freshness. She owned to twenty years of age, but it was hard to believe her more than seventeen. Her fragile figure, which she loved to dress in heavy velvets and stiff rustling silks, till she looked like a child *tricked out for a masquerade* [my emphasis], was as girlish as if she had just left the nursery. All her amusements were childish. She hated reading, or study of any kind, and loved society; . . . [she would] loll on one of the sofas in her luxurious dressing-room, discussing a new costume for some coming dinner party, or sit chattering . . . , with her jewel box beside her, upon the satin cushions, and Sir Michael's presents spread out in her lap, while she counted and admired her treasures. (90)

Lucy is indeed tricked out for a masquerade: a masquerade as Lady Audley. The mask of child-bride is a well-executed persona. By adopting it, Lucy seems to fulfill the norms of compliant, passive femininity.[64] Meanwhile, Alicia Audley has "undisguised contempt for her step-mother's childishness and frivolity" (90) and reveals this contempt in conversation with Robert: "I'm sorry to find you can only admire wax dolls" (93). In observing that her stepmother's beauty is the "ideal of beauty [that is] to be found in a toy-shop" (280), she suggests Lucy's status as an artificial, even commercial product. Whereas consumer culture might manufacture images of femininity that perpetuate stereotypes and fixed roles, women's strategic uses of consumer culture do not necessary replicate such norms. Lucy might appear obedient and ornamental, and thus harmless, but in fact "she threatens bourgeois culture by too closely parodying its ideal, and revealing it as a hollow idol."[65] Lucy actively exploits the appearance of innocence, and it becomes a good cover for this deliberate, calculating woman. Not the childish doll she appears to be, Lucy is a sensational confection, the sort of unlikely lady criminal that Linton identifies as a new breed of heroine in sensation fiction: "Instead of five foot ten of black and brown, they have gone in for four foot nothing of pink and yellow; instead of tumbled masses of raven hair, they have shining coils of purest gold. . . . In daily life, who is the really formidable woman to encounter?—the . . . broad-shouldered giantess, . . . or the pert, smart, trim little female?"[66]

Lucy's unlikely weapons include her clothing and frequent wardrobe changes that highlight the way in which her manicured persona is secured through repetition, through the seriality of the latest fashion.[67] Throughout the novel, her dress and accessories are almost obsessively detailed, from her beloved sable furs that she proudly reveals "cost sixty guineas" (140), to an artfully unassuming but clearly costly "morning costume of delicate muslin, elaborate laces, and embroideries" (338), to "her most gorgeous silk; a voluminous robe of silvery, shimmering blue, that made her look as if she had been arrayed in moonbeams" (347). Rather than inert, feminized miscellany, Lucy's dress and toilet, right down to her "pencilled eyebrows" (114), are central to her masquerade. The text at one point actively discloses the ways in which a lady is an artificial phenomenon who is manufactured through cosmetics, false hair and teeth, and the invisible labors of her maid:

> Amongst all privileged spies, a lady's-maid has the highest privileges. It is she who bathes Lady Theresa's eyes with eau-de-cologne after her lady-ship's quarrel. . . . She has a hundred methods for the finding out of her mistress's secrets. . . . [S]he knows when the ivory complexion is bought and paid for—when the pearly teeth are foreign substances fashioned by the dentist—when the glossy plaits are the relics of the dead, rather than the property of the living; and she knows other and more sacred secrets than these. She knows when the sweet smile is more false than Madame Levison's enamel, and far less enduring—when the words that issue from between gates of borrowed pearls are more disguised and painted than the lips which help to shape them. (346)

That female gentility is a matter of performance is not a secret to the maid who assists Lady Audley by adding false hair or enameling her skin with cosmetics. What is concealed from others is actually working-class knowledge, and the novel implies the classed implications of this artificial and commercial self-production. The text also knowingly casts Phoebe, Lucy's maid, as a double who, "under the shrouded avenues in the garden, you might have easily mistaken . . . for my lady" (138), suggesting that with the right accessories, working-class Phoebe could look just like Lady Audley.

Perhaps the most striking representation of the excessively constructed nature of femininity is found in another of Lucy's accessories, the Pre-Raphaelite portrait of her that stands on an easel, as yet unfinished, in the antechamber of her private rooms:

> No one but a pre-Raphaelite would have so exaggerated every attribute of that delicate face as to give a lurid lightness to the blonde complexion, and a strange, sinister light to the deep blue eyes. No one but a pre-Raphaelite could have given to that pretty pouting mouth the hard and almost wicked look it had in the portrait. . . .
>
> Her crimson dress, exaggerated like all the rest in this strange picture, hung about her in folds that looked like flames, her fair head peeping out of the lurid mass of colour, as if out of a raging furnace. Indeed, the crimson dress, the sunshine on the face, the red gold gleaming in the yellow hair, the ripe scarlet of the pouting lips, the glowing colours of each accessory of the minutely-painted background, all combined to render the first effect of the painting by no means an agreeable one. (107)

At first the painting might seem offered up—even fetishized—by a narrative gaze mediated through Robert Audley's attempts to read his young aunt. The painting might appear to package her as a consumable object, an advertisement for the accomplished, genteel woman. The Pre-Raphaelite aesthetic seems consistent with such a woman, for such portraiture often presents images of women that lend themselves to a consuming gaze. Indeed, Robert and George anticipate viewing this painting so much that they defer the pleasure of consuming it and "looked at the [other] paintings on the walls first, leaving this unfinished portrait for a *bonne bouche*" (106).

But the endless repetitions of flowing hair and sensuous lips that we associate with the Pre-Raphaelite subject actually construct not a readily reducible image but an exaggerated version of femininity that calls attention to its constructedness. As Robert catalogues the details of the painting, this blazon does not finally fragment Lady Audley into body parts for easy consumption, does not finally produce an anatomization of her. Instead, the blazon is excessive and hyperbolic. Her dress color is "lurid," her eyes "sinister," and her mouth "almost wicked." The painting is both her and not her. "It was so like and yet so unlike; it was as if you had burned strange-coloured fires before my lady's face, and by their influence brought out new lines and new expressions never seen in it before" (107). Rather than the childish woman Robert is accustomed to, the portrait has "something of the aspect of a beautiful fiend" (107). This ghastly vision disturbs Robert's attempts to master the image, a parody of femininity that cannot easily be consumed or mastered by the male gaze. No *bonne bouche*, the painting proves indigestible. The shock of this painting derives not only from the fact that it will eventually reveal to George that his wife is not dead but also from its nature as a testament to the unstable nature of femininity. The same woman who seems in life an angel is here a fiend. Alice remarks, "*We* have never seen my lady look as she does in that picture; but I think that she *could* look so" (108), suggesting that Lucy can knowingly adopt and deploy looks. If Lucy can adopt an innocent guise, she may well be able to deploy this more sinister one. This is not a painting to be viewed effortlessly; rather, it highlights Lucy's status as the active manipulator of her self-presentation rather than the object of a mastering gaze, as consumer rather than consumed.

When Robert later examines the painting following its completion, the narrator moves from the view of Lucy in the painting to Lucy in the flesh, as she bends over her bedridden husband in a room adjacent to the antechamber that houses the portrait. It is easy to substitute her here for the painting, for even in the flesh, she seems like a model who is posing for a painting: "Lucy Audley, with her disordered hair in a pale haze of yellow gold about her thoughtful face, the flowing lines of her soft muslin dressing-gown falling in straight folds to her feet, and clasped at the waist by a narrow circlet of agate links, might have served as a model for a mediaeval saint" (236–37). Her "disordered hair"—Lucy's most serialized accessory and perhaps the novel's most persistent token of her hyperfemininity—emerges here again where, once more, we get the sense that Lucy is consciously posing. As a facsimile of Woman, Lucy is a copy or a duplication. Lady Audley is her painting, and her painting is she. Both are copies without an original. A later description of the painting plays upon this notion of reproduction: "If Mr. Holman Hunt could have peeped into the pretty boudoir, I think the picture would have been photographed upon his brain to be reproduced by and bye upon a bishop's half-length [that is, upon a canvas] for the glorification of the pre-Raphaelite brotherhood" (308). The image of Lady Audley is marked by what Walter Benjamin terms an absence of "aura"—as a product of the emergent age of mass production, she is not endowed with a sense of the original or unique. She seems, rather, an image that might be endlessly repeated, much like a photograph. "By making many reproductions," writes Benjamin, a "technique of reproduction" such as photography "substitutes a plurality of copies for a unique existence."[68] Already a copy and never an original—not even on canvas—Lucy is always a pose, an advertisement, an image ready-made for the replicating processes of mass culture.[69] Just as Lucy is associated with brand names such as "Pompadour china, Leroy's and Benson's ormolu clocks, or my Gobelin tapestried chairs and ottomans" (316), the name of Lady Audley might well be included as a brand for female gentility.

As a sensuous and excessive display of Lady Audley's aspect, the painting cannot contain Lucy. Her personal effects and the painting alike encode a sense of the deliberate display by which she fashions herself. In *The Art of Decoration* (1881), Mrs. Haweis argues that clothing and interior décor are analogous: "Furniture is a kind of dress, dress is a kind of furniture, which both mirror the mind of their owner, and the temper of the age; which both minister to our comfort and culture, and they ought to be considered together."[70] Lucy's self-adornment is not limited to dress but extends to her ornamental surroundings. While Lucy's genteel performance depends on home furbishings as much as clothing, neither mirrors her in the sense that Mary Eliza Haweis imagines, for there is no essential self at the heart of Lady Audley to be reflected. Lucy's private rooms, which include her dressing room and boudoir, are an excessive extension of her dress and self-display that rehearses the nature of her branding: there is no primary self, only a contingent one formed through a relationship to commodity goods. These further implications of Lucy's artful self-presentation are made explicit in the ways in which she is associated with the "elegant disorder" (105) of her dressing room. That is to say, Lucy's consumer-driven self-fashioning not only reveals the constructed nature of gender and class but also inscribes a particular model of subjectivity and the possibilities of this attendant commodified self. If Lady Audley is a brand for whom there is no original, her affiliation with a world of objects underscores the way in which there is no subjectivity prior to these objects:

> Beautiful in herself, but made bewilderingly beautiful by the gorgeous surroundings which adorn the shrine of her loveliness. Drinking-cups of gold and ivory, chiselled by Benvenuto Cellini; cabinets of buhl and porcelain, bearing the cipher of Austrian Marie Antoinette, amid devices of rose-buds and true lover's knots, birds and butterflies, cupidons and shepherdesses, goddesses, courtiers, cottagers and milkmaids; statuettes of Parisian marble and biscuit china; gilded baskets of hot-house flowers; fantastical caskets of Indian filigree work; fragile tea-cups of turquoise china, adorned by medallion miniatures of Louis the Great and Louis the Well-beloved . . . ; cabinet pictures and gilded mirrors, shimmering satin and diaphanous lace; all that gold can buy or art devise had been gathered together for the beautification of this quiet chamber. (308–9)

Lucy is even more beautiful, even more herself when she is accompanied by her objects. She is not overwhelmed by the goods that are displayed in her boudoir; instead, she is all the more present and embodied when she is surrounded by the signs of her consumption.

In *Middlemarch*, by contrast, Dorothea's boudoir is a place of meditative retreat; it is the space in which she imagines her ideal life, and it is also often the scene of her despair that she may not live such a life. Dorothea does not wish to decorate the blue-green boudoir when Casaubon first shows it to her, despite the fact that it is "[a] little bare" and has not been updated since its previous occupant, Casaubon's mother, used it.[71] "Pray do not speak of altering anything," she tells her husband (100). The room is the fitting setting for *Middlemarch*'s ascetic heroine, while Lucy's boudoir admits of the impulses of a consumer eager to acquire almost redundantly, not out of need but for the sake of acquisition.

The commodity display of Lucy's rooms is equally different from the carefully acquired objects laid out in a collector's cabinet. Her boudoir houses the plunder of a compulsive consumer, not the prized treasures of the connoisseur, who selects each item both for its singularity and for its thematic relationship to a whole collection. We are told that Lucy is impulsive by nature (311), and the random contents of her boudoir would seem to confirm this. The contents exceed the terms of utility and instead comprise a bursting stock-list whose individual items are subsumed by the tangle of the whole. According to an 1863 article in *Queen*, the boudoir of the period was quickly becoming "a philippie on bad taste." "[Y]ou paid a heap of money," the article continues, "and yet, after all, you had nothing out of the way," such that one woman's boudoir looked like any other. The ideal boudoirs were those that truly "reflected the owner, and took a personality derived from those who dwelt in it." But since there is no essential core to Lady Audley, her boudoir, like the generic one *Queen* describes, "bear[s the] trace of no one."[72] Lucy's overfilled rooms also lack the restraint and purpose of what Charles Eastlake would term "taste" in *Hints on Household Taste*, first published in 1868; indeed, her rooms are an example of a feminized, commercial extravagance that Eastlake objects to. Eastlake singles out the boudoir as a particular malefactor because it is so often the scene of women's decorating excesses. He charges that "the extravagant and graceless appointments of the modern boudoir" disrupt a sense of the uniform aesthetic that should be executed and maintained in a consistent way throughout the rooms of the home.[73] Arguing that good taste is often falsely attributed to women, Eastlake suggests that women falter in their aesthetic vision for the home because they are vulnerable to the latest fashion. Imagining a scenario in which a woman is about to make her decorating choices in a shop, Eastlake's shopper "looks from one carpet to another until her eyes are fairly dazzled by their hues."[74] Here, Eastlake sounds much like writers in the popular press who argued that women were too easily dazzled by the wares of the department stores. For them, as for Eastlake, the consumer sphere exerts a negative influence on women's good judgment. A woman's idea of elegance in home furnishings is tainted by the atmosphere of the shop: "[E]legance means nothing more than a milliner's idea of the beautiful, which changes every season."[75] His cry against the common appeal for the latest fashion sounds very much like Mansel's against the novelty of serial fiction.

Later, in a discussion of bedroom furbishing, Eastlake once again addresses women's serial desire for the new. He is appalled by bedroom décor that looks like the contents of a hodgepodge shop: "[I]n the midst of lace bed-curtains, muslin toilet covers, pink calico, and cheval glasses, one might fancy oneself in a milliner's shop."[76] There is better design in "the servant's coal-box," he sniffs, "than the illuminated scuttle in my lady's boudoir."[77] The boudoir is a problem for Eastlake, an instance of undisciplined and feminized commodity display. Without the intervention of taste or restraint, this room is barely distinguishable from a crowded shop display.

Eastlake was not alone in his attempts to manage the boudoir to produce it as an orderly space. At one point in *The Bedroom and Boudoir* (1878), a title in the popular decorating series Art at Home, Lady Barker suddenly halts her instructions on how to choose an appropriate sofa and addresses connotations of the word *boudoir*, "a word signifying a place to idle and sulk in, instead of a retreat in which to be busy and comfortable."[78] The boudoir was a space coded as indolently female, a room that Lady Barker felt she needed to reclaim as a space in which "to be busy" and usefully occupied. Lucy's boudoir would not pass such a test, for it is a room that eschews function and utility. Lucy's boudoir is an excessive space in which the display of the commodity is foremost, where cultivated taste is displaced by the bourgeois shopper's taste for shopping.

Lucy has taken her shopping home, as it were, and commodity objects appear almost magically in her rooms. Within that series of connective spaces of boudoir and dressing room, her accessories and furbishings garner attention the way a shopwindow or department display might. Thad Logan has shown that the Victorian parlor "was a site of collection and display comparable to the museum, department store, and trade fair."[79] More than any other room at Audley Court, however, Lucy's dressing room and boudoir represent a particularly feminized version of commodity display. If the department store was in many ways modelled on the home—often with departments that corresponded to a particular domestic need or type of feminine dress and the supporting infrastructure of restrooms and cloakrooms—Lucy's rooms certainly recall these emporia. The commodity spectacle of her boudoir makes visible this porous divide between marketplace and home and point up the ways in which women's identification with goods was altering their normative status as domestic subjects.

We know that Lucy goes shopping and in doing so moves freely between the home and the shop; the town of Chelmsford is a nearby shopping destination for her (270). London is also within Lucy's sphere of consumption. On one occasion, Lucy tells her maid, Phoebe, that a dress is ready to be picked up from Madame Frederick (96) in London. Regular day-trips to London to shop were not unusual for women by the 1860s, when the railways were already providing out-of-town shoppers with access to the West End. And yet for a woman who has accumulated so much and for whom shopping is a regular practice, the actual labors of Lucy's consumption are not directly represented. It is as though her rooms contain the signs of her plunder, both concealing and revealing the terms of her stolen identity. Her consumption is conspicuous as this amassed plunder, the ill-gotten wares of someone who is guilty of identity theft. They are the secreted goods of a shoplifter, who quietly lifts them without detection, amassing them not because she needs them but from a compulsive need to acquire more. Objects are not so much carefully arranged as stashed like the hastily gathered booty of a shoplifter. The seriality of the objects of Lucy's rooms is reproduced as so much textual kleptomania, as the text works to compulsively detail the objects. The result is the affecting sensation of "formless desire." In all of its excess and redundancy, the boudoir is a space that eschews utility, arrests the narrative, and inscribes an economy of pure desire.[80]

In this chapter, I have been suggesting that the commercial display of Lucy's rooms encodes forms of identity that emerge through the subject's encounter with a world of goods. The continuous (re)production of Lady Audley relies so heavily on this condition of serial desire that she seems to occupy her rooms even when she is absent from the scene:

> Every evidence of womanly refinement was visible in the elegant chamber. My lady's piano was open, covered with scattered sheets of music and exquisitely-bound collections of scenas and fantasias which no master need have disdained to study. My lady's easel stood near the window, bearing witness to my lady's artistic talent.... My lady's fairy-like embroideries of lace and muslin, rainbow-hued silks, and delicately-tinted wools littered the luxurious apartment; while the looking-glasses, cunningly placed at angles and opposite corners by an artistic upholsterer, multiplied my lady's image, and in that image reflected the most beautiful object in the enchanted chamber. (307–8)

The spatial relationship of her rooms (her boudoir, dressing room, and the antechamber where the painting hangs are all connected) and the objects crammed therein suggest that Lady Audley is a product of contiguous spaces and a surplus of objects. There is a seriality not only to her possessions but also to her identity. The state of her boudoir, with its emphasis on multiplied or reproduced images, implies the production of identity without reference to an original. In the middle of this boudoir is not the woman, but her manufactured image. Recalling the model of commodified identity suggested by the department store where the self forms through a proximity to goods, Lucy is also produced through her objects. Whether Lucy is present when others trespass into her rooms matters little, for, as we have seen, her objects stand in for her. Lady Audley is an object among objects. A deliberate surface, a manufactured effect, she exists through the play and repetition of the polished surfaces of her boudoir looking glass and the other commodities of her "enchanted chamber."

Lucy's consumer compulsion hints at the possibilities of shopping disorders for the construction of feminine identities. The self that forms contingently through consumer encounters is a version of femininity that is not static or originary, that does not limit women to the spatial and economic norms of bourgeois domesticity. A woman without origins, Lucy's uses of consumption enable her elaborate, ongoing masquerade. Although her fraud will eventually be discovered, her consumer disorders persist to disrupt the operations of patriarchal inheritance and the production of bourgeois masculinity on which it depends. The boudoir and dressing room, the scene of her production as Lady Audley, attest to the condition that Lucy exploits: there is no self prior to objects. The "formless desire" of the disorderly shopper is directed not to any particular object that would guarantee the self; rather, the pleasures of consumption are such that the borders of the self are no longer maintained. The rooms are a space of pure desire and excess, one in which the boundary between subject and object is collapsed. In a novel where much knowledge is withheld, where secrets are kept, Lucy's rooms are a remarkable site of plentitude, attesting not only to the artificial labels of class and gender but also to the ways in which the work of consumption produces identity as an excessive, commodified form.

"An Unreasoning Rage": Masculinity and Consumption

As part of its economy of secrets, the text reserves the problem of reading Lady Audley's self-fashioning and acquisition, of accounting for her "formless desire." It actively constructs the problem of making meaning out of the seriality of her consumption and the intensity of her compulsions and points up the difficulty of deciphering the implications of her covert operations. Her shopping disorders are a problem for Robert Audley to detect and assess.

Rather than a purely private retreat inside Audley Court, Lucy's boudoir seems an almost public space of commercial display. Among the visitors to this unusual shop are Phoebe and her sweetheart, Luke; the latter is dazzled by Lucy's jewels (he wishes "to handle" them and "find out their mercantile value" [70]) before discovering the hidden tokens of hair and a baby shoe that are clues to Lucy's past as Helen Talboys. Robert Audley and George Talboys are likewise overcome by the tangle of goods on display in Lucy's rooms. Although these visits are conducted without Lucy's knowledge, they underscore the public nature of her rooms and a remarkable commodity display that Robert, in particular, attempts to interpret.

Like a shop detective trying to discern the movements of a suspicious customer, Robert tries to plumb the depths of Lucy's secret, but in doing so he will discover that this form of knowledge is not tenable in the age of consumerism, in which identity is no longer founded on interiority and history. When Robert enters Lucy's chambers secretly with George, "the elegant disorder of Lady Audley's dressing-room" (105) comes to exert its influence on them: "The atmosphere of the room was almost oppressive from the rich odours of perfumes in bottles whose gold stoppers had not been replaced. A bunch of hothouse flowers was withering upon a tiny writing-table. Two or three handsome dresses lay in a heap upon the ground, and the open doors of a wardrobe revealed the treasures within. Jewellery, ivory-backed hair-brushes, and exquisite china were scattered here and there about the apartment. George Talboys saw his bearded face and tall gaunt figure reflected in the cheval-glass, and wondered to see how out of place he seemed among all these womanly luxuries" (105). Amidst this material redundancy in which Lady Audley is not supplemented but produced, the men are confronted with an excessive scene of feminized objects. Although they have entered these rooms to plumb the enigma of Lucy, they find themselves in danger of being subsumed by her possessions.

The threat of feminized objects seems at first a manageable one for Robert, for he comes eventually to learn how to read his aunt in a way that reveals not merely a former or original identity but her condition as a layered and fabricated subject. When Robert unravels the nature of Lucy's secret, it is not from discerning something in her portrait, nor does he gain some form of deep knowledge by penetrating her apartments. Instead, he reads the labels on her hatbox. He unwittingly predicts this moment when he says to her in volume 1, "Upon what infinitesimal trifles may sometimes hang the whole secret of some wicked mystery, inexplicable heretofore to the wisest upon the earth!" (152). In this case, everything depends on the comings and goings of Lady Audley's hatbox.

In this key moment in his investigations, Robert reads the labels of an old bonnet-box left in the Peckham Grove residence of Mrs. Vincent, where Lucy (then Helen Talboys) had lived under the alias of Miss Lucy Graham:[81]

> Mr. Audley knelt down to examine the scraps of railway labels and addresses which were pasted here and there upon the box. It had been battered upon a great many different lines of railway, and had evidently travelled considerably. Many of the labels had been torn off, but fragments of some of them remained, and upon one yellow scrap of paper Robert read the letters TURI.
>
> "The box has been to Italy," he thought. "Those are the first four letters of the word Turin, and the label is a foreign one."
>
> The only direction which had not been either defaced or torn away was the last, which bore the name of Miss Graham, passenger to London. Looking very closely at this label, Mr. Audley discovered that it had been pasted over another. (256–57)

Peeling off two labels, Robert reveals the layers of deception that Lucy has fashioned herself upon. Later, Robert confronts Lucy with "'[t]he evidence of two labels, pasted one over the other, upon a box left by you in the possession of Mrs. Vincent, the upper label bearing the name of Miss Graham, the lower that of Mrs. George Talboys.' My lady was silent . . . and he knew that the shot had gone home to its mark" (287). While this evidence establishes that Lady Audley is Helen Talboys, and before that Helen Maldon, it does more than that. For Robert's ability to read Lucy through a hatbox is not an instance of revelation; rather, it shows that he has been inducted into a knowledge of the commodified self. The knowledge that the hatbox produces about Lucy is analogous to what the reflective surfaces of her boudoir say about her. Lucy's self-production, as we have seen in the description of her boudoir, points to the absence of a primary self and in its place an identity that emerges from the layers of a manufactured one. Central to the discovery of Lucy's fabricated identity is this hatbox, itself an empty shell, a carrying-case she has disposed of. The commodified self is one whose outlines can be read; it is a matter of peel-away surfaces. This well-traveled box, moreover, is the inscription of a form of subjectivity in flux, one as mobile as the rail travel it is associated with, the fast world of frequent stops and exchanges that Henry Mansel also ascribed to railway book-stalls and the commercialization of fiction. There is no original self, only one that leaves its trace as the accretion of labels that register one's comings and goings.

Being able to read Lucy does not inoculate Robert from the suffocating threat of consumption, however. Although Robert is inducted into knowledge of the commodified self and develops the ability to interpret it, the terms that offer Lucy an alternative to self-regulating femininity pose a threat to the consolidation of bourgeois masculine identity for Robert. If the novel imagines subversion for the disorderly woman consumer, it is arguably more muted in its vision of the ways in which the male consumer might pose a challenge to prevailing gender norms.[82] It instead places emphasis on both an incompatibility between normative masculinity and consumerism and the inevitability of men's contact with a feminized world of objects despite their attempts to renounce it.

Lucy, then, is not the novel's only consumer; before Robert undertakes the project of reading Lady Audley, he is a consumer. The Robert we see at the beginning of the novel is an idler whose feminized role is legible as his consumer and leisure practices. Although he is preparing to pass the bar, he admits to little professional ambition and has such a surplus of leisure time that he can while away hours as "an idle *flaneur* upon the smooth pathways that have no particular goal" (438). Early in the novel, when Robert visits Audley Court for the hunting season, he "show[s] no inclination for any of these outdoor amusements" (146–47) and comes prepared instead to lounge in the drawing room, bringing with him "half-a-dozen French novels, a case of cigars, and three pounds of Turkish tobacco in his portmanteau" (145). He is often seen reading decadent French novels, such as are also associated with Lucy's own trivial tastes in literature, which include "yellow-paper-covered novels . . . from the Burlington Arcade" (138). Robert's bachelorhood, idleness, and lack of vocational drive are not only markers of his marginal masculinity but also suggest his status as consumer. Robert's consumption threatens to emasculate him, and so he must manage it—as well as a related condition, his concealed but all-consuming homoerotic attachment for George Talboys, which drives his quest to reveal Lucy's secrets[83]—so that his social identity as a proper Victorian man, one whose desires are vocational, familial, and heterosexual, ultimately can be guaranteed. Among the most pronounced fears regarding consumer culture and the specter of the woman as extravagant consumer were ones that concerned the potentially feminizing affects of consumption on Victorian manliness. The novel uses Robert Audley's narrative to stage the vexed relationship between consumer culture and masculinity: while the effete man was languorously mired in a world of commodities, the manly man worked to keep this suffocating sphere at bay by emphasizing his mastery over consumption and leisure. His dedication was directed to active, vocational pursuits and the (re)productive desires associated with heterosexual relations rather than the unproductive, consuming, "formless desires" of same-sex desire.

In the course of investigating Lucy, Robert comes to shed his unproductive vocation as a decadent consumer and the idle pursuits of French novels, Turkish tobacco, and leisure time. As he does so, his animosity toward consumerism and women becomes more pronounced. If the "elegant disorder" of Lucy's boudoir troubles and threatens to suffocate Robert, the objects of his bachelor lodgings come to exert a psychic burden on him that must be cast off. Heavy with the knowledge that George may have been murdered, Robert returns to his rooms in the Middle Temple, where the material effects of everyday life seem to exert a cruel strain on him. Here, the narrator dilates upon this burden of objects as a condition of the Victorian age: "Who has not felt, in the first madness of sorrow, an unreasoning rage against the mute propriety of chairs and tables, the stiff square-ness of Turkey carpets, the unbending obstinacy of the outward apparatus of existence? We want to root up gigantic trees in a primeval forest, and to tear their huge branches asunder in our convulsive grasp; and the utmost that we can do for the relief of our passion is to knock over an easy chair, or smash a few shillings'-worth of Mr. Copeland's furniture" (226–27). The narrator underscores the affective properties of objects and how their status as the "outward apparatus of our existence" torques the self away from a comforting sense of interiorized subjectivity. Indeed, for Eastlake, a tastefully decorated bedroom was the correlative of a mind at peace with itself: "A room intended for repose ought to contain nothing which can fatigue the eye by complexity."[84]

Robert's animosity toward the commodities that press on his sense of interior cohesion is coupled, in the paragraphs that follow, with a misogynist rant that concludes, "I hate women. . . . They're bold, brazen, abominable creatures, invented for the annoyance and destruction of their superiors. Look at the business of poor George's! . . . He goes to a woman's house and he is never seen alive again" (229). If a world of objects threatens to overwhelm, so do women threaten to consume men. Robert rails against consuming women as the ruiners of men, as "graceful automaton for the display of milliners' manufacture" whose "spells" render men "powerless to escape" (265).

The "convulsive" (226) affects produced by a world of objects and by voracious femininity seem to be ameliorated by Robert's gradual repudiation of consumption as a vocation. He enacts his own version of the Great Masculine Renunciation, divesting himself not so much of sartorial excess, a dominant feature of this phenomenon in Britain from midcentury on, as of the signs of his consumption.[85] Whereas he was formerly consumed by reading decadent novels and other leisurely practices, he now can only faintly recall his earlier, consumerist self: "[H]ow can I believe that it was I who used to lounge all day in the easy-chair reading Paul de Kock, and smoking mild Turkish, who used to drop in at half-price to stand amongst the press men at the back of the boxes, and see a new burlesque, and finish the evening with the 'Chough and Crow,' and chops and pale ale at Evan's" (405). Robert thus seems to have cast off the feminizing affects of consumption that threaten his constitution as a proper masculine subject.

For Eastlake and other advocates of tasteful interior decorating, the bourgeois domestic interior is where the redemption of the individual occurs.[86] But Braddon's novel inverts this logic, such that the commodified bourgeois interior can never fully duplicate and ensure the condition of interiorized subjectivity. While Robert comes to master one mystery of the self in the consumer age—how to solve the puzzle of Lady Audley by learning to read the terms of her manufactured surface—the other part of his education is that of being inducted into the reality of a consumer society where the self cannot maintain its borders, where desire is not directed at a fixed object that will guaranteed the self. What is an opportunity for Lucy to remake her social and economic position is for Robert a crisis in the production of normative heterosexual masculinity, a crisis that can only be forestalled and never fully assuaged.

The Sensational Remainders of Consumption

At first, it might seem that Robert accedes to normative masculinity at the end of the novel. He ensures that open scandal at Audley Court is averted by seeing that Lucy is banished to a Belgian asylum, and he substitutes his obsession for George Talboys by redirecting it toward the appropriate object of George's sister, Claire, whom he marries and has a son with. Not only a family man, Robert also becomes dedicated to his work; as "a rising man upon the home circuit" (445), he is rewarded for his newfound vocational commitment with the prospect of a great career. Despite these corrective measures, the disordering affects of female consumption on men are not entirely expunged from the novel. The effete male consumer, despite appearances to the contrary, is always being replicated. His presence remains an unspoken threat to proper patriarchal inheritance, a threat that is concealed by the more obvious confinement of the novel's ostensible women consumer. Whether Robert will carry on the family name, however, is unclear, for the way in which Lucy's consumer legacy persists despite her exile suggests that Robert's inculcation as proper masculine subject can never be entirely ensured and always stands open to the disordering ruptures of consumption. The final pages of the novel imply that Robert's legacy is not so much his biological son as the other bachelor who inherits Robert's earlier decadent tendencies: "The meerschaums and the French novels have been presented to a young Templar, with whom Robert Audley had been friendly in his bachelor days" (446). Thus, one of the final exchanges that the novel alludes to is the one in which Robert passes on the signs of his consumerism and leisure to another bachelor. Robert bequeaths his novels and smoking pipes to another version of his former self, another indolent barrister who conducts his life of leisure from the very same rooms in the Inns. There is the sense that for every man, such as Robert, who is inducted into proper manhood, there is another who is lounging about somewhere who will assume his former profession as a consumer. The novel ends not with full domestic reinscription and consolidated masculinity but with the idea that the male consumer, too, is always being generated at the expense of proper patriarchal inheritance.

Nor is Lucy entirely expelled: once a disorderly consumer, she is always one. Even as she is leaving Audley Court, Lucy thinks obsessively about her things. As she wraps a hundred-guinea Indian shawl around her, she hopes that she will not need to abandon the booty she acquired as Lady Audley: "[A]nd do not wonder if she clung with a desperate tenacity to gauds and gew-gaws in the hour of her despair" (380). As her maid packs her trunks, Lucy is relieved that she will not be sent away without at least some dresses, jewels, and millinery: "It seemed a pleasant excitement to her, this folding and refolding of silks and velvets, this gathering together of jewels and millinery. They were not going to rob her of her possessions, she thought" (387). But some is not enough, and Lucy's consumer desires are such that she is compelled to steal from the splendor of her former rooms: "[S]he had not forgotten her favourite Russian sables even in this last hour of shame and misery. Her mercenary soul hankered greedily after the costly and beautiful things of which she had been mistress. She had hidden away fragile tea-cups and covered vases of Sèvres and Dresden among the folds of her silken dinner dresses. She had secreted jewelled and golden drinking cups amongst her delicate linen. She would have taken the pictures from the walls, and the Gobelin tapestry from the chairs, had it been possible for her to do so" (388). Tucking these objects into her dresses, she becomes like a shoplifter who stashes stolen plunder in her skirts to conceal her final crime.

While one might not be surprised that Lucy leaves Audley Court as much a shoplifter as ever, what is remarkable is that the affects of consumption remain there as an excess that spills over into the economic domain of patrimony. The revelation of Lucy's bigamy disorders the operations of proper exchange on the marriage market. Earlier, the novel casts marriage as a commercial enterprise when Sir Michael makes the arrangement between himself and Lucy in the language of a business contract: "Is it a bargain, Lucy?"(53). Having already been married, Lucy does not observe the proper limits of the contract, and her serial relationship to consumer objects thus extends to serial marriage. Her kleptomania includes the acquisition of more than one husband, a form of redundancy in the marriage market that disorders the house of Audley to the extent that its patriarch becomes physically displaced. Sir Michael vacates Audley Court and goes on to purchase a much smaller house "on the borders of his son-in-law's [Sir Harry's] estate" (446), living out his days as a neighbor to Lord Tower and as a visitor to Robert's comfortable but by no means grand "fairy cottage" (444).

Ultimately, it is Lady Audley who occupies Audley Court after Sir Michael leaves. The relationship between the great house and the commercial sphere is secured when it becomes a museum of sorts, with the story of Lady Audley as its main attraction. Audley Court is not a grand, dignified private home that can exist apart from an association with public consumption; after Sir Michael leaves, it becomes like a kind of exhibition, a popular stop for tourists who are eager to view the portrait and admire Lucy's old rooms: "The house is often shown to inquisitive visitors, though the baronet is not informed of that fact, and people admire my lady's rooms, and ask many questions about the pretty, fair-haired woman, who died abroad" (446). Since Lady Audley was always the sum total of her effects, she is there as much as she ever was through her possessions; indeed, she has ousted everyone else and has taken over Audley Court for herself and for the promotion of her legend. The fact that a curious public comes to see Lucy's rooms suggests that her image continues to be reproduced. Lady Audley cannot be banished, for she was always a fabrication, and her compulsive consumption lives on in serial form as popular myth.

The novel concludes not with Robert's bourgeois domestic reinscription and consolidated masculinity, then, but with the sensational reiteration of Lady Audley's commodified self. Rather than a triumphal inscription of Robert's narrative of self-constitution, the ending that lingers is one that emphasizes the disorders of consumption. The circulation of Lady Audley's legend emphasizes how identity, never stable, has become as much a commodity as the gewgaws of her former apartments. Resembling the "elegant disorder" of a ransacked department store display, Lucy's rooms remain, as it were, beyond the ending of the novel as its most affecting scene of disorderly consumption. Such a scene attests to the condition of mid-Victorian consumerism. Commodities were not so much assigned or imbued with social meanings as they were a means through which identity was being constructed and the materials through which the meanings of class and gender were being disturbed, contested, and remade. Moreover, this world of consumer objects had never been more proximate, despite the popular and professional discourses of orderly shopping and tasteful decoration that sought to manage it. Henry Mansel's observation that sensation fiction depended on proximity to the stimulations of commercial life for its "electrifying" affect was perhaps as much about this commercially successful genre as about how the sphere of consumption was bound up more than ever in the formation of the subject.[87] A disruptive presence in Britain's urban shopping districts, the shopper was bringing her disorders home, where, increasingly and uncannily, the Victorians were finding that they were never more themselves than when they were surrounded by their things.

Three

MIDDLEMARCH AND THE EXTRAVAGANT DOMESTIC SPENDER

Managing an Epic Life

As George Eliot prepared to publish the first edition of *Middlemarch* in 1871, she was also poised to take a gamble. Eliot's ambitions for the novel extended beyond the scope of its composition, with its nuanced understanding of social relations and complex intertwining of multiple plots. She also entertained the possibility of a radically new format of publication in parts.[1] Acting on an earlier suggestion from John Blackwood, George Henry Lewes wrote to him on May 7, 1871, asking if he would consider this publishing experiment: "Mrs. Lewes finds that she will require 4 volumes for her story, not 3. . . . [A]s you have more than once spoken of the desirability of inventing some mode of circumventing the Libraries and making the public *buy* instead of borrowing I have devised the following scheme, . . . namely to publish it in *half-volume parts* either at intervals of one, or as I think better, two months. The eight parts at 5/- could yield the 2£ for the four volumes, and at two month intervals would not be dearer than Maga [*Blackwood's Magazine*]. Each part would have a certain unity and completeness in itself with separate title."[2] To secure these terms, the matter of who would shoulder the risk had to be determined. Either the publisher could assume it and offer the novelist £6000 cash or a four-year English copyright, or Eliot could take the chance and accept a 40 percent royalty on each part. Eliot chose the latter, and this risk earned her the distinction of being known as the first author to turn down a flat fee in favor of a royalty.

There were reasons why Blackwood, Lewes, and Eliot had attempted to "circumvent[ ] the Libraries" and the standard three-decker. Blackwood, as David Carroll points out, was still fuming over the lending libraries' refusal "to buy [*Felix Holt* in] either [its] three-volume or the 12s. edition," a factor in its failure, and wished to bolster himself against a system that had too much of a hand in determining the fate of his business. Lewes, for his part, was keen to find a means of publication that could turn a greater profit.[3] With such a share of the market, lending libraries such as Mudie's and W. H. Smith kept the price of fiction artificially inflated, ensuring that the price of new fiction remained high and preventing a market for cheap literature from taking hold. This obstruction was in the libraries' interest, for they received a sizable discount by buying directly from publishers; cheap editions would not only lure the lending public away but also dampen sales in the libraries' second-hand trade, through which they sold off used three-deckers to the public. By offering each of the volumes of *Middlemarch* at a lower price than usual, Lewes hoped to extend readership beyond the subscription system and induce readers "to buy rather than borrow."[4]

If these were the motivations of her publisher and of her companion-cum-literary agent, what were Eliot's reasons for this scheme? Tiring of hearing that single copies of her novel were passed from one reader to the next until they became threadbare, Eliot evidently wished to put more copies of her novels into more readers' hands.[5] But her investment in shaping the terms of *Middlemarch* as a commodity to be purchased was arguably most directed toward her continued efforts to accrue status as an preeminent author, one who would not be constrained by the terms of received publishing formats. Turning down an invitation in 1853 to contribute to the *English Woman's Journal,* Eliot wrote that she had "given up writing 'articles'" for others and was eager instead to build her "own house" by writing books.[6] Eliot's concern was "to have freedom to write out one's own varying unfolding self, and not be a machine always grinding out the same material or spinning the same sort of web."[7] By playing the publishing market in 1871, Eliot was doing so in the interest of once again ensuring her currency as a professional author, one whose narrative ambitions could only be realized through the epic space of four volumes.

Eliot's textile metaphor for the publishing market evokes her most famous pronouncement on dress in relation to market-driven literature, "the *mind-and-millinery* species" of novels that she wished to distinguish from her own. Despite her dismissal of such "silly" novels—one echoed in G. H. Lewes's disparaging of "waist-coats" and "pots and pans," or that "*detailism* which calls itself Realism"—*Middlemarch* makes much of household matters and the semiotics of dress.[8] Eliot's text inscribes the risks and rewards of women who extend themselves into an economic domain, whose spending what they do not have is a way to borrow against dividends that may or may not pay off in the future.

At first glance, it is Rosamond Vincy rather than Dorothea Brooke who seems to offer the novel's most obvious woman consumer. Recalling Lucy Audley, Rosamond is an iteration of familiar cultural anxieties surrounding women's status as household spenders, for how the Angel in the House's spending might affect the integrity of the very private finances of the bourgeois home. Rosamond's expensive tastes for fashion and furnishings for the home contribute to placing her husband, Lydgate, on the brink of financial ruin. By contrast, Dorothea Brooke seems indifferent to dress and ornamentation, were it not for the ways in which the novel makes a display of her sartorial restraint and makes a value of this spectacular simplicity. Although *Middlemarch* might appear to conform to high Victorian cultural constructions by making its heroine an apparently fiscally responsible wife who is a help rather than a hindrance to her scholar-husband, Casaubon, the novel departs from the cultural norms of its day. To assume that Rosamond stands as a voracious consumer in stark contrast to a more restrained Dorothea would be to reinscribe the commonplace assumptions concerning domestic economy: the belief that women possessed a consumerist appetite that must be fiscally disciplined.

Instead of rejecting the extravagant woman spender or constructing Rosamond and Dorothea as polar opposites, *Middlemarch* suggests how spending might be put to both social and personal uses. Rosamond negotiates class standing through the acquisition of consumer goods for the household, while Dorothea, who appears to eschew materiality and ornamentation, invests riskily in the uncertain venture of her husband's scholarship, hoping that her labors will pay her vocational and intellectual dividends in the future. Dorothea emerges, then, as a most unusual domestic manager. The opposite of the middle-class mode of management constructed in Victorian domestic advice literature, her management style is extravagantly, even perversely restrained. Unlike Rosamond, who works the loopholes of bourgeois household spending by overspending her husband's capital, Dorothea takes the logic of thrift to its limits, locating in her economies of restraint a form of surplus and in her spending an ethical imperative. From her radically understated dress to her risky investment in Casaubon and finally to the "unhistoric acts" (896) that the novel imagines will characterize the everyday endeavors in the community following marriage to Ladislaw, Dorothea is willing to borrow against the future. In doing so, she makes self-management into an "epic life" (25).

Domestic Economy and the Extravagant Woman

Set in the early 1830s but first published in Blackwood's from December 1871 to December of the following year, Middlemarch demonstrates a retrospective understanding of how the locus of the small provincial town was poised to be altered by the economic and industrial shock waves of the mid-nineteenth century. As though to anticipate the getting and spending of the decades to follow, the novel addresses such developments as the incursion of the railways to the countryside, the spread of mass journalism, and the rise of Reform politics. Moreover, through the shady dealings of Nicholas Bulstrode and the debts of Fred Vincy, it also registers the much-publicized financial failures on the horizon, such as the 1847 fallout of the "Railway Mania" speculation schemes, when shares imploded, or "Black Friday" on May 11, 1866, when the supposedly stable credit bank of Overend, Gurney and Company collapsed and brought a series of other financial houses down with it.[9]

Fears of personal bankruptcy and national solvency already loomed large in Britain in the earlier decades of the nineteenth century; from 1800 to 1850, there were 1,000 to 1,500 bankruptcies in trade each year, many of which were publicly reported weekly in the newspapers. In the 1850s and 1860s, the list grew still longer, such that the *Times* devoted up to six pages in its quarterly index to a registry of declared bankrupts.[10] Such fiscal anxiety took on a new valence with the growing specter of women's household debt. While married women were ostensibly authorized to spend in the interests of maintaining the home, their shifting legal status following the midcentury mark made unclear to what extent they were responsible for their own debt. A whole host of Lucy Audleys, it seemed, posed a threat to the stability of one of the most fundamental of Victorian political arrangements: the bourgeois household.

Written in the wake of the financial panic of the late 1860s, *Middlemarch* is attendant to how the status of the domestic woman consumer was to alter following the mid-nineteenth century.[11] As the Women's Property Acts were formulated and revised between the 1850s and 1880s, the terms of women's economic agency were changing, with women gradually gaining better access to their own assets.[12] Over these same decades, so too was popular print returning to the idea of a consuming woman whose household expenditures had to be carefully managed to maintain the financial health of the middle-class household. Since the 1830s, advice literature in Britain had been configuring women as an extension of their husbands' resources. Through a discourse of domestic economy, which would later include the virtues of thrift, middle-class etiquette manuals and household guides acknowledged women's commercial sway by calling women to account over the dangers of excessive household spending.[13] Advice literature for middle-class women readers, such as Anne Cobbett's *English Housekeeper* (1835) and Sarah Stickney Ellis's *Women of England: Their Social Duties and Domestic Habits* (1839) on the household, manners, and dress, that had begun to appear earlier in the century was followed by such publishing phenomena as Isabella Beeton's *Book of Household Management* (1861) and Samuel Smiles's *Thrift* (1875).[14] Although, as Clair Hughes points out, Dorothea Brooks and Rosamond Vincy embody "ideals of womanhood" including ones of dress in keeping with the 1830s, the ways in which consumerist femininity is constructed in *Middlemarch* are more contemporary with those following the 1850s, by which time a discourse of domestic economy had been well articulated.[15]

In the late 1860s and 1870s, household guides were rehearsing what had become a familiar contrast in domestic advice literature: on the one hand, household managers who practiced an economics of thrift; on the other, extravagant women spenders who spent resources allocated for the home on themselves. *Cassell's Household Guide*, whose final volume appeared the same year *Middlemarch* was published, calls the household "the most important of all human institutions.... It is there that the fruits of man's labour are ultimately enjoyed; there that woman finds her chief sphere of duty, as the helpmeet of man.... Domestic comfort ... centres in the practice of a wise ECONOMY—in the thoughtful and intelligent fitting of means to ends."[16] In *Warne's Model Cookery and Housekeeping Book*, first published in 1868, Mary Jewry urges that it is the task of "the 'Lady' of the house" to take "care that no waste or ignorant misuse shall squander the property of her husband.... She is to take care that there is no lack through fault of hers, nor any drawback to domestic comfort through injudicious rule.... It is her thoughtfulness that provides—very often her self-denial that purchases—the comfort of others."[17] Similarly, Samuel Smiles insists in his bestseller *Thrift* that frugal wives are crucial to ensuring domestic financial stability: "There can be no thrift, nor economy, nor comfort at home, unless the wife helps.... If she be thriftless, putting money into her hands is like pouring water through a sieve. Let her be frugal, and she will make her home a place of comfort, and she will also make her husband's life happy, if she do not lay the foundation of his prosperity and fortune."[18]

Among the household guides that had already begun to establish this mid-Victorian sense of female financial prudence was *A Manual of Domestic Economy: Suited to Families Spending from £100 to £1000 a Year* (1856), written by J. H. Walsh and "assisted in various departments by a committee of ladies."[19] Walsh's *Manual* was addressed to a middle-class audience, a broad readership with household spending ranging from more-modest outlay to the larger household budgets of upper-middle-class houses. The *Manual* proceeds to examine the proper running of a household in close detail, addressing the specific concerns related to each of four income levels.[20] As it does so, the *Manual* periodically revisits the figure of the ideal domestic woman who must choreograph the running of a successful household, a wife who is a good manager and whose restrained dress, quiet home, and charity work are the markers of a respectable middle-class homemaker. In doing so, it imagines women as economic agents who shop, buy, and procure for and on behalf of the household. Yet they must not spend for the sake of spending. Purchase must be translated into use; items bought must be deployed in a practical manner within the home. In the process of constructing domestic spending as a problem that must be carefully managed, *A Manual of Domestic Economy* locates women's excesses as potentially disruptive to the household budget. "It is truly astonishing," the *Manual* observes, "how much a woman will contrive to spend upon herself, when she is encouraged in extravagance.... I think it may be maintained, that female extravagance is now more common than of yore, as compared with the similar quality in the male sex."[21] As though to anticipate the domestic spending of Rosamond Vincy, the guide states that such a woman is more prevalent "in the large provincial towns, where dinner-parties . . . , carriages and horses, [and] expensive clothes . . . help to swell the Christmas bills."[22]

Despite shoring up the model of the ideal household spender, the spendthrift or extravagant wife is a recurring figure to whom household guides return time and again, particularly concerning the topic of women's finery. The extravagant woman whose clothing expenditures must be curtailed was already a familiar figure in advice literature earlier in the century. In *The Women of England*, Ellis had warned that "admiration is not to be obtained by the display of any kind of extravagance in dress. . . . [T]he praise most liberally and uniformly bestowed by men upon the dress of women, is, that it is neat, becoming, or in good taste."[23] When *A Manual of Domestic Economy* addresses the mysterious topic of securely middle-class ladies' dress, however, it seems unequal to the task. Although acknowledging that women must spend on dress as a mark of their station, the *Manual* is unsure of how such expenditures can be accounted for in domestic economy, which is premised ultimately on saving rather than spending. "Female dress," the *Manual* notes, "is a constant source of domestic jars, inasmuch as the master is not always aware of the necessary expenditure. . . . [I]t is also the case that he often grumbles at, or refuses to pay for, what is really required to make a proper and respectable appearance." In the end, the *Manual* retreats from matters of women's dress to pronounce that "it is not a part of domestic economy to enlarge upon such a gratification of taste, which is more fit for the pages of a book of fashions; and all that will be here attempted will be the best and cheapest method of effecting what is necessary."[24]

Like the bewildered husband in *A Manual of Domestic Economy*, who is often advised of his wife's clothing purchases belatedly, if at all, the guide cannot account for the sudden appearance of the conspicuously dressed woman in the midst of a text condoning restraint. Despite an attempt to anticipate the woman spender at the beginning of the manual, and so contain her, her appearance during a discussion of dress ruptures the text that would seek to limit her extravagant appearances. Her dress is not economical but informed by conspicuous consumption—a new outfit for each day, if possible. Walsh, like the husband of the scenario, retreats by claiming ignorance of the subject, a topic that he demurs is more appropriately discussed in fashion magazines. The woman who spends more than she needs to on dress, that is, who possesses more (or more elaborate) clothing than is needed to perform her domestic and social duties, constitutes for Walsh a spurious interruption in a manual on domestic economy.

The *Manual* thus rests uneasily upon a contradiction endemic to advice literature on domestic spending: to be a proper middle-class woman, the literature concedes, is to spend something on dress. A woman must buy clothing for herself if she is to be a sign of her husband's economic power, but this spending is to be distinguished from careful household management. Thus, the problem of how to distinguish between the two kinds of spending remains. Some household guides attempted to negotiate this difficulty by calling for the mistress of the house to spend efficiently and strategically in all her expenses, to manufacture the outward appearance of extravagant spending for guests.[25] This is very much the spirit of Eliza Warren's 1864 guide, *How I Managed My House on Two Hundred Pounds a Year*, which advises the reader that "by close attention to *trifles*, I was ultimately able to *appear* a very liberal housekeeper; indeed, 'extravagant' was the gratuitous title I earned."[26]

When the domestic woman spender refuses to balance the books carefully and even indulges in the use of credit to supplement her prescribed household budget, she becomes a particularly transgressive figure. During the 1830s during which *Middlemarch* is set, credit comprised a loosely arranged agreement between a shopkeeper and a customer based on the aristocratic patronage of the previous century. Even prior to legal reforms that granted women the right to enter into contracts for which they were personally liable, women's access to credit was a long-established tradition. Under common law, the "law of necessities," as it was known, "empowered [women] to make contracts on their own behalf for necessaries, as agents of their husbands." As Margot Finn further notes, women deployed common law strategically using "the law of necessities as an instrument of credit."[27] As Erika Rappaport has demonstrated, credit arrangements between women and shopkeepers continued throughout the nineteenth century, although they were altered by the arrival of the department store. The proprietors of these large emporia, unlike small shopkeepers, rarely knew their vast clientele personally and could place little confidence in whether items bought on credit would ever be repaid. Department stores such as Whiteley's, and later Harrods, owed much of their success to a ready-money policy. By insisting on cash payment, large stores reduced losses from unpaid credit accounts and could then afford to lower their merchandise costs overall, attracting shoppers with their competitive prices. Meanwhile, some smaller shops continued to offer credit because they depended on trade with customers who continued to expect it.[28]

Both advice literature and the popular press regularly warned against the dangers of credit. One early warning, "Observations on Credit," an 1819 article in the *Pamphleteer*, cautions that credit is "the parent evil not only of Bankruptcy, but of that Insolvency which abounds in our country."[29] Later in the century, Lady M. Jeune criticizes the abuse of credit in "The Ethics of Shopping": "The system of credit which was the foundation of extravagance and recklessness, could only exist, when one paid a higher price for any article than it was worth, on the understanding that one would pay for it at a later date." "To many people," she continues, describing someone who sounds much like William Makepeace Thackeray's Becky Sharpe, "the system of credit was a very convenient one because they had no ready money and could buy on no other terms; and if they put off indefinitely the hour of payment, why not then have everything they fancied or liked to buy?"[30] Credit ran counter to principles of thrift, deferring payment rather than deferring spending.

In *Thrift*, Smiles underscores how women's access to credit poses particular problems. Credit creates domestic discord as well as the accumulation of serious debts. Smiles even imagines a scene in which a disgruntled husband confronts his wife upon her return from a shopping trip:

> "Is that dress paid for?" asked a husband. "No." "Then you are allowing yourself to be clothed at another man's expense!" No woman is justified in running into debt for a dress without her husband's knowledge and consent. If she do so, she is clothing herself at the expense of the draper. This is one of the things that worry a man who is trying to keep his head above water; and it is often sufficient to turn his heart against his wife and her extravagances.... By running into debt yourself, or by your allowing your wife to run into debt, you give another person power over your liberty.... [Credit] is the shop-keeper's temptation; and we fall before it.... By giving credit, by pressing women to buy fine clothes, [shop-keepers] place the strongest temptation before them. They inveigle the wives of men who are disposed to be honest into debt, and afterward send in untruthful bills. They charge heavier prices, and their customers pay them—sometimes doubly pay them; for it is impossible to keep a proper check upon long-due accounts.[31]

Women, Smiles contends, are apt to run into debt because of an irresponsible use of credit. They purchase items that their husbands are not aware of and enter into financial contracts without their husbands' knowledge or approval. Shopkeepers might tempt wives to buy goods by extending credit to them, then cheat the unknowing wives by charging high interest and by keeping dishonest records of payment. Perhaps most threatening of all, a woman who enters into a credit agreement with a shopkeeper becomes beholden to him and forms a relationship dangerously resembling that of adultery.[32] As in Gustave Flaubert's *Madame Bovary*, a man other than her husband clothes her, and this impropriety dissolves masculine proprietorship over the bourgeois household.

The extravagant household spender troubled the norm of a self-regulating domesticity in which middle-class women's household labor was to be invisible. Domestic ideology, as Nancy Armstrong has shown, depended on a disciplined female body: "Self-regulation alone gave a woman authority over the field of domestic objects."[33] The self-regulating domestic woman reaches her apotheosis when her labors become invisible, and her vigilance over the household comes to stand in for labor itself. She becomes a figure through which to translate her husband's income, that is, she comes to occupy no material body of her own.[34] The woman who consumes makes a spectacle of herself, becomes visible when her spending is unregulated or excessive. "[A]s an object of display," Armstrong writes, "she . . . loses value as a subject."[35] The extravagant woman—as household mismanager, credit user, or potential debtor—thus constitutes a transgressive figure within domestic economies. Her financial dealings and dalliances with credit, as a reading of *Middlemarch* will illustrate, render material the gendered, desiring body of an economic agent whose mobility between the household and the marketplace reveals the limits of nineteenth-century domestic ideology. Eliot's novel explores these limits and in doing so redefines thrift to make a unexpected virtue of spending.

Rosamond's Transactions

Middlemarch reprises the extravagant woman not as a figure to be repressed or rehabilitated through the discipline of saving but as one who secures social meanings through spending, including forms of overextension such as debt. In a novel replete with men's financial secrets, stakes, risks, failures, and disclosures, women's foray into economic spheres provides an illuminating counterpoint.

The shameful source of Bulstrode's wealth, Will Ladislaw's grandfather's pawnshop, Farebrother's two wills, Mr. Vincy's tenuous business success, Caleb Garth's struggle to provide for his family, and Fred Vincy's gambling debt are obvious instances of the economic dealings that help structure the action of the novel. But the novel positions women's conflicted relationship to domesticity in equally material and economic terms, as Rosamond's bid in the marriage market also becomes a matter of playing the field of consumerism.

The novel's introductory portrait of Rosamond initially suggests her similarity with the extravagant women of Smiles's *Thrift* and of household and etiquette manuals. Like Herodotus, "a maiden apparently beguiled by attractive merchandise" (123), Rosamond, we are told, "had excellent taste in costume, with that nymph-like figure and pure blondness which gave the largest range to choice in the flow and colour of drapery" (123). Her education has prepared her for the role of decorative wife: "She was admitted to be the flower of Mrs. Lemon's school, the chief school in the county, where the teaching included all that was demanded in the accomplished female—even to extras, such as the getting in and out of a carriage. Mrs. Lemon herself had always held up Miss Vincy as an example: no pupil, she said, exceeded that young lady for mental acquisition and propriety of speech, while her musical execution was quite exceptional" (123). Rosamond is clearly motivated by class interests, which her taste for "attractive merchandise" helps secure. Her expectations for success on the marriage market are high, and she states emphatically to her mother, "I shall not marry any Middlemarch young man" (125). Her determination to marry outside of local provincial society betrays her embarrassment over her social standing. Her mother, who has humble roots as an innkeeper's daughter, has a tendency to use "shopkeepers' slang" (126), which Rosamond detests. Rosamond thinks she "might have been happier if she had not been the daughter of a Middlemarch manufacturer" (128) and aspires, through marriage, to something more. Mary Garth's favorable "inventory" (141) of Lydgate's appearance is confirmed by Rosamond, who likes what she sees and imagines herself married to the doctor, "rid . . . of all the visitors who were not agreeable to her at her father's; and she imagined the drawing-room in her favourite house with various styles of furniture" (300). Such is the extent of Rosamond's preparation for overseeing her own household.

Although Elizabeth Langland argues that *Middlemarch* largely occludes the representation of domestic management and household labor, and Langland concludes that the effect of the mystification of women's domestic labors is "to reinforce our sense of women's disability in patriarchy," Rosamond's example of how not to run an efficient household remains striking as a version of the extravagant housewife who haunts advice literature of the period.[36] She has no knowledge of running a household, since Mrs. Vincy "resigned no domestic function to her daughter" (187), who "never thought of money except as something necessary which other people would always provide" (301).

The novel's more conventional practitioner of household management is, of course, Mrs. Garth. A model of efficiency, Mrs. Garth seems to surpass the ideal, single-minded housewife of guidebooks. The former governess flawlessly executes the role of domestic multitasker: "She had sometimes taken pupils in a peripatetic fashion, making them follow her about in the kitchen with their book or slate. She thought it good for them to see that she could make an excellent lather while she corrected their blunders 'without looking',—that a woman with her sleeves tucked up above her elbows might know all about the Subjunctive Mood or the Torrid Zone—that, in short, she might possess 'education' . . . without being a useless doll" (275). If Mrs. Garth is careful to display the extent of her usefulness, Mrs. Vincy is, by contrast, an example to her daughter of how to produce the mere effect of a well-run household by keeping "those running accounts with tradespeople, which give[s] a cheerful sense of getting everything one wants without any question of payment" (262).

As soon as she is engaged to Lydgate, Rosamond begins to accumulate her trousseau and buys "the best linen and cambric for her underclothing" (377), hopes to secure a good house, and has Mrs. Garth's daughter, Mary, double-hem a requisite half-dozen "first-rate pocket handkerchiefs" (389). As the couple discusses a wedding date, Rosamond looks serious, but "in fact, she was going through many intricacies of lace-edging and hosiery and petticoat tucking, in order to give an answer that would at least be approximate" (386). Believing that a dowry is forthcoming from Rosamond's father, Lydgate assumes that "[m]arriage, of course, must be prepared for in the usual way" (382), and, as Rosamond expects, he sees to the house, furniture, and housewares although he does not care for such things: "He would have behaved perfectly at a table where the sauce was served in a jug with the handle off, and he would have remembered nothing about a grand dinner except that a man was there who talked well" (382).

Following the marriage, for which Lydgate receives no dowry, Rosamond is unaware of her husband's slide into debt, although she has some sense that his medical practice is not a great financial success. Rosamond "had not yet had any anxiety about ways and means, although her domestic life had been expensive" (626). She busies herself during her pregnancy by collecting "embroidered robes and caps," only to have a baby that is stillborn. Rosamond sees the visit of Captain Lydgate and his sister, Mrs. Mengan, as an opportunity to entertain guests in their honor and an occasion "to take pains with . . . the careful selection of her lace" (627). She hopes that following the visit, she will in turn be invited to visit Lydgate's relations, where she would be "a much more exquisite ornament to the drawing-room there than any daughter of the family" (632).

Rosamond's material and social aspirations, and her unchecked spending, make it all the more difficult for Lydgate to confess the extent of his financial woes. The novel goes on to explain, rather economically, the conditions that led to Lydgate's circumstances: "When a man in setting up a house and preparing for marriage finds that his furniture and other initial expenses come to between four and five hundred pounds more than he has capital to pay for; when at the end of a year it appears that his household expenses, horses and et caeteras, amount to nearly a thousand, while the proceeds of a practice reckoned from the old books to be worth eight hundred per annum have sunk . . . and make hardly five hundred chiefly in unpaid entries, the plain inference is that . . . he is in debt" (633). Eighteen months before his marriage, we are told, Lydgate was poor—he enters into the marriage with no significant assets (633). Banking on the hoped-for success of his new practice, he spends generously in readying a home for his bride who expects no less, spending, in fact, several hundred more pounds on furniture and setting-up costs than he possesses. In addition to these initial costs, Lydgate discovers, after marriage, that it would take nearly one thousand pounds in regular household expenditures to keep his home with Rosamond running in style. He feels that he is obliged, as a professional man, to keep two horses and a well-supplied table and to pay a high rent on an attractive house and garden. But his income, in the best of circumstances, will not permit this level of living. Although the practice that he has taken over normally yields eight hundred pounds a year in income, this amount drops to five hundred when Lydgate assumes the practice, and, owing to the practice of patients deferring their payment for his medical services, he has received very little of that five hundred.

Household management guides of the 1830s were already devising systematic and tabular means by which to account for household expenditures. *The Family Exchequer Book* (1838), for example, claimed to offer a "plan . . . for the first time devised and submitted to public use" that would enable families to "obtain a minute and perspicuous synopsis" of their monetary affairs.[37] *The Family Exchequer Book* merely provided a system for domestic bookkeeping; later guides such as *A Manual of Domestic Economy* proffered suggestions of what appropriate middle-class spending levels should be. If we take the recommendations of the *Manual* as an approximate guide, the Lydgates are apparently living well beyond their means. Book II, the penultimate book of the *Manual*, provides a chart that subsumes all household expenditures, including clothing, to a master budget (fig. 3.1).[38] The *Manual*'s upper limit for household spending is £1,000 a year. This amount accords with a high standard of upper-middle-class living and would require an annual income of more than £1,000 for the prudent running of a household. The couple cannot afford to live on more than twice as much as Lydgate earns, but in effect, this is what they have been attempting to do. The guidelines for Walsh's *Manual* were created in reference

TABLE OF EXPENDITURE.

	ANNUAL INCOME.			
	No. 1, £1000.	No. 2, £500.	No. 3, £250.	No. 4, £100.
	£ s.	£ s.	£ s.	£ s.
Housekeeping:—				
Butcher's meat and bacon	75 0	40 0	30 0	18 0
Fish and poultry ...	30 0	10 0	7 0	—
Bread	20 0	16 0	14 0	10 0
Milk, butter, and cheese	20 0	18 0	16 0	8 0
Grocery	30 0	20 0	18 0	8 0
Italian goods	8 0	5 0	3 0	—
Greengrocery	20 0	12 0	10 0	6 0
Beer	20 0	12 0	10 0	5 0
Wine and spirits ...	50 0	15 0	8 0	1 0
Coals	25 0	15 0	12 0	5 0
Chandlery	12 0	7 0	7 0	2 0
Washing	40 0	30 0	15 0	2 0
	350 0	200 0	150 0	65
Carriages and horses ...	150 0	50 0	—	—
Rent and taxes	125 0	62 10	31 5	12 15
Clothing	125 0	62 10	31 5	12 10
Wages & incidental expenses	125 0	62 10	18 15	5 0
Illness and amusements	125 0	62 10	18 15	5 0
	£1000 0	£500 0	£250 0	£100 0

3.1 "Table of Expenditure." J. H. Walsh, *A Manual of Domestic Economy: Suited to Families Spending From £100 to £1000 a Year* (London: G. Routledge, 1856, 606)

to costs and to the value of currency in the 1850s; presumably, £1,000 is worth even more in the 1830s of *Middlemarch*. According to the chart, the Lydgates' actual income of £500 would at best permit them to afford only a modest horse and carriage. Clearly, Lydgate also spent beyond his means in furnishing a home. The *Manual* calculates the total cost of purchasing all the furniture needed for a home that runs on £1,000 a year to be £1,391.[39] Lydgate's resources would permit them to spend no more than £584 to furnish their home, according to Walsh's manual. We are told that Lydgate has spent what capital he has on furniture, plus another £400–£500 on credit, again exceeding the recommended amount for his income level.

While it was Lydgate who financed the furniture before the marriage and watched mounting household bills accrue following it, Rosamond is complicit in this accumulation of household debt. She is "accustomed from her childhood to an extravagant household, thought that good housekeeping consisted simply in ordering the best of everything—nothing else 'answered'" (634). She apparently keeps no accounts and provides little or no direction as to an economical running of the household. Her household consumption is justified as necessity—she is a well-attired wife of a doctor, a hostess in a well-appointed home that is commensurate with such a social standing. We do not see Rosamond placing an order in the text to supply the house or prepare it for guests; the transactions she makes "in ordering the best of everything" are not represented. The novel's refusal to represent this spending, however, does not suggest necessarily an affinity with ideals of domestic economy to conserve; rather, this is a showy omission in the manner of what we shall see is the excessive nature of Dorothea's sartorial understatement. But some traces of household consumption remain legible in Rosamond's dress and the parties she gives, for she "was fond of giving invitations" and "[t]he sociability seemed a necessary part of professional prudence, and the entertainment must be suitable" (634). Lydgate, who was not unhappy as a poor man before he was married and cares little for his dress, has deferred to Rosamond's material standards. That is, to secure the goods that she would like, Rosamond need not pledge Lydgate's credit herself to shops and tradesmen, though the law of necessities would permit this under common law. Lydgate, who has internalized Rosamond's material expectations, does it for her, furbishing her with amethyst jewelry, the best in furniture and dishes, and a house whose rent is more than he can afford.

Since Rosamond has concealed her consumption as social necessity, she is able to distance herself from responsibility for the debt. When Lydgate at last tells Rosamond about the debt, her deflective response is that of the extravagant woman in domestic advice literature who expects that her husband will pay up on her behalf: "What can I do, Tertius?" (640). The "neutrality" of Rosamond's words "fell like a mortal chill on" Lydgate (640). Rosamond is secure in the fact that she is not liable for the debt although it has accumulated because of her expensive tastes. The husband is the one who must pay, and Rosamond expects Lydgate to find a discreet way to do so. To satisfy the most pressing debts, Lydgate proposes to return as much of the plate as possible to the Brassing tradesman who sold it to him on credit. Also, he arranges for an inventory of the household furniture so that he may offer the bill of sale on the furniture to a second creditor as security and obtain in exchange more time to pay his debt. He urges economy, cuts the household staff to one servant, trims the stable to only one horse, and investigates both renting a smaller house that lets for thirty pounds a year and turning over the current lease of ninety pounds and furniture to Ned Plymdale.

These terms are unacceptable to Rosamond, whose solution is to act as unauthorized agent on behalf of her husband. In an attempt to prevent Lydgate from passing the lease of their home to Plymdale, she deliberately withholds the news that their home is available to let. Having prevented another couple from taking over the house, Rosamond visits Borthrop Trumball, who has a cheaper house to let, and interferes with Lydgate's arrangements to secure affordable housing: "It was the first time in her life that Rosamond had thought of doing anything in the form of business, but she felt equal to the occasion" (704). Having successfully forestalled plans to give up their expensive home, Rosamond plunges deeper into financial arrangements that place her outside of a normative domestic role. Having no direct access to capital, she writes secretly to Lydgate's uncle, Sir Godwin Lydgate, requesting to borrow one thousand pounds, the amount needed to substantially offset the debt. Lydgate receives a scathing letter from his uncle in response: "Don't set your wife to write to me when you have anything to ask. It is a roundabout wheedling sort of thing which I should not have credited you with. I never choose to write to a woman on matters of business. As to my supplying you with a thousand pounds, . . . I can do nothing of the sort" (715). The letter clearly indicates that Rosamond has overstepped the bounds of bourgeois domesticity as a woman who takes private financial matters outside the home.

Lydgate's bad credit comes to carry further social meanings that make him a suspect figure in Middlemarch. Following his decision to abandon gambling as a possible way to raise capital, Lydgate at last borrows money from Bulstrode. But his association with the latter sullies his reputation in the community when Raffles, whom Lydgate treats, dies under suspicious circumstances under Bulstrode's roof. Lydgate and Rosamond are snubbed by their neighbors, for there persists among them the notion that Lydgate was bribed to keep the source of Bulstrode's wealth a secret. He is only finally saved by Dorothea, who not only provides financial support so that he can be relieved of any obligation to Bulstrode but also restores his social currency—his reputation in the community.

Despite Lydgate's eventual financial recovery, Rosamond's invasive actions have a lasting effect. Exerting her economic agency in ways that displace her husband's authority, "she had mastered him" (719). While the novel by no means advocates women's extravagant household spending, nor does it portray Rosamond as an admirable figure who secures commodity goods at the expense of her husband, it nevertheless uses feminine material culture to register social relations and the production of identity. Dress and household items conceal class aspirations and, in the case of clothing, attest to how "sexual desire itself is always mapped within a social grid, and feminine beauty is inscribed onto the body through signifiers of social status."[40] Rosamond is more than just another extravagant woman; she proves to be a shrewd reader of signs and in the end gains the social standing she has always pursued. Indeed, after Lydgate's financial restitution through Dorothea's assistance and the ensuing financial success of his practice, Rosamond goes on to enjoy marriage to a man who can now provide her with a home "all flowers and gilding, fit for the bird of paradise that she resembled" (893). The implication is that Rosamond has enjoyed greater success than has her husband, who, "[a]s the years went on . . . opposed her less and less, when Rosamond concluded that he had learned the value of her opinion" (893). Lydgate ultimately "regard[s] himself as a failure" (893), professionally, and dies at the age of fifty. Rosamond outlives him, marries "an elderly and wealthy physician," and is last seen making "a very pretty show . . . driving out in her carriage" and speaking "of her happiness as a 'reward'" (893). While Rosamond may not have undergone the transformation that is usually associated with the successful rounding of a character, she has reached her objective of social solvency not through the economies of thrift recommended in household management guides but through the manipulation of material culture and its signs on the marriage market.[41]

Dorothea's Gambles

Although Rosamond and Dorothea might apply different approaches to the management of their domestic affairs, they are similar in that they both construct identities through credit and risk rather than through economy, recalling the risks that Eliot was willing to take in the publication of *Middlemarch*. If Rosamond seems a dubious model of femininity to the reader, she differs from Dorothea primarily because of her different uses of credit. In their similar enterprise to maximize debt, both women are a departure from the extravagant woman constructed through contemporary advice literature on etiquette and domestic economy, for together they demonstrate how household management and spending are not contradictory pursuits. Although their forms of credit may vary—Rosamond discovers more-immediate rewards, while Dorothea's must be deferred—both women challenge Victorian notions of separate spheres, revealing the extent to which the bourgeois domestic sphere was a porous space extending into a futurity that only the strategic deployment of credit can ensure.

Rosamond and Dorothea, then, share a vested interest in spending, albeit it to different ends. If Rosamond's marriage to a poor doctor was a risky venture, Dorothea's union with the pedantic Casaubon seems even more so. Although Casaubon suffers from no financial difficulties, he does not provide the emotional or intellectual stimulus that Dorothea banks on in marriage. Investing in Casaubon's scholarly work as his amanuensis, she spends her marriage indentured to his dubious enterprise to enumerate a Key to All Mythologies. However, she hopes to gain substantial returns that will enable her to formulate her own vocation, even if it means that she must defer the rewards.

But before Dorothea enters into this marriage contract, the novel produces Dorothea as a woman whose ascetic aspirations might make a union with Casaubon—whom Sir James calls "no better than a mummy" (81)—initially seem an attractive one. Although Dorothea's lofty aims for "an ideal life" (68) might seem to place her beyond matters of dress, Andrew H. Miller has rightly pointed out that "[w]omen's dress is the paradigmatic instance of material culture in *Middlemarch*, the emblem of its structural importance for Eliot's understanding of subjectivity and social relations."[42] Rather than seeing dress as an instance of the "compromise" that Eliot must reach—that "women should attend to it enough to effectively limit its importance"—the novel's recurring interest with what Dorothea is wearing indicates something other than an attempt to escape commodification through repression or renunciation.[43] Instead, the concerted plainness of her attire is indicative of the degree to which Dorothea takes the logic of thrift to its limit.

Middlemarch regards Dorothea's relationship to materiality with fascination, particularly in its frequent reflections upon her restrained dress and ornamentation. Indeed, the novel opens with an exploration of Dorothea's clothing, one fashion show of many to follow that leads Ellen Moers to declare that Dorothea "has what must be the most stunning wardrobe in Victorian fiction."[44] "Miss Brooke had that kind of beauty which seems to be thrown into relief by poor dress. Her hand and wrist were so finely formed that she could wear sleeves not less bare of style than those in which the Blessed Virgin appeared to Italian painters; and her profile as well as her stature and bearing seemed to gain the more dignity from her plain garments, which by the side of provincial fashion gave her the impressiveness of a fine quotation from the Bible,—or from one of our elder poets,—in a paragraph of to-day's newspaper" (29). Although Dorothea's ascetic style might seem far from Rosamond's obviously commodified one, the text produces plainness and understatement as a fetish. If her appearance is to be read as a paragraph from the daily newspaper, then Dorothea is an advertisement for an aesthetic of sartorial restraint, one that is no less an effect of commodity culture for its effort to efface that relation.

One obvious value of such restraint is how it conveys an upper-class standing, in contrast to Rosamond's class ambitions concerning her clothing. Whether originating in the 1830s, during which *Middlemarch* is set, or the 1870s, when the novel appeared, advice literature often echoes the sentiment that a lady should avoid showy dress. *Etiquette for the Ladies* (1837) warns, "Never allow your pursuit after fashion to be so eager, as to make people suppose that you have nothing better than the mode of your dress to recommend you."[45] In reference to self-presentation, Beeton advises that "it is better to be under-dressed than over-dressed," a directive echoed in *Etiquette for Ladies and Gentlemen* (1876), which recommends that "it is better to be too plainly dressed than too much dressed. Nothing has a more vulgar appearance than being too fine."[46] With her aspirational fashion sense, Rosamond looks like the women Beeton criticizes, women "who love to appear in a variety of suits every day new, as if a gown, like a stratagem in war, were to be used but once."[47] Dorothea and her sister Celia, in contrast, need not impress through dress, since "the Brooke connections, though not exactly aristocratic, were unquestionably 'good': if you inquired backward for a generation or two, you would not find any yard-measuring or parcel-tying forefathers. . . . Young women of such birth, living in a quiet country-house, and attending a village church . . . naturally regarded frippery as the ambition of a huckster's daughter. Then there was well-bred economy, which in those days made show in dress the first item to be deducted from, when any margin was required for expenses more distinctive of rank" (29). Overly decorative dress is associated with the social ambitions of daughters of drapers and tradesmen, of the likes of Rosamond. By contrast, Dorothea's and Celia's clothing would never be confused with the "frippery" of the arriviste.

While Celia dresses with a certain understatement in keeping with her class, she does not carry this understatement to the extremes of Dorothea's sartorial reserve. She is the model of upper-class dress, whereas Dorothea's plainness conveys the intensity of another economy at work. As Clair Hughes points out, Dorothea's plain sleeves were not in fashion in the 1830s, when the elaborate gigot, or leg-of-mutton sleeve, was a mark of the latest style.[48] Her apparent indifference to the latest fashion and to the allure of material objects in general is apparent when Dorothea and her sister divide their late mother's jewels between them. Refusing an ornamental cross "with careless deprecation" (34), Dorothea agrees at last to take a matching ring and bracelet, "trying to justify her delight in the colours by merging them in her mystic religious joy" (36). Later, in a scene that rewrites *Jane Eyre*'s disavowal of consumer goods when Rochester takes her shopping, Dorothea and Will Ladislaw look over some cameos that Dorothea has purchased by Celia's request while on her honeymoon in Rome. But if the episode in *Jane Eyre* raises the specter of seduction, Ladislaw proves an amiable and helpful shopping companion for Dorothea, who has brought the cameos back to her honeymoon quarters to inspect. Feeling "uneasy" about the choices she has made for her sister (251), she asks Ladislaw for his opinion. Learning that Dorothea has not purchased them for herself, wishing instead "to make life beautiful," Ladislaw affirms Dorothea's aesthetic nature over her self-described asceticism, telling her, "You *are* a poem," and urging that "[t]he best piety is to enjoy" (256, 252).

Indeed, for a woman who claims to be unable to "reconcile the anxieties of a spiritual life involving eternal consequences, with a keen interest in guimp and artificial protrusions of drapery" (30), Dorothea undergoes a number of extraordinary costume changes throughout the novel. Arguably, the narrativization of her dress is far more detailed and memorable than is Rosamond's. We are aware that Rosamond "has excellent taste in costume," yet the plainness of Dorothea's clothing is what is most sensuously catalogued. In each instance, Dorothea's "anti-fashion," to use Hughes's term, seems not merely a fulfillment of advice literature's dicta that women avoid frivolous dress but a form of understatement that takes such advice to its limits. For the dinner party at which Casaubon is a guest, Dorothea wears a "silver-grey dress . . . in keeping with the entire absence from her manner and expression of all search after mere effect" (114). During her honeymoon in Rome, gray is again her color of choice, and the effects are stunning. Dorothea is "clad in Quakerish grey drapery; her long cloak, fastened at the neck, was thrown backward from her arms, and one beautiful ungloved hand pillowed her cheek, pushing somewhat backward the white beaver bonnet which made a sort of halo to her face" (220). As Will Ladislaw and his artist friend, Naumann, see her standing by a nude statue of Ariadne, the latter is struck by the "fine bit of antithesis" between the stillness of the one form and the "breathing life" of the other (220). In this remarkable juxtaposition, Dorothea's austere dress outshines the more overt display of a nude Ariadne.

In chapter 43, the text cannot resist one other important comparison, as Dorothea and Rosamond are finally placed side by side. Dorothea is clothed ethereally, in "that thin white woollen stuff soft to the touch and soft to the eye. It . . . was always in the shape of a pelisse with sleeves hanging all out of the fashion. Yet if she had entered before a still audience as Imogene or Cato's daughter, the dress might have seemed right enough" (470). Rosamond's "pale-blue dress [is] of a fit and fashion so perfect that no dressmaker could look at it without emotion, a large embroidered collar which it was to be hoped all beholders would know the price of, her small hands duly set off with rings, and that controlled self-consciousness of manner which is the expensive substitute for simplicity" (471). Rosamond is always up-to-date, and her fashion sense is the textile equivalent of another text, that of the elaborately decorated *Keepsake* annual that Lydgate had dismissed as a "sugared invention" (303) near the beginning of their courtship. While Rosamond, a product of the latest fad, flaunts expensive clothing, it is Dorothea who arguably comes up trumps. Dorothea's appearance is valued for its plainness, for how it resists classifications, for its antifashion stance, and it is placed within the realm of value precisely because it cannot be priced. This "Christian Antigone," as Naumann earlier describes her, anticipates the "Aesthetic or 'reformed' dress of Eliot's own time."[49] Dorothea's clothing is at once anachronistic and ahead of its time. A style that seems to belong to no particular era or fad, it is nevertheless the result of a residual relation to the consumer world it would seem to ignore.

If Dorothea's self-fashioning suggests a way to manage the ephemeral nature of commercially driven tastes, one final costume change brings home the nature of her investments. Following Casaubon's death, Dorothea is said to look "handsomer than ever in her mourning" (582) in "this heavy solemnity of clothing [which] made her face look all the younger, with its recovered bloom" (585), and she must be prodded to remove her cap in her sister's company, for she claims to be "so used to the cap—it has become a sort of shell. . . . I feel rather bare and exposed when it is off" (592). Her widow's garb exerts a powerful attraction for Will Ladislaw, who "never quite knew how it was that he saved himself from falling down at her feet, when the 'long while' came forth with its gentle tremor. He used to say that the horrible hue and surface of her crape dress was most likely the sufficient controlling force" (587). In a performative gesture that recalls Lucy Audley's manufactured appearance, it is finally Dorothea's mourning dress that makes the extremes of her economy of restraint most visible. On Dorothea, the black crape of the widow's mourning is hyperbolic, and this emphatic display stands in for the grief that she does not truly feel over the death of Casaubon.[50] Dorothea's sartorial restraint and her indifference to the latest style do not mark a retreat from material culture but indicate the weighing and measuring of a set of very different economic concerns. What is striking about Dorothea's parade of Quakerish, even funerary clothing is the excessive nature of its plainness. Such dress would hardly be noticeable on humble Mary Garth, for example; on Dorothea, in contrast, plainness takes on real value. The signs of her clothing acquire meaning in reference to others in the marketplace, notably Rosamond. But while Dorothea does not directly engage a world of commodities as Rosamond does, she is not entirely unlike Lydgate's spendthrift wife, for she constitutes an unexpected version of the extravagant woman constructed in advice literature. Dorothea's dress is crowded with the signs of a form of surplus, the excess of her own reserve. These are not the signs of a miser or a hoarder. Unlike Silas Marner, whose body, Jeff Nunokawa notes, "is invulnerable to any sensation at all," Dorothea's elegant understatement makes her an object of desire not only for Will Ladislaw but also for the text, which digresses time and again to enumerate the extent to which she is unadorned.[51]

If dress is the novel's most recurring instance of material culture, Dorothea's managed fashion sense finds its corollary in a related set of investment practices that seem conservative but are actually risky. Both Dorothea's investments in clothing and her role as her husband's amanuensis entail forms of withholding that are epic in their scope. For her, the reserve that is produced through the economies of thrift is a form of credit, and she hopes that her indenture to Casaubon's work will translate into her own vocational dividends in the future; by spending herself for Casaubon, she aims to shore up the experience for an epic life. Entering into marriage with Casaubon and assisting him in his scholarly endeavors, Dorothea hopes to fulfill her intellectual goals: "'I should learn everything then,' she said to herself, still walking quickly along the bridle road through the wood. 'It would be my duty to study that I might help him the better in his great works. There would be nothing trivial about our lives. Everyday-things with us would mean the greatest things. It would be like marrying Pascal. I should learn to see the truth by the same light as great men have seen it by. And then I should know what to do, when I got older: I should see how it was possible to lead a grand life here—now—in England'" (51). By demanding an epic life, Dorothea determines to exceed the usual limitations of married domesticity. The preface of the novel, we recall, likens her to a modern St. Theresa who tries to shape for herself some noble aspiration to follow. But lacking vocational definition and confined by nineteenth-century notions of separate spheres, such women have "no coherent social faith and order which could perform the function of knowledge for the ardently willing soul" (25). While a day-to-day interest in domestic arrangements might be more the province of lower-middle-class Mrs. Garth and middle-class Rosamond, even an upper-class Dorothea would be expected to take some interest in the affairs of a household. Instead, Dorothea attempts to surpass the usual role of wife and mistress of the house.

After accepting Casaubon's offer of marriage, Dorothea imagines she is "a neophyte about to enter on a higher grade of initiation. She was going to have room for the energies which stirred, uneasily under the dimness and pressure of her own ignorance and the petty peremptoriness of the world's habits. Now she would be able to devote herself to large yet definite duties; now she would be allowed to live continually in the light of a mind that she could reverence" (68). Dorothea hopes Casaubon will permit her to assist him in his research, teach her classical languages, and provide her with the opportunity to embark upon scholarly pursuits for which few women had opportunity. An initial visit to Casaubon's melancholy house reveals, however, that there will be "nothing for her to do in Lowick" (103). Casaubon prefers to work in isolation, does not delegate any duties to Dorothea, and assigns her a boudoir where he imagines she will occupy herself. Following the wedding and a joyless honeymoon, during which Casaubon is cloistered in the Vatican Library nearly every day, Dorothea retreats to this boudoir. Spending idle hours here, she discovers that she is "not yet freed . . . from the gentlewoman's oppressive liberty" (307). Marriage has not improved her opportunity "to lead a grand life."

With some persistence, Dorothea persuades Casaubon to permit her to perform some clerical work in connection with his research, "making it a matter of course that she should take her place at an early hour in the library and have work either of reading aloud or copying assigned to her" (315). But as she undertakes these tasks for him, the bankrupt nature of his emotional resources gradually becomes apparent to her. Casaubon clearly believes that he has garnered a considerable equity through his scholarship and bachelorship that would permit him now to enjoy the companionship of Dorothea as his wife: "Poor Casaubon had imagined that his long studious bachelorhood had stored up for him a compound interest of enjoyment, and that large drafts on his affections would not fail to be honoured" (111). As early as his engagement, however, he is surprised that the depth of his feeling amounts to "an exceedingly shallow rill" (87). Casaubon's work also lacks vision. It is a losing venture, and Eliot puts it in economic language to highlight the unprofitable undertaking into which Dorothea has cast her lot. The research is not only anachronistic in its revisiting of eighteenth-century debates but also ignores developments in German higher criticism. Casaubon's work amounts to little more than "the surplus stock of false antiquities kept in a vendor's back chamber" (237). In the current marketplace of ideas, such scholarship has little currency. So dubious is Casaubon's undertaking that the research can only be described in terms of a negative economics, that is, said to possess a "surplus" of worthlessness.

In a desperate bid to compensate for a disappointing marriage, Dorothea draws further upon her own resources. Indeed, her reasons for investing in the union in the first place appear to be altruistic. Dorothea does not want "any share in Casaubon's learning as mere accomplishment. . . . All her eagerness for acquirement lay within that full current of sympathetic motive in which her ideas and impulses were habitually swept along" (112). Dorothea attempts to translate a bankrupt marriage and her husband's fruitless scholarship into a deeper capacity to empathize. Earlier, when the first dissatisfactions with marriage emerge during the trip to Rome, Dorothea summons "a current into which all thought and feeling were apt sooner or later to flow. . . . There was clearly something better than anger and despondency" (235). With this hope intact, Dorothea resolves to demonstrate greater empathy toward Casaubon and the "sad consciousness in his life" (243).

Dorothea's reserves are nearly depleted, however, when Casaubon asks her to honor his dying wish: that she continue his work by carrying on with the outlines he has been producing as the framework of his study. This constitutes a kind of debt or obligation, a bill of credit that she must fulfill. As such, it is a reversal of the legal situation in which a husband may be held responsible for his wife's debts. Dorothea shudders to think how her consent to continue Casaubon's work would ensure an indebtedness that would weigh her down well into the future, for the task will be as pointless as it is endless: "She had no presentiment that the power which her husband wished to establish over her future action had relation to anything else than his work. . . . And now she pictured to herself the days, and months, and years which she must spend in sorting what might be called shattered mummies" (519). Dorothea's efforts in Casaubon's venture have all along been a gamble. As with any financial risk, such a gamble is premised on a conception of time and how time is spent. With all her "passion . . . transfused through a mind struggling towards an ideal life," Dorothea borrows against the future, projecting herself into a time when she will have "learn[ed] everything" (68, 51). Consistent with the operations of market capital, Dorothea's version of a credit economy is a notably mercantile subversion of a Christian ethos in which one's present suffering cannot be compared to a future reward yet to be revealed.[52]

When Dorothea is mercifully released from obligation to Casaubon's work following his death, she reorganizes her portfolio and focuses instead on the prospect of how to spend now, instead of later. And so she reprises her earlier interest in establishing a model workers' colony. Having spent freely of herself while married to Casaubon, with little hope of returns, her vocational goals, significantly, become increasingly identified as the problem of spending. Her contribution of two hundred pounds a year—a significant portion of her personal annual income of seven hundred—to Lydgate's New Fever Hospital is not simply a philanthropic act but a great relief for Dorothea. She desires "something good to do with [her] money" (822), "to buy land . . . and found a village which should be a school of industry" (822), and she informs Lydgate that "it would be like taking a burden from me if you took some of it every year" (825). If Dorothea evinces little attention for the operations of her household, she is certainly interested in bettering the domestic experience of local cottagers. Her plans to improve cottagers' housing in the parish are excessive in that they place her in a public role. She prefers poring over her architectural plans, ensuring that she has "not got incompatible stairs and fireplaces" (37), to the duties attendant to being mistress of a well-appointed home. Indeed, her investment is political: "I think we deserve to be beaten out of our beautiful houses with a scourge of small cord—all of us who let tenants live in such sties as we see round us. Life in cottages might be happier than ours, if they were real houses fit for human beings from whom we expect duties and affections" (54).

In life, "Mr Casaubon apparently did not care about building cottages . . . [but] he would not disapprove of her occupying herself with it in leisure moments, as other women expected to occupy themselves with their dress and embroidery" (56). But with his death, Dorothea can renew her desire to execute her housing scheme. Like household manuals, she approaches spending as a problem, but she locates the solution not in saving but in an ethical form of spending: "She sat down in the library before her particular little heap of books on political economy and kindred matters, out of which she was trying to get light as to the best way of spending money so as not to injure one's neighbours, or—what comes to the same thing—so as to do them the most good. Here was a weighty subject which, if she could but lay hold of it, would certainly keep her mind steady" (863). A far better prospect than Casaubon's Key to All

Mythologies, an exercise in interpretation in which signs are merely matched to their signifiers, Dorothea's housing project is the province of a true manager, in which organizing, sorting, and allocation are valued in themselves. When such energies are directed by the imperative of social spending, they are consistent with the ideal life Dorothea imagines. If Dorothea has been a gambler, the prospect of a life of philanthropy marks her emergence as an ethical spender.[53]

Some difficulties remain for Dorothea, however. She has the capital to dispense but not the cultural authority to formulate a vocation commensurate with her ability to spend. Like many other women of property, as Tim Dolin has considered, Dorothea presents a narrative challenge: how to write the solvent *feme sole*. For Dolin, the nineteenth-century novel returns time and again to "courtship and marriage as a powerful set of conditions for narrative resolution, whether those conditions are to be resisted, subverted, or rejected outright."[54] For Dorothea, the resolution comes not through marriage but remarriage. But even when the novel goes on to locate Dorothea's vocational fulfillment in marriage to Will Ladislaw, it does so in terms of spending. Believing Rosamond and Will to be romantically linked, a jealous Dorothea discovers the fullness of her emotional reserves and weighs this against what she believes have been Ladislaw's overextended or counterfeit attentions toward her: "The fire of Dorothea's anger was not easily *spent*, and it flamed out in fitful *returns* of spurning reproach. . . . Why had he brought his *cheap* regard and his lip-born words to her who had nothing paltry to give in *exchange*. He knew that he was deluding her—wished, in the very moment of farewell, to make her believe that he gave her the whole *price* of his heart, and knew that he had *spent* it half before" (845; emphasis added). When Rosamond assures Dorothea "that no other woman exist[s] for him besides you" (856), there still are economic impediments to their union. Ladislaw's fear is that Dorothea will not have him if she believes that he was willing to accept a quiet financial settlement from Bulstrode in exchange for suppressing knowledge of Ladislaw's grandfather's ill-gotten wealth. Furthermore, Casaubon's codicil to his will stipulates that his estate will not go to Dorothea, should she marry Ladislaw.

In addition to these problems, which Dorothea and Ladislaw overcome by renouncing any claim to Casaubon's fortune, the novel also suggests that Dorothea must overcome an additional impediment related to the problem of spending. At the moment of declaring her desire to be with Will, she makes this disclosure using notably economic language: "Oh, I cannot bear it—my heart will break. . . . I don't mind about poverty—I hate my wealth. . . . We could live quite well on my own fortune—it is too much—seven hundred-a-year—I want so little—no new clothes—and I will learn what everything costs" (870). This pivotal declaration is couched in terms of dress, appropriate dress, and its attendant costs. Having invested in marriage to Casaubon and in Casaubon's scholarly work, Dorothea has discovered deep losses whose cost she now begins to count. That Dorothea's declaration is couched in terms of dress points to how very material her objectives for an epic life are.

Although mid-nineteenth-century conventions of the domestic novel might not permit Dorothea's self-realization through anything other than marriage and construct Ladislaw as her appropriate love-object, Eliot's novel preserves Dorothea's relationship to spending both as constitutive of an expansive subjectivity and as ethical. This spending amounts to her everyday practices, which extend her into the future of the text as it imagines her life beyond it, crediting her with small, "unhistoric acts" (896) that are nevertheless generous. The novel figures her final act discursively as a form of extravagant spending of herself: "Her finely-touched spirit had still its fine issues, though they were not widely visible. Her full nature, like that river of which Cyrus broke the strength, spent itself in channels which had no great name on the earth. But the effect of her being on those around her was incalculably diffusive: for the growing good of the world is partly dependent on unhistoric acts; and that things are not so ill with you and me as they might have been, is half owing to the number who lived faithfully a hidden life, and rest in unvisited tombs" (896). As Gillian Beer observes, this spending is a form of absolute expenditure, not exchange.[55] It is giving in which indebtedness is not possible, for nothing is expected in return.

If advice literature cautioned against women's expenditures, in *Middlemarch*, spending enables Rosamond and Dorothea to reformulate and even transgress the terms of their economic standing in the domestic sphere. Spending on credit—spending what one does not have—may extend women, such as Rosamond, into masculine spheres where they may manipulate their limited liability for debt to further their social standing. Women's spending here functions not as a simple, emancipatory practice but as a disruptive element within masculine economies that disinters Woman from an identification with the commodity form. Furthermore, the woman creditor stores up future dividends in the production of female identities. That is, instead of a female subjectivity produced through the limits of the disciplined female self of Victorian sexual economies, women's spending in *Middlemarch* enables strategic forms of mobility through its reconceptualization of time. In representing women with either limited access to capital or limited ways to dispose of it, *Middlemarch* figures spending discursively in an economy that forms a striking contrast to Samuel Smiles's economies of thrift, imbedding within the text a gendered ethic of spending that informs and revises the apparently nonmaterial aim of the novel's famous exploration of the terms of an epic life for women as one that is thoroughly bound up with commercial and material concerns.

Women's expenditures, whether in the home or poised just beyond in new forms of commercial philanthropic ventures, extend female subjects and guarantee them through the prospect of a future return. Dorothea's economic dealings translate the ideology of thrift into a practice that makes an excessive display of its own accumulated resources. Even through the practice of dressing down, Dorothea negotiates the terms of everyday life on vast scale. From a sartorial economy fashioned through restraint to a marriage contract whose payoff could only be realized in the remote future, her investments resemble what Alfred Tennyson called the "far-off interest of tears."[56]

Dorothea's gambles return us to Eliot's publishing venture, and its particular costs. In the end, the sales figures for the four-volume edition of *Middlemarch* turned out to be a disappointment. Book 1 sold only about 6,000 copies, while the other parts came in at about 5,000 copies each;[57] this was 2,000 to 3,000 fewer per part than Lewes had anticipated.[58] Despite these mediocre results, Eliot could not resist another similar wager, repeating the same format of eight half-volume parts for the publication of her final novel, *Daniel Deronda*, in 1876. Recalling that novel's memorable opening scene, where we find Gwendolen Harleth seated at a roulette table and engaged in a desperate bid to reverse her fortunes, one can almost imagine Eliot's speculations in the literary marketplace running concurrently with those of her heroine. In the closing sentences of *Middlemarch*, where Dorothea too is all in, her actions retain a notably ethical dimension, suggesting that there is much that connects the ambitious woman in pursuit of an ideal life to the woman as thrill-seeking spender. Managing an epic life in this way is not without its costs, but as Dorothea makes herself felt by those around her in an "incalculably diffusive" way, those efforts have produced a life that is nonetheless extravagant for having been "unhistoric."

Four

TO THOSE WHO LOVE THEM BEST

The Erotics of Connoisseurship in Michael Field's Sight and Song

*I*n his cover design for the first prospectus for *The Yellow Book*, Aubrey Beardsley depicts the front of the Bodley Head's shop in Vigo Street, including its large windows stocked neatly with books for sale (fig. 4.1). Standing in the background of the picture and in the shop entrance is Bodley Head cofounder Elkin Mathews, who is caricatured "as a round-faced, wizened, and bespectacled pierrot."[1] Although this depiction of Mathews, who would sometimes escape to a storeroom rather than deal with difficult customers, is amusing in itself, more engaging still is the larger figure who occupies the foreground of the drawing.[2] The subject of Mathews's scowling gaze is a woman shopper who rummages through a bin of aesthetically designed books. Ignoring the disapproving looks of the proprietor, the woman continues to browse at her leisure. Despite her fashionable dress and the intellectual refinement of an "advanced" or New Woman, she proceeds like any bargain shopper, jumbling up the stock as she goes along.[3] Although this woman, as

4.1. Aubrey Beardsley front cover design of the prospectus for *The Yellow Book*, 1894.
V&A Images/Victoria and Albert Museum, London

Sally Ledger points out, is "on the streets alone at night in the West End, quite close to the notorious Burlington Arcade," she seems less a figure of vulnerability than a potential nuisance to the shop owner.[4] Will she purchase one of the many volumes, or is she another version of the errant shopper, who looks but does not buy and leaves the merchandise in disarray when she finally moves on?

With her command of the scene and her cool disdain for the male bookseller, this browser is emblematic of women's problematic relationship to aestheticism in the 1890s, including the world of aesthetic book collecting. As part of the Bodley Head roster, so too did Katharine Bradley and Edith Cooper, the aunt and niece who wrote collaboratively as "Michael Field," disturb in their own way the gendered practices of aestheticism, connoisseurship, and publishing. In *Sight and Song*, their 1892 volume of poems published in the Bodley Head's belles lettres series, they present thirty-one ekphrastic lyrics. The poems were based primarily on Renaissance paintings with classical themes, many of which the women viewed together in British and Continental museums and galleries, especially during an excursion abroad in 1891. Through a series of lyrics that focus particularly on images of women, *Sight and Song* contends with what it means to consume a feminized object of the gaze. Michael Field's emphasis on the discursive formation of shared pleasure rather than possession rewrites consumption as desire instead of erasure, presenting possible ways of extending the boundaries of identity through consumption to achieve an expansive female subjectivity. Harkening back to the homoeroticism of exchange in *Goblin Market*, *Sight and Song*'s consumable bodies become the visible surfaces onto which women's same-sex pleasures might be inscribed apart from masculine viewership.

In such a discursive economy, desire between women figures as a transaction that reveals the continuities between aestheticism and consumption. Studies of fin-de-siècle British aestheticism of late have shifted from an earlier interest in models of production to the relationship between cultural production and consumption.[5] Regenia Gagnier, for example, identifies an "emerging service and consumerist economy that determined late-Victorian aestheticism" and emphasizes, not unlike Michel de Certeau, that categories of production and consumption are not mutually exclusive.[6] Consumption models have enabled an analysis of aestheticism that considers how, despite an apparent retreat from the materialities of the marketplace, the content of aestheticism constitutes a reflection upon this very retreat. The art for art's sake credo of the aesthetes attests to aestheticism's dependence on the very commercial forms it would seem to renounce. As Jonathan Freedman has observed, the aesthetic practices that pertain to collectible objects, clothing, interior decoration—even to the social currency obtained from the repetition of a perfectly packaged Wildean witticism—come to resemble Marx's understanding of commodities in the ways in which they circulate meanings apart from their means of production.[7] By locating desire in a world of objects, the aesthete was engaged in social practices that enacted the conditions of Marx's commodity. Thus, for the aesthetes, "the loftiest notion of cultural superiority still depend[ed] on the vulgar act of shopping."[8] As Kathy Alexis Psomiades has shown, eroticized feminine images typically function in male aestheticism as the crucial mediation between the economic and the aesthetic to suspend contradictions inherent in the relationship between art and commodity culture.[9] Such images operate differently in Michael Field's commodity aesthetics, which depends on an economy of pleasure in which there is no feminized, compensatory object of exchange.

We can understand Bradley and Cooper's literary collaboration not only in terms of the modes of authorship that generate a nonobjectifying consumption of female portraiture in *Sight and Song* but also as part of a set of lived practices and publishing endeavors that constructed aestheticism as a consumer enterprise. These aesthetic practices were by no means separate from the writing of *Sight and Song*, for, as de Certeau reminds us, "'ways of operating' or doing things, no longer appear as merely the obscure background of social activity."[10] The images that occasioned the poems of *Sight and Song* were carefully organized and translated as text within the women's leisure pursuit as museumgoers, rather than being incidental to the poems. As a result of such practices, the couple, who lived together as lovers in aesthetically decorated homes in Reigate and Richmond, came to reconstitute literary aestheticism as a same-sex enterprise for women, a space where both writing and pleasure could be exchanged and circulated between themselves.

Bradley and Cooper, however, were not merely writing for themselves. Their distinction as Bodley Head writers meant a certain entrée into elite company; among the other authors that Elkin Mathew and John Lane published were Arthur Symons, John Addington, and Oscar Wilde.[11] As a material object, *Sight and Song* was the result of the Bodley Head's unique production methods and its marketing appeals to a refined readership. However, the economies of female pleasure that it discursively inscribes complicate the idea of the book as commodity to be owned. As though in dialogue with the book's status as a consumer item, sought after for its elegance and daintiness, the poems of *Sight and Song* acquire a sense of concreteness, often as an effect of layout and typographical design—an autonomy that departs from Walter Pater's subjectivist adaptation of Matthew Arnold's concern for the viewer "to see the object as in itself it really is."[12] In a series of lyrics that highlight the refusal of the female subject to be mastered and offer instead the possibilities of female homoeroticism and a shared gaze between women, the text constitutes a rejoinder to the impulse to collect. Through a self-conscious display of its own material status, *Sight and Song* pressures the aesthetic economies that produced the feminized book-as-object as that which is exquisitely bound, as it were, only to be possessed.

Michael Field at the Bodley Head

Following moves from earlier residences in Birmingham and Bristol, where they lived with family members, the women established a home together in suburban London, first in Reigate beginning in 1888, and later in Richmond from 1899 until Cooper's and Bradley's deaths in 1913 and 1914, respectively. The fashioning of both of these homes attests to the women's consumerist relationship to aestheticism. The Reigate house, called Durdans, featured a drawing room decorated with Morris wallpaper and carpet. Here, photographs of themselves and of Robert Browning and a William Rothenstein drawing of their friends Charles Ricketts and Charles Shannon shared space with Botticelli and Titian prints.[13] No less charming was the next residence, an eighteenth-century house decorated by Ricketts. In the 1933 preface to Michael Field's journals, *Works and Days*, the editors include this recollection of the home's décor:

> [The Paragon's] eighteenth-century doors and mouldings were painted white, the walls of the small room to the right on entering were silver. . . . There were two Hiroshigi prints in this room and several lithographs by Shannon. . . . The furniture was eighteenth-century satinwood. . . . Shannon's lithographs, dignified, for the first time, with gilded frames of beautiful proportions, made walls, distempered a warm grey, exquisite;

among them hung two of Ricketts' *Hero and Leander* woodcuts and a drawing of two heads of wild garlic. . . . On the dainty, polished table-tops stood several pieces of white porcelain and rare glass, or old plate, and a tangle of necklaces or other jewels displayed with artful carelessness.[14]

In their aesthetically appointed space, Bradley and Cooper wrote and entertained. By the time the women had settled in the Paragon, a daily routine had already been established. The women would often begin by reading letters and the *Times* over a long breakfast before beginning to write. Cooper worked in the "Silver Room" amid "Japanese prints and Shannon's lithographs," while Bradley wrote just a flight of stairs away in a green room "with blue silk cushions"; each wrote alone between nine and one, and following lunch the women often compared work and made suggestions for one other, as they put it, "breaking bits off for each other to do."[15] In the afternoon, they might garden or pay visits to friends. In the evening, they often wore formal clothing and invited friends such as Bodley Head illustrators Shannon and Ricketts, Logan Pearsall Smith, and on one occasion, a nervous young William Butler Yeats to dinner.[16] Far from being defined by these secluded and rarefied quarters, however, the women's identity as Michael Field was an effect of what Ana Parejo Vadillo calls "the dialectic city-suburb," as Bradley and Cooper moved freely between the spaces of their home and the metropolitan experience of London, including public lectures and museums, as well as the cosmopolitan pleasures of the Continent during their excursions abroad.[17]

The considerable energies the women devoted to their everyday aesthetic lives were equaled by the care they took in their commercial publishing enterprises. Their exacting standards extended to their specifications for the physical appearance of *Sight and Song*. Mary Sturgeon, Michael Field's early biographer, notes that

> we may find, in [Michael Field's] correspondence with Mr Elkin Mathews about *Sight and Song* in 1892, one proof out of many which the poets' career affords of their concern for the physical beauty of their books. They desired their children to be lovely in body as well as in spirit; and great was their care for format, decoration, binding, paper, and type: for colour, texture, quality, arrangement of letterpress, appearance of title-page, design of cover. In every detail there was rigorous discrimination:

precise directions were given, often in an imperious tone; experiments were recommended; journeys of inspection were undertaken; certain things were chosen and certain others emphatically banned.[18]

"We know," wrote Michael Field to Mathews, that "you will share our anxiety that the book should be as perfect as art can make it."[19]

As poets interested in the production values of their work, Bradley and Cooper found a suitable venue in the Bodley Head publishing house. John Lane, who had witnessed the growing taste for exotic, antiquarian books over the course of the 1880s, realized "that there was a public for daintily produced books."[20] Capitalizing on this ready market, he and Elkin Mathews launched the Bodley Head in 1887, and the firm soon became synonymous with aesthetically designed books. By producing a select number of volumes as limited editions, the Bodley Head meant to appeal to the growing number of readers who were seeking out beautifully decorated first editions in the rare book market. If George Eliot's publishing scheme with Blackwood's had been a gamble, so too was the Bodley Head venture a risk, banking on the hope that antiquarian book buyers would also be intrigued by tastefully decorated volumes written by new and innovative writers, especially poets.[21] The success of the first Bodley Head book boded well for the firm. Richard Le Gallienne's poems, *Volumes in Folio*, sold briskly in 1889, and fifty copies were bought up in the United States by Scribner's for an eager American readership.[22] This early success was followed by others, as when just over two hundred of Oscar Wilde's *Poems*, originally published by Brogue and Company in 1881, were transferred to the Bodley Head's belles lettres list. Reissued with a new title page and cover designs by Charles Ricketts, the new 1892 edition of *Poems* sold out in just days.

As James G. Nelson has recounted, the Bodley Head's "calculated risk" to supply books for a collector's market was carefully calibrated, paying attention to the smallest of production details.[23] Rarely exceeding five hundred copies for any one edition, the firm managed its outlay while creating demand for this small stock. Through deliberate production practices such as using a font size larger than ten point, wide margins, and extra leading between lines, Mathews and Lane managed to keep typesetting costs down while producing a striking effect on the page. Also, by buying up remaindered paper from manufacturers at a discount rate, they were able to print the books on good-quality paper. Leaving the pages unopened instead of machine-cut, they reduced costs further, even as they ensured what Margaret D. Stetz calls "a deliberate bow to nostalgia for the style of the past" by enabling the book's buyer to cut the pages by himself or herself.[24] While Bodley Head books looked expensive, with their cloth binding and illustrated title pages by artists such as Aubrey Beardsley and Selwyn Image, they were actually comparatively affordable. Mathews and Lane often set the price below the five shillings typically charged by other publishers and still ensured a profit. As a further inducement to buyers, many of the books came with a statement of limitation and were signed by the author. For those readers willing to pay more, the Bodley Head offered some volumes in large-paper special editions; these issues were more elaborately bound, sometimes in a run of only three to forty copies done with handmade Japanese paper.[25]

Although Bodley Head books were readily distinguished by these physical characteristics, Stetz argues that "what was really most distinctive about a book published by Mathews and Lane was the way it was marketed."[26] Mathews and Lane placed advertisements in journals such as the *Academy*, the *Athenaeum*, and the *Spectator*, where the ad copy was careful to announce the details that would matter to a connoisseur, such as the quality of the paper, the typeface, and the name of the printer and illustrator.[27] Perhaps most important, Bodley Head promotions "developed a philosophy of limitation" that announced the number of limited copies that were available, translating scarcity into an aesthetic value.[28] The most significant and compendious of the Bodley Head advertisements, which likewise emphasized the limited stock, were bound into the back of each volume. These detailed lists of "Books in Belles Lettres" had reached fifteen pages' worth by 1895. In addition to the titles of books in the series, the lists also included other materials, such as excerpts from newspaper reviews, sometimes written by Bodley Head writers, that emphasized aesthetic values of beauty and taste and attributed these to the firm itself.[29] "To buy a Bodley Head book," Stetz writes, "was to obtain 'culture'—in the social, as well as the intellectual, sense—at rock bottom prices (often, for a mere three shillings and sixpence) and to feel part of a 'choice' and 'rare' population oneself."[30] Stetz finds in the Liberty catalogues of the 1880s a precedent for the lists and prospectuses that Mathews and Lane produced to announce their offerings. "[W]ith their engravings, decorative borders, ornaments, and subtle merchandising," Stetz writes, "one can find the model for the Bodley's 'List of Books in Belles Lettres.'"[31] Following the notably aesthetic values of such Liberty advertisements as seen in figure 1.2 ("Quaint!—Artistic!—Original!—Beautiful—and Useful!"), the Bodley Head's belles lettres catalogues "featured the very same elements of language and idea" in their concern to market the books as new, rare, elegant, and alluring, and to suture in this advertising sleight of hand the domains of aestheticism and commercialism.[32]

A survey of the material aspects of *Sight and Song* suggests that Bradley and Cooper's desire that their "book should be as perfect as art can make it" was likely met, in part because of Bradley's frequent letters to Elkin Mathews (whom the couple liked to refer to as "The Elk") regarding the publication details.[33] It was Lane's idea, however, that *Sight and Song* should be done in the manner of Graham R. Tomson's popular volume of poems, *A Summer Night*, which had been published in 1891 by Methuen and Company.[34] That book had been bound in blue boards covered in paper and decorated on the cover with a gold moon-and-star design. While adapting the same format, size, and typeface, *Sight and Song*, bound in an elegant olive-green cover, was a higher-quality production. Printed by T. A. Constable, *Sight and Song* was limited to four hundred copies, a number announced on the page facing the title. The title page consisted of a bold, wood-engraved design by Walter Biggar Blaikie (fig. 4.2). Perhaps the best of his title-page designs for the Bodley Head, it is "[s]trikingly asymmetrical in its disposition of type," as Nelson observes; the page is organized around a circular, botanical design that incorporates flowers, leaves, and berries and is printed in red. By having the name of the volume and author in two lines at the top of the page and the publisher, place, and date of publication below "in a tight block," all in black type, the design plays "three geometric forms—rectangle, circle, and square—against one another" to produce energy and interest and, one might add, an aesthetic play on the organic as artifice.[35] Inventory sheets from the Bodley Head in 1894 indicate that 400 copies were printed; 165 were sold by subscription, and 94 were bound in cloth. The trade price is listed as £4/2/0, much in keeping with the firm's other offerings, and Bradley and Cooper were contracted to earn 10 percent of the royalties.[36] Although *Sight and Song* would not be published until May 1892, Mathews and Lane launched it in March of that year, placing an "Announcement for the Season" in the *Publisher's Circular* that listed *Sight and Song* as one of five new titles that also included Arthur Symons's *Silhouettes* and

SIGHT AND SONG WRITTEN
BY MICHAEL FIELD

ELKIN MATHEWS
AND JOHN LANE
AT THE SIGN OF
THE BODLEY HEAD
IN VIGO STREET
LONDON 1892

4.2. Title page of *Sight and Song* (London: Elkin Mathews and John Lane, 1892). ©
British Library Board. All Rights Reserved 011653.n.18

Oscar Wilde's *Poems*.[37] When *Sight and Song* came off the presses a few months later, a review in the *Academy* praised it for its sensuous echoes of Keats.[38]

Sight and Song had all the visible and tactile trappings of one of Mathew and Lane's desirable belles lettres. Boasting high production values and backed by a shrewd advertising campaign, Bodley Head books were indeed objects of consumer desire. "What the Bodley Head was really selling," Stetz maintains, "were books that were marketed both as status objects and as sex objects."[39] Indeed, the books, described as a "pretty little volume," "delicate," "fanciful," and "dainty" by 1894 reviewers, were "culturally marked as feminine."[40] Although a Bodley Head book, *Sight and Song* offers through its poems a form of desire that refuses objectification. By materializing a new theory of visuality that emphasizes the value of reciprocity and exchange between women, this *belle lettre* disturbs "the rhetorical linking of women and books as objects of desire [that] was particularly pervasive in aesthetic circles of the Eighties and Nineties."[41] On the cover of *Sight and Song*, there is an early, material indication of the ways in which the poems to follow in this volume may be poised to disrupt the usual terms of this connoisseur-book relationship. The cover first provides the title of the volume in large type. Following this, we read that the volume is

> Written by Mi-
> chael Field

Interestingly, the name Michael is bifurcated, as the second part of the name falls on a separate line (fig. 4.3). This divided name is also repeated on the spine of the book. Through typography, the cover inscribes the volume's dual authorship and begins to establish the nature of a shared viewership that the poems will encode. Moreover, as the hyphen "calls attention to the die-stamped binding itself, [it] simultaneously transform[s] the human subject ("Michael") into a formalist object composed of line and color," drawing attention to what Nicholas Frankel sees as the constructivist nature of the book and of the language of the lyrics to follow.[42] *Sight and Song* reveals the extent to which the collecting enterprise that would seek to make a singular possession of the feminized book is similarly culturally constructed. As we shall see, by granting autonomy to the female objects it represents, *Sight and Song* rearranges the usual terms of connoisseurship by critiquing ownership as a prerequisite value in the aesthetic-commercial project.

4.3. Front cover of *Sight and Song* (London: Elkin Mathews and John Lane, 1892).
© British Library Board. All Rights Reserved 011653.n.18

Consuming Pleasure in Sight and Song

While the ekphrasis of Michael Field's volume might recall such earlier works as Dante Gabriel Rossetti's *Sonnets for Pictures, Sight and Song* is an experiment that more immediately addresses Walter Pater's subject-centered criticism and more broadly responds to the ways in which feminine images have historically functioned under the consuming gaze of male viewership. In the preface to *The Renaissance: Studies in Art and Poetry* (1873), Pater insists that the goal of aesthetic criticism "is to know one's own impression as it really is." Pater's revision of Arnold's objectivism emphasizes subjective response and pleasure: "What is this song or picture, this engaging personality presented in life or in a book, to *me*? What effect does it really produce on me? Does it give me pleasure? and if so, what sort or degree of pleasure? . . . The aesthetic critic, then, regards all the objects with which he has to do . . . as powers or forces producing pleasurable sensations, each of a more or less peculiar or unique kind."[43] Pater's subjective response to art, however, has the potential to devalue the autonomy of art objects. In the conclusion to *The Renaissance*, Pater writes, "Experience, already reduced to a group of impressions, is ringed round for each one of us by that thick wall of personality through which no real voice has ever pierced on its way to us. . . . Every one of those impressions is the impression of the individual in his isolation, each mind keeping as a solitary prisoner its own dream of a world."[44] Here, Pater's aesthetics seems positioned to devolve into a form of solipsism.

In the brief preface to *Sight and Song*, which begins to establish a collaborative, intersubjective model of pleasurable consumption, Michael Field economically lays out a "method of art-study" that includes another way of seeing. In a sense, this preface positions the volume as a guidebook for visual consumption: "The aim of this little volume is . . . to translate into verse what the lines and colours of certain chosen pictures sing in themselves; to express not so much what these pictures are to the poet, but rather what poetry they objectively incarnate. Such an attempt demands patient, continuous sight as pure as the gazer can refine it of theories, fancies, or his mere subjective enjoyment."[45] Although this might sound at first like Arnoldian objectivism—the division of ideas from knowledge that in turn informs Pater's belief that art should remain separate from social conditions—Michael Field's insistence on something other than Pater's subjective enjoyment invites women's pleasures and gazes that are refined of masculine specular economies. The "theories, fancies, or his mere subjective enjoyment" are the master narrative of representations of women in Western culture and the universalizing male gaze that has historically commodified these images. In response, Bradley and Cooper, as Michael Field, insinuate themselves into the discursive production of art as gendered commodity: in a self-conscious rewriting of viewership, the poems will introduce alternative forms of consumption.

As Julia F. Saville observes, Field's preface is a direct response not just to *The Renaissance* but to one of Pater's public lectures. This preface was written with a lecture that the women attended in London in November 1890 in mind, where Pater had discussed Prosper Mérimée, the German critic whose practices were "another version of the artistic self-discipline referred to in the preface to *The Renaissance*."[46] Field's preface is thus offered with a view to Pater's reflections on what he called in that lecture the "self-effacement" and the "impersonality" of the observer, even as it is the broader culmination of what Saville calls "the product of an energetic program of art appreciation on which the two women embarked in the early 1890s" that included trips to museums and galleries both at home and in Europe.[47]

Michael Field's use of the ekphrastic object is indebted to Pater, but it also signals an important departure from Pater's philosophy. In illustrating the ways in which the poems constitute a rereading of Pater's aesthetic subjectivism, Vadillo has argued that Michael Field rewrites Pater by positing the autonomy of objects, concluding that Michael Field's visual aesthetics grant agency to gendered forms of representation that "refuse the gaze of the avid and always consuming subject."[48] To this, one could add that Field's difference from Pater stems from a recognition, rather than an obscuring, of the object as commodity; what these ekphrastic poems, these autonomous objects resemble, significantly, are commodities. One way in which *Sight and Song* encodes the object as commodity is evident through a governing aspect of its organization: by recording the museum location of each source painting as part of the apparatus of the text. Below the title of each poem, the name of the artist and host museum or gallery is listed. While every poem credits its source, so to speak, by citing the artist's name and the location of the painting, the poems are a commodified version of the paintings in the sense that the commodity is that which has been removed from its usual context, from that which has produced it. In other words, the images are exchanged for text and detached from the scene in which they were originally produced as paintings on view in various prominent institutional settings.

It remains for Michael Field to reveal how such commodities may be consumed without cost. But objects, granted their own forms of agency in *Sight and Song*, come to constitute a significant challenge to masculine aestheticism's colonization of the feminine. Together, the poems revise the condition whereby the feminine is constituted as an exchangeable or commodified object, part of aestheticism's attempt to consolidate male subjectivity and conceal its relationship to commercial culture. As the poems translate image into text, *Sight and Song* mediates and amends the usual optics of a masculine gaze. Michael Field's discursive viewership enables a mode of female connoisseurship that is marked by an absence of possession or ownership. By rendering image as text, Michael Field evades and elides the power relations of the subject-object encounter in which a collectible woman is gazed upon by a man. Whereas in Wilde's *The Picture of Dorian Gray* male-authored aestheticism often includes a collectible painting that functions as a means to consolidate male subjectivity, *Sight and Song* troubles this usual prescription in which women have historically occupied the position of mediating possession.[49] As connoisseur of the female form, Michael Field reorders female desire in the poems, configuring it as desire between women who deploy nonpossessive desires between them. Michael Field's feminized viewing thus radically reconfigures consumption into a "feast on the female form" that recalls Lizzie and Laura's erotic encounter in *Goblin Market* in which one woman turns her desiring gaze upon the other.[50] *Sight and Song* does not merely lead us to consider the peculiarities or agencies of female viewership. It also explores how alternative female sexualities might be formed in and through consuming practices and how such identities might be rendered material in a mode of lyric that, as Frankel discerns, has replaced the lyric "I" with a sense of the poem's own concrete properties.[51]

Although the poems of *Sight and Song* do not appear to be organized in any particular thematic order or recurring lyric form, among the most striking are those that deal in homoerotic images of women and engage in a doubled strategy: crucial poems, such as "La Gioconda," stage the problem of the collectible woman who is readily consumed by the interests of masculine aestheticism, then go on to offer strategies to resist this commodification.[52] Other poems, such as "The Sleeping Venus," posit alternative modes of consumption by offering female economies in which women obtain pleasure in themselves or among other women, often through the homoerotic rendering of a Venus figure; these economies do not figure women as the object of exchange. This double movement in the poetry from resisting to desiring, which in turn brings mobility to a reading of ostensibly static images, does not simply enact visual pleasures that feature a female gaze but also performs a conspicuous consumption of female bodies wherein women spend and desire freely.

"La Gioconda" is a brief lyric written in response to not only Leonardo da Vinci's *Mona Lisa* of the Louvre but also, implicitly, Pater's reflections on his "Lady Lisa" in *The Renaissance*. Indeed, Bradley and Cooper ensured that Pater would see the poem, sending a copy of *Sight and Song* to him, for which he offered a muted thanks.[53] Although this poem neither begins nor ends the collection, it is perhaps the central poem of the volume, for like the preface, it dismantles the privilege of male gaze to enable the freely spent desire that marks many of the other poems. When Pater casts a connoisseur's eye toward Lady Lisa in *The Renaissance*, his detailed and lingering description reveals how easily Woman and commodity are interchangeable within aestheticism, such that a trade in images of women has been central to the production of masculine subjectivity:

> From childhood we see this image defining itself on the fabric of [Leonardo da Vinci's] dreams. . . . The presence that rose thus so strangely beside the waters, is expressive of what in the ways of a thousand years men had come to desire. Hers is the head upon which all "the ends of the world are come." . . . She is older than the rocks among which she sits; like the vampire, she has been dead many times, and learned the secrets of the grave; and has been a diver in deep seas, and keeps their fallen day about her; and trafficked for strange webs with Eastern merchants: and, as Leda, was the mother of Helen of Troy, and, as Saint Anne, the mother of Mary. . . . Certainly Lady Lisa might stand as the embodiment of the old fancy, the symbol of the modern idea.[54]

With no explicit reference to commercial culture, Pater succeeds in providing a gloss to the work of commodities through the self-referential world of art and the insular discourse of aesthetics. Pater's Lady Lisa, whose identity seems interchangeable throughout the centuries, resembles a commodity. She is, as Psomiades writes, "a container for desires of all kinds; she holds the history of sexuality itself in her capacious depths. . . . [She] is explicitly an embodied abstraction, her flesh made up of ideas."[55] She is something more than a painting, a trivial thing; rather, like Marx's commodity, she is "abounding in metaphysical subtleties."[56] Pater's Lady Lisa is that standard trope in aestheticism, the collectible woman. But she must be carefully managed, for in addition to being lovely and timeless, she is also termed a vampire in Pater's text, as though she is able to shift from the position of object to be consumed to that of subject that consumes. In so doing, Lady Lisa also threatens to destabilize the terms that so carefully conceal aestheticism's proximity to commercial culture.

Michael Field's "La Gioconda," however, escapes Pater's ekphrastic silencing:

> HISTORIC, side-long, implicating eyes;
> A smile of velvet's lustre on the cheek;
> Calm lips the smile leads upward; hand that lies
> Glowing and soft, the patience in its rest
> Of cruelty that waits and doth not seek
> For prey; a dusky forehead and a breast
> Where twilight touches ripeness amorously:
> Behind her, crystal rocks, a sea and skies
> Of evanescent blue on cloud and creek;
> Landscape that shines suppressive of its zest
> For those vicissitudes by which men die.[57]

This Mona Lisa is not Pater's idealized lady on which to map male desire. Rather, she is an unreadable text, unreassuring, disturbing, refusing to reflect a male gaze, "implicating" such a gaze that would seek to interpret her. In eleven pentameter lines, some of which are regularly iambic, others not, any irregularity in the poem becomes all the more noticeable. Indeed, the graphic features of the poem duplicate the Lady's gesture of resistance; while the poem on the page admits of regular left margins and lines of comparable length, the subtle graphic disruptions of semicolons (lines 1–3, 6, and 9) and a colon (line 7) arguably determine, and thus bracket and limit, the access to this Lady Lisa. At first she seems eroticized but not completely fragmented, through close-ups of lips, a hand, forehead, and breast. This familiar cataloguing of a woman's qualities "break[s] the Lady down into her component parts, . . .

mak[ing] her cease to be a lady, . . . reveal[ing] the creakiness of the old form, the way the femme fatale tends to fall apart when you look at her for too long."[58] Then, following the colon of line 7, the scene shifts abruptly to what lies beyond her, the landscape that does nothing to reveal her own interiority, as though Michael Field's "La Gioconda" has shown all that she will allow and will refuse a final, totalizing gaze by forcing the viewer's attention to a far less satisfying elsewhere. There is nothing to be read behind her that might grant the viewer a clue as to what resides inside her. She proves to be an unreadable surface, guaranteeing not a sense of the eternal but, rather, hinting at the failure to master her—those "vicissitudes by which men die"—to function as Pater's commodified surface that "is expressive of what in the ways of a thousand years men had come to desire [and] the head upon which all 'the ends of the world are come.'" "La Gioconda" constitutes a refusal for women to remain Pater's universalized "embodiment of the old fancy, the symbol of the modern idea."

"A Portrait" is, like "La Gioconda," a critique of masculine representations of women. Based on a painting of the same name by Bartolommeo Veneto and housed by the Städel'sche Institut at Frankfurt, it is composed in seven stanzas of rime royal that confront the ways in which portraits of women traditionally have been painted in service of a male viewer. In the first four lines of the opening stanza, the regular rhyme seems to intone the plasticity and the nearly mass-produced ways by which women have been represented:

> A CRYSTAL, flawless beauty on the brows
> Where neither love nor time has conquered space
> On which to live; her leftward smile endows
> The gazer with no tidings from the face[.]
>
> (lines 1–4)[59]

Veneto's woman gazes, and pays for this transgression not so much through fading beauty as through the deathly capture of representation. The woman of Veneto's painting is that gendered stereotype that has been "painted . . . for centuries," a "vacant eminence persist[ing] for all men to behold!" (lines 29 and 35). She is another iteration of Pater's Lady Lisa that Field will contest.

After alluding to the historical problem of masculine representations of women, "A Portrait" goes on to construct an alternative space in which female desires might be explored apart from a male gaze. The woman depicted flees the interior spaces in which she is artificially constructed to explore a natural world:

> Forth to the field she goes and questions long
> Which flowers to choose of those the summer bears;
> . . . .
> She sets the box-tree leaf and coils it tight
> In spiky wreath of green, immortal hue;
> Then, to the prompting of her strange, emphatic insight true,
> She bares one breast, half-freeing it of robe,
> And hangs green-water gem and cord beside the naked globe.
> (lines 17–18, 24–28)

Outside of the confines of traditional, domestic representation, where she enjoys what Chris White calls a "sensuous, self-directed relationship with the natural world," another "relationship is established between the woman and the fluid elements, water plants becoming the tool for realising female self-pleasuring and representation of her sexuality to herself, while the indoor mirror can only represent to her the social meaning of her body and sexuality."[60] The fluidity of this association is also duplicated in the typographical layout of the poem. Whereas the first four lines of each of the poem's seven stanzas share carefully ordered left margins, the fifth and final lines of each rime royal stanza break into a more ecstatic heptameter, as in lines 26 and 28 above, where these fourteeners graphically inscribe the unchecked flows of this woman's self-directed desire.

Although the natural world might constitute an essentialized space, as constructed as any feminized domestic space, the point is that the woman in the poem creates for herself a sensory realm in which a male gaze apparently cannot place limits on feminine sexuality. This is a space not merely for one woman's sexual awakening, but one in which the possibility exists for pleasures to be exchanged between women. Nature, like a second woman, responds to the first in an ecosystem where fluidity is not only generated but also reciprocated. The poem ends with the woman "conquer[ing] death" (line 49), exceeding the confines of masculine representation through her sensual retreat.

Although the woman in "A Portrait" is not identified, she has much in common with the many Venus figures who populate *Sight and Song*. This recurring

Venus figure is often emblematic of women's homoerotic and autoerotic pleasure apart from heterosexual relations. "The Birth of Venus," for example, based on Sandro Botticelli's painting in the Uffizi, rehearses, in luxuriant ten-line stanzas, the familiar scene of Venus rising from the sea in notably sensual terms:

> Coiling hair in loosened shocks,
> Sways a girl who seeks to bind
> New-born beauty with a tress
> Gold about her nakedness.
>
> (lines 7–10)[61]

This sensual scene then becomes thoroughly homoerotic. Michael Field shifts the focus to another female figure who occupies the scene, the goddess Flora, who rushes to meet Venus to shroud her with a robe:

> And her chilled, wan body sweet
> Greets the ruffled cloak of rose,
> Daisy-stitched, that Flora throws
> Toward her ere she set her feet
> On the green verge of the world:
> Flora, with the corn-flower dressed,
> Round her neck a rose-spray curled
> Flowerless, wild-rose at her breast,
> To her goddess hastes to bring
> The wide chiton of the spring.
>
> (lines 11–20)

Whereas regular lines and carefully maintained left margins are a graphic condition that the woman of a poem such as "A Portrait" must exceed, the symmetrical layout of "The Birth of Venus" seems rather to encode the sameness, reciprocity, and homoerotic exchange that the poem represents. Michael Field focuses initially on composing an eroticized portrait of Venus but then redirects the scene toward an encounter between two women, as Flora rushes to meet Venus and cover her with a cloak. Botticelli's well-known image of Venus rising from the sea for all to behold becomes recast as a homoerotic exchange between two women who greet each other, hastening not only the arrival of a fertile spring but also their own union.⁶² Rather than placing Venus on display, the poem makes explicit a production of desire between women.

The homoeroticism of "The Birth of Venus" is translated into autoeroticism in another poem, "The Sleeping Venus." The female figure in "The Sleeping Venus," based on the painting by Giorgione, is one of the most prominent of the Venus figures in *Sight and Song*. A favorite painting of Bradley and Cooper's, which they viewed in the Dresden Gallery, "The Sleeping Venus" recalls the woman of "A Portrait" who escapes to a space of female erotic pleasures. Like her, the sleeping Venus steals away from the usual terms of her representation, leaving the confines of "her archèd shell" for the more expansive space of the cornfields (line 4). The stanzas that follow indulge in a sensual description of the Venus. The poem lauds the fidelity between her "curves" (line 15) and those of the surrounding pastures and sky and praises the erotic landscape of her body:

> With desirous sway, each breast
> Rises from the level chest,
> One in contour, one in round—
> Either exquisite, low mound
> Firm in shape and given
> To the August warmth of heaven.
>   (lines 37–42)

At the heart of the poem, in the fifth stanza, Venus revels in unreserved sensual pleasures in a display of conspicuous consumption:

> Her hand the thigh's tense surface leaves,
>   Falling inward. Not even sleep
>   Dare invalidate the deep,
>   Universal pleasure sex
>   Must unto itself annex—
>   Even the stillest sleep; at peace,
>   More profound with rest's increase,
>   She enjoys the good
>   Of delicious womanhood.
>   (lines 62–70)⁶³

Here, the concave right-hand margin of the poem—as it curves inward following line 62—suggestively reproduces the curves of Venus's body. Each of the fourteen-line stanzas of this poem visually inscribes this sense of self-contained enclosure; following the first six lines in each stanza, the remaining eight lines are indented, as though such a bracketing preserves a space in the poem for pleasure. Indeed, this Venus enjoys the autoerotic pleasures of "delicious womanhood" and thus challenges the collecting and commodifying enterprise of masculine aestheticism. These pleasures are notably self-referential, suggesting an economy of expenditures in which excess is valued over the utility of procreative sex, in which pleasure is obtained autoerotically.

Works and Days includes an account of Bradley and Cooper's journey to view Giorgione's "Sleeping Venus" in the Dresden Gallery during their 1891 continental excursion. The trip, however, was soon interrupted because of illness. After seeing only a few galleries in Belgium and Germany, Cooper fell ill, and both women were confined to a fever hospital at Dresden. As Cooper became delirious, an effect of the scarlet fever, she recorded an almost stream-of-consciousness reflection on Botticelli's painting *Venus and Mars*: "I determine I will have as much pleasure as I can. I dance at balls, I go to Operas, I am Mars and, looking across at Sim's [Bradley's] little bed, I realise that she is a goddess, hidden in her hair—Venus. Yet I cannot reach her. . . . I grew wilder for pleasure. . . . Sim comes to quiet me and assure me."[64] This vision suggests the ways in which paintings, even ones that featured heterosexual desire, could function for the couple as scenes they could revise to play out their same-sex desires for each other. Practising what Hilary Fraser has recently termed a "dynamic stereoscopic gaze," one that is also "intersected by homoerotic desire," Bradley and Cooper's visual engagement in *Sight and Song* is a collaborative "gaze of gays" that ruptures the premise of both the male/female binary and the monolithic viewer.[65]

The journal extracts in *Works and Days* also note Bradley and Cooper's particular praise of Giorgione's painting for the ways in which it resists an ornamentalized male gaze: "Giorgione's *Venus* [is] that ideal sympathy between woman and the land, which nations have divined when they made their countries feminine. . . . No stranger from the sea, no apparition, no enchantress, but simple as our fields, as nobly lighted as our harvests, pure as things man needs for his life that use cannot violate. No one watches her."[66] What is significant, the journal entry suggests, is that this portrait does not garner a continuous gaze: "No one watches her." The poem, indeed, goes on to acknowledge the ways in which the Venus figure resists capture and selects her own pleasures:

> Eyelids underneath the day
> Wrinkle as full buds that stay,
> Through the tranquil, summer hours,
> Closed although they might be flowers;
> The red lips shut in
> Gracious secrets that begin.
>
> (lines 79–84)

Michael Field's version of "The Sleeping Venus" does not permit wholesale consumption but enables pleasure on Venus's own terms. This pleasure, as the end of the poem predicts, will not be forestalled, but will remain ongoing: "She is of the things that are; / And she will not pass / While the sun strikes on the grass" (lines 124–26). The poem's resistance to an acquisitive gaze, then, is what confers on it, and the other poems, the concreteness that is often inscribed through the poems' arrangements—the use of punctuation, indentations, expansive lines, and stanzaic forms. The aims of Field's ekphrastic project and the poetic discourse of shared female pleasure that results contribute to the sense of the poems as uncolonized objects. In a series of gestures that anticipate Imagism, the poems acquire a thickness that Frankel calls an "artefactual presence," as Field puts a visual theory into practice through the graphic possibilities of the text.[67]

"A Pen-Drawing of Leda," inspired by the painting by Sodoma, a Sienese contemporary of Raphael, also suggests an economy of autoeroticism that is materialized on the page. In this two-stanza poem, Leda's pleasure, like that of the Venus in "The Sleeping Venus," is not reserved or diminished. The Swan and its nest become the extension of Leda's own body: "Drawing her gracious Swan down through the grass . . . / . . . / One hand plunged in the reeds and one dinting the downy neck, / . . . / She draws the fondled creature to her will" (lines 2, 4, 7). The second stanza points not only to Leda's sexual ecstasy but also to how she has authored her own pleasure:

> She joys to bend in the live light
> Her glistening body toward her love, how much more bright!
> Though on her breast the sunshine lies
> And spreads its affluence on the wide curves of her waist and thighs,
> To her meek, smitten gaze
> Where her hand presses
> The Swan's white neck sink Heaven's concentred rays.
>
> (lines 8–14)[68]

The irrepressible, wandering left margins of the poem typographically inscribe the poem's exuberant frisson and emphasize the curves of Leda's body. The poem, which revises the myth of Leda as victim to produce her instead as sexual agent, does not curtail female pleasure and represents desires that exist apart from mastery, possession, or objectification. Consumption is a condition of the pleasures located in the female body, rather than those replicated and propagated through the universalizing masculine aestheticism.

Michael Field places no limits upon female desire; indeed, some of the poems go beyond consolidating female pleasure through a single Venus figure to indulge in sensual portraits of groups of women, celebrating the proliferation of women's shared homoerotic pleasures. In doing so, they anticipate Luce Irigaray's vision of commodity exchange as the realization of jouissance or absolute desire. Irigaray muses, "[W]hat if these 'commodities' [women] refuse[ ] to go to 'market'? What if they maintained 'another' kind of commerce, among themselves? Exchanges without identifiable terms, without accounts, without end. . . . Use and exchange would be indistinguishable . . . , exempt from masculine transactions."[69] A painting by Benozzo Gozzoli displayed at the Campo Santo at Pisa inspired one such poem, "Treading the Press," which envisions a scene in which women exist as commodities among themselves, their value residing solely in the pleasure they ensure each other. In three brief stanzas, the poem depicts a group of women in the act of pressing grapes, an exuberant dance that is reproduced visually on the page through indented margins that also seem to dance on the page:

> From the trellis hang the grapes
> Purple-deep;
> Maidens with white, curving napes
> And coiled hair backward leap,

> As they catch the fruit, mid laughter,
> Cut from every silvan rafter.
>
> (lines 1–6)

The scene is one of excess, with teeming baskets "over-filled with fruit" (line 7) and the unrestrained "smashing" and "thrashing" (lines 11 and 12) of the group of women, who labor together with hedonistic abandon. The activities of these women, which recall Lizzie and Laura sharing stolen goblin fruit, are thoroughly sexualized at the end of the poem, when "Wild and rich oozings pour / From the press" (lines 13–14). The "oozings" that remain are indicative of the unchecked pleasures and surplus of pleasure that are possible in such an economy.

As *Sight and Song* constructs a discourse of female consumption based on reciprocal desire rather than possession and on the continued production of these forms of pleasure, the implied viewer of the text rarely intrudes. Women, such as those in "Treading the Press," seem to exist only for themselves. One important exception occurs in the final poem. Prompted by Antoine Watteau's *L'Embarquement pour Cythère* in the Louvre, this poem depicts Venus as she draws lovers to the island of Cythera on a quest for love, a sight that causes the speaker to exclaim:

> I see it now!
> 'Tis Venus' rose-veiled barque
> And that great company ere dark
> Must to Cythera, so the Loves prevail,
> Adventurously sail.
>
> (lines 22–26)[70]

This glimpse is deferred, however, as the postscript of the poem positions Venus as the final observer in the text:

> Now are they gone: a change is in the light,
> The iridescent ranges wane,
> The waters spread: ere fall of night
> The red-prowed shallop will have passed from sight
> And the stone Venus by herself remain
> Ironical above that wide, embrowning plain.
>
> (lines 141–46)

In keeping with the aims set out by Michael Field in the preface, to view art objects "in themselves," Venus persists as a remainder, beyond capture, after *Sight and Song* has come to an end: a female figure from the text comes to acquire the powers of gaze.[71] Recalling the earlier portrait of "La Gioconda," which refuses a male gaze, and the ongoing, uninterrupted pleasures of "The Sleeping Venus," the Venus of the postscript persists beyond the capture of the reader's gaze to ensure the continuous production of images of desiring women. The italicized font, moreover, disrupts a sense of conventional temporality in the poem to signal, in this concrete way, a shift to an expansive future that will guarantee Venus's self and her gaze beyond the text.

Michael Field's visual aesthetics grant agency and autonomy to gendered forms of representation, visualizing scenes in which women refuse to go to market but instead exist as commodities to be traded for pleasure among themselves. Such an aesthetics goes beyond rewriting Pater in positing the autonomy of objects. The object is constituted not in itself but through non-possessive viewing, and sometimes touching, that is discursively deployed in the poems. The autonomous art object resembles the commodity form but is reimagined as that which functions as the pure pleasure of exchange value. *Sight and Song*'s female erotics constitute Michael Field's version of commodity aesthetics, suggesting a place for not only the feminine but also dissident femininity in fin-de-siècle culture. Whereas Woman was often appropriated by masculine aestheticism, Michael Field's consumption enables the inscription of women's same-sex desires as distinct from the collecting impulse of masculine connoisseurship, rendering those desires as material.

If women are not the typical object of exchange in *Sight and Song*, what of these economies of pleasure—is women's condition finally fixed or bound, so to speak, as a Bodley Head book? The persistence of the book/Woman conjunction, as Stetz points out, is evident in Kenneth Grahame's 1894 essay "Non Libri Sed Liberi," from *Pagan Papers*, itself a Mathews and Lane publication. Here, Grahame considers not just shopping for a beautiful book but also what follows that transaction:

> The process of the purchase is always much the same, therein resembling the familiar but inferior passion of love. There is the first sight of the Object, accompanied of a catching of the breath, a trembling in the limbs.... But once possessed, once toyed with amorously for an hour or

two, the Object . . . takes its destined place on the shelf—where it stays. And this, saith the scoffer, is all; but even he does not fail to remark with a certain awe that the owner goeth thereafter as one possessing a happy secret and radiating an inner glow."[72]

Once purchased, once collected, the initial ardor for the book/Woman may fade, but the male owner possesses her all the same.

If Katharine Bradley and Edith Cooper were also devoted to the aesthetic object, one particular episode demonstrates not a mastery of the object but how very fluid and arbitrary the terms of possession can be. While visiting Bernhard Berenson and Mary (Costelloe) Berenson in Surrey in 1903, the women collaborated in an act resembling shoplifting. They relate in their journal an incident involving a painting belonging to Logan Pearsall Smith that his sister, Mary, had hung in their vacation cottage. So much did they admire this painting that they took it home with them, apparently in accordance with "that law of ownership," as Pearsall Smith later put it to them, in which "objects of beauty belong to those who love them best."[73] Bradley and Cooper, who did feel that they loved the painting best, only grudgingly returned the painting to Pearsall Smith, who demanded it back. Instead of buying the aesthetic object to possess it as Grahame professes, Bradley and Cooper are more like Beardsley's woman shopper who flirts with the prospect of purchasing, jumbling up the displays or otherwise disrupting the prescribed ways in which one is supposed to behave within authorized systems of exchange. The couple's art heist, moreover, operates much like *Sight and Song* in the aesthetic book marketplace, its fluid economies of pleasure jamming the premise of possession that often underwrote masculine connoisseurship, in which an object that is purchased free and clear is thought to be owned absolutely. If Bradley and Cooper, as women aesthetes, confounded the rules of proprietorship in and through the pages of their Bodley Head production *Sight and Song*, another species of "advanced" women, the suffragettes (with their more overtly political agenda), were in a few short years to take position in front of as well as behind the shopwindows of the West End and beyond, where they would use the sphere of consumption dramatically to announce women's autonomy and entitlement as citizens.

Five

VOTES FOR WOMEN AND THE TACTICS OF CONSUMPTION

With many others she had been ordered to patrol Bond Street, and to watch her opportunity of doing as much damage as she could to the shop-windows. . . . The orders were that the women should distribute themselves throughout the street so that at half-past five . . . simultaneous attacks should take place at intervals of about twenty yards. Each woman carried a muff or a bag in which a hammer was concealed. . . . Una's heart was beating fast as she took her stand opposite a fashionable haberdasher's shop, pretending to look with interest at the scarves and gloves and white shirts displayed in the windows, while her hand was nervously playing with the hammer in her muff. . . . Would the time never come? . . . Slowly the minute hand [of the shop clock] reached the half-hour, and then Una . . . pulled out the hammer and dealt one resounding blow on the plate-glass.[1]

In W. L. Courtney's short story "The Soul of a Suffragette" (1913), Una Blockley is one of a group of suffragettes who, disguised as ordinary shoppers, have gathered to vandalize the windows of the shops of Bond Street. Although this is a fictional account, Courtney likely had in mind the events of Friday, March 1, 1912, when militants from the Women's Social and Political Union quietly converged at 5:45 p.m. on the streets of London's West End. Posing nonchalantly as shoppers, they suddenly produced hammers and stones and began to smash one pane of shopwindow glass after another. As Emmeline Pankhurst would later recall, this carefully planned and executed tactical strike was carried out in "intervals of fifteen minutes" by "relays of women who had volunteered for the demonstration."[2] The first wave occurred in the Haymarket and Piccadilly, where the disruption led to a number of arrests. Soon after and without any warning, a second attack took place in Regent Street and the Strand, followed by a third in Oxford Circus and Bond Street. Although few businesses escaped vandalism, the large windows of big drapers such as D. H. Evans, Jay's, Liberty's, Marshall and Snelgrove, and Swan and Edgar's "suffered special attack," as one tradespaper put it.[3] In its own press, the WSPU reported that "[i]n front, behind, from every side it came—a hammering, crashing, splintering sound, unheard in the annals of shopping."[4] Over the next several days, the results of this ambush became more widely known: the WSPU had smashed close to four hundred shopwindows, causing damages of up to five thousand pounds. More than a hundred women were arrested; some of them were fined, while others were committed to prison with sentences ranging from one week to two months.[5]

By relating this drama as fiction from the point of view of Una, one of the vandals, "The Soul of a Suffragette" not only lends heart-pounding, psychological realism to an actual occurrence but also taps into the political urgency on the part of these suffragettes that had prompted their extreme actions in real life, an urgency that tended to be eclipsed by public reaction and the sensational tone of newspaper reports that followed. Popular response to these events ranged from outrage to disbelief. Representatives from more-moderate suffrage groups such as the National Union of Women's Suffrage Societies (the NUWSS) spoke out to condemn the raids for targeting private property, thus distancing themselves from the WSPU's willingness to use violence.[6] Voicing the consternation of many retail business owners, Arthur Lasenby

Liberty wrote a letter to the *Standard*, in which he called WSPU founder Emmeline Pankhurst to account, calling on her to show how breaking the windows "of the very shrines at which [you] worship will advance [your] cause."[7] Compounding the disbelief and confusion of such retailers as Liberty was the fact that many of the large drapers who had been attacked were also faithful advertisers in the WSPU's weekly newspaper, *Votes for Women*. In widespread reports of the incident, the mainstream press, too, was perplexed. Accounts of the events in several papers could not reconcile the image of the leisurely shopper with that of the politically motivated vandal. One report, for example, stated that "[s]uddenly women who had a moment before appeared to be on peaceful shopping expeditions produced from bags or muffs, hammers, stones and sticks, and began an attack upon the nearest windows."[8] Similarly, the *Daily Mail* remarked that during the rampage, "any unaccompanied lady in sight, especially if she carried a hand bag, became an object of menacing suspicion."[9]

Established in 1903, the Women's Social and Political Union was among the most publicly provocative of the many suffrage societies that sprung up in Britain at the turn of the century.[10] Although the WSPU participated in peaceful demonstrations and street processionals alongside other moderate or constitutional societies such as the NUWSS, it had grown increasingly impatient with pageants and exhibitions. In 1905, it had adopted a policy of what it called "militant tactics." In a 1909 pamphlet, Christabel Pankhurst argued that force was being used only when necessary and that when it was used by the WSPU it was always proportional, "using just so much force, and no more, as is necessitated by the action of the Government."[11] Between 1905 and 1914, the Women's Social and Political Union deployed a host of these militant tactics to agitate for the cause. The first window-breaking incident occurred in 1908 when the Liberal government refused to receive a WSPU delegation. That same year, the Pankhursts and other members attempted to storm or "rush" the House of Commons. In two further incidents, also in 1908, women chained themselves to the railings of No. 10 Downing Street and to the grille of the Ladies' Gallery in the House. During the following year, the WSPU increased its agitation, breaking windows of government offices and organizing demonstrations. Over the next few years, it incorporated further forms of protest that targeted both public and private property, committing various acts of arson and vandalizing golf greens and telegraph wires. Of the many women who were arrested and imprisoned for their acts of civil disobedience, a significant number continued to agitate in prison by engaging in protracted hunger strikes, often enduring painful forced-feedings as a result.[12] After truces for part of 1910 (because of hopes over the Conciliation Bill, which were dashed months later) and 1911 (in observance of the coronation), the WSPU escalated its campaign in 1912 and began to vandalize pillar boxes to disrupt the postal service. Not until 1914, when national attention became focused on the specter of a world war, did Emmeline Pankhurst declare a suspension of all militant activities.

The WSPU ostensibly used one of its most spectacular demonstrations, the West End window-smashing campaign in 1912, to protest what it felt was retailers' political indifference to the issue of women's franchise. In doing so, it clearly did not consider the world of retailing as somehow disjunct from its campaign to win women the vote. In a handbill entitled "Window Breaking: To One Who Has Suffered," the WSPU addressed shopkeepers, urging them to direct their anger not at those who broke their windows but at the Liberal government, which continued to deny women the right to vote. "[T]he women," the handbill reminds shopkeepers, "are good friends to you, and without them . . . what would become of that flourishing business of yours? . . . [Y]ou can't get on without the women who are your good friends in business."[13] West End proprietors were not third-party victims of indiscriminate guerrilla attacks; rather, they had been singled out because they were part of the commercial sector affiliated with the political sphere. The WSPU reasoned that shopkeepers were not politically neutral; they were business owners who should leverage their enfranchisement and influence members of Parliament to pass a bill for women's suffrage. If retailers wished to keep their female customers, they would have to support the campaign for the vote, for the same women who frequented their shops were among those who were demanding the franchise.

In a sense, those who witnessed the events of March 1, 1912, had not really mistaken political activists for shoppers, for the women who smashed the windows were doubly inscribed as militants and consumers on that evening in the West End. This incident, then, does more than suggest how suffragettes sought to secure the political clout of the businesses from whom they bought dresses and hats. For this window smashing might be characterized more significantly as a moment in which activist feminism visibly marked its relationship with consumer culture. Far from outright rejection, militant tactics on this occasion rehearsed the complex ways in which British first-wave feminism formed through encounters with the marketplace rather than apart from it.

As Lisa Tickner and Barbara Green have shown, suffrage societies engaged in the production of mass spectacles that sought to ensure the visibility and strategic promotion of first-wave feminist politics in the public sphere.[14] Green, in particular, argues that the orderly suffragist street theater that is often associated with an earlier phase in the campaigns, from about 1905 to 1911, was coextensive with rather than distinct from the militant suffragette activism that followed. While Green's contention rests upon the similarities between the "spectacular politics" of both street pageantry and such commodified images as those of imprisoned suffragettes, there is another way to conceptualize the affinities between the shared performative politics of moderate and militant suffrage. What these approaches had in common was their inscription within what Guy Debord has termed "the society of the spectacle," a structuring of commodity relations that ultimately maintains, rather than transforms, the fundamental workings of capitalism to project a uniform and totalizing vision of social life. In a world dominated by the circulation of images, the "principle of commodity fetishism" is one in which the commodity "reaches its absolute fulfillment in the spectacle."[15] Images of suffrage, including those spectacles carefully manufactured by suffragists, could become fodder for mainstream public consumption. Even such incidents as the 1912 shopwindow vandalism—which would appear to diverge radically from mass events such as the nonmilitant 1908 Hyde Park demonstration and 1911 Coronation procession—were ultimately contained by the degree to which they answered to a public appetite for outrage. Sensationalized in the mainstream press, the spectacle of shattered glass did not end when it was directed at its intended target, the shopkeepers and their political clout. Instead, as the event was seamlessly integrated within the popular press, it became part of a sign system of commodified images that absorbed scenes of suffrage and turned them into commodities that ensured the "monopoly of appearance" that characterizes capitalism, a homogeneity that is complicit with the machinery of capitalism and helps to maintain it.[16]

To see how the militant suffrage movement perforated the fiction of a uniform spectacle that capital seeks to uphold, we turn not to the drama of mass spectacle but to a version of the tactical in which the WSPU observed the outward forms and exchanges of conventional consumer culture even while disrupting it from within. The WSPU's entrepreneurial activities can be understood in light of what Michel de Certeau calls "[t]he tactics of consumption, the ingenious ways in which the weak make use of the strong, [and] thus lend a political dimension to everyday practices."[17] The militant suffrage campaigns, then, can be characterized not only as the choreographed, spectacular politics of both orderly and disorderly street spectacle but also as persistent tactics that inscribed gendered, political identities in contingent, local, and improvised ways through engagements with shopping as a mode of the everyday. For de Certeau, a tactic is an operation that defies spatialization, that refuses the kinds of borders and fixity that we associate with the state and with monolithic institutions. "A tactic," de Certeau writes, "insinuates itself into the other's place, fragmentarily, without taking it over in its entirety."[18] What is significant is not so much the appropriation of consumer culture as the ways in which it is used, hacked into, derailed, and redeployed from moment to moment.

To locate the most properly tactical of the WSPU's activities, then, we need to look not at its militant tactics of public disorder and vandalism but at a more subtle set of practices that were produced through its appropriations and uses of consumer culture, particularly as these were constructed discursively in the WSPU's newspaper, *Votes for Women*. Together, these forms of consumption imagine shopping for the vote as an everyday, even playful activism in which suffragettes participated as both shoppers and shopkeepers. Rather than its shopwindow vandalism, the WSPU's most striking intervention in consumer culture was setting up its own shops and using these windows to sell its own goods. Moreover, by imagining shopkeeping as a form of political buying and selling, the WSPU effected a radical revisioning of the public sphere as a marketplace of ideas where the terms of citizenship could be actively contested.

Votes for Women *and the Fashioning of Consumer Feminism*

Nowhere was this tactics of consumption made more visible than in the pages of the WSPU's newspaper, *Votes for Women*, which began its run in 1907.[19] More than a simple record of the life of one of Britain's best-known suffrage societies, *Votes for Women* documents even as it constructs the WSPU's engagements with consumer culture. An extended political advertisement for first-wave feminism, the newspaper represented a mode of engagement that was activist and politically motivated yet also disarmingly middle class, appealing and consumable. Maria DiCenzo and Simone Murray are among those who have considered *Votes for Women* as an important instance of the WSPU's material production and explore how the newspaper was central to the dissemination of suffrage politics.[20] At the same time, however, the newspaper also produced consumption as a means to negotiate women's full recognition in civic life. During the five years that *Votes for Women* was the WSPU's official organ, the call for urgent and militant action ran alongside fashion columns, shopping directories, advertisements from West End retailers, and articles concerning the WSPU's fleet of shops. Here, one could buy not only books, pamphlets, and treatises published by its Woman's Press but also licensed suffrage merchandise such as scarves, badges, tea, soap, and games. Politics and pleasure were not separate strands in the newspaper's ongoing discussion about how best to secure the franchise for women; instead, they were mutually constitutive discourses.

An early refrain in the pages of *Votes for Women* was the need to fashion a feminine image of the suffragette. Soon after the beginning of its run in 1907, the paper identified a public relations crisis, which it termed "the suffragette and the dress problem." This problem concerned popular conceptions of suffragettes as humorless, unattractive frumps who were impervious to the pleasures of consumerism. In 1907, a writer in *Votes for Women* pointed out that the same general public who imagined suffragettes to be "masculine women . . . with short hair, billycock hats, and other articles of masculine attire . . . [considered this unfeminine appearance] another argument against giving women the vote."[21] The writer was responding to well-known caricatures of suffragettes. Among these was a 1906 *Punch* caricature called "The Shrieking Sister" (fig. 5.1). It represents a suffragette as an unattractive, shabbily dressed woman who hysterically brandishes a "female suffrage" flag and threatens to burst into a meeting of the Liberal Party. She is restrained by a younger, moderate or constitutional suffragist called "The Sensible Woman," who appears feminine and composed and disassociates herself from her militant "shrieking" sister by stating, "*You* help our cause? Why, you're its worse enemy." Another caricature, a 1910 anti-suffrage postcard, "Always Make Room for a Lady," takes the unfeminine appearance of a group of suffragettes a step further, giving them "mannish" features and dress. Brandishing Votes for Women signs, they stomp along in huge boots and leave a wake of terrified policemen in their merciless path (fig. 5.2).

Although the WSPU grew out of labor organization in Manchester and its membership did not lack diversity, the union was keen to avoid the stereotype of the so-called unsexed woman and therefore embraced the more politically *(right)* 5.1. "The Shrieking Sister," by Bernard Partridge (*Punch,* January 17, 1906, 39)

(below) 5.2. "Always Make Room for a Lady" postcard, ca. 1910

efficacious image of the middle-class "womanly" woman.[22] It did not wish to equate radical politics with a radical departure from gendered norms. Partly because of popular lampooning, many suffrage groups—both militant and moderate—came to adopt a "costume code." The WSPU's third annual report notes that the union policy of wearing league colors for public events was in place in the spring of 1908.[23] For large street processions and pageants, the various suffrage groups would often dress in white and adorned themselves with ribbons, banners, scarves, jewelry, belts, and hats in their union colors. Each suffrage society adopted its own official colors; the WSPU came to be recognized for its tricolor scheme of purple, white, and green (which symbolized freedom, purity, and hope).[24]

Conscious of the power of a corporate image, *Votes for Women* urged its members to dress as well as they could afford and wear the official colors of purple, white, and green to suffrage events or simply as a matter of course. In an article about one major gathering of suffrage groups, the 1908 demonstration in Hyde Park, *Votes for Women* coeditor Emmeline Pethick-Lawrence includes a detailed section on popularizing the colors. "You may think that this is a small and trivial matter," she writes, "[b]ut there is no action and no service that can be considered as small or trivial in this movement. I wish I could impress on every mind as deeply as I feel myself the importance of *popularising the colours* in every way open to us. If every individual woman in this union would do her part, the colours would become the reigning fashion."[25] Similarly, in 1909, Christabel Pankhurst addressed the political importance of the colors in a *Votes for Women* article, identifying them as one of the tactics by which the suffrage movement ensured its visibility: "The colours," she insists, "enable us to make that appeal to the eye which is so irresistible. The result of our processions is that this movement becomes identified in the mind of the onlooker with colour, gay sound, movement, beauty."[26]

By July 1908, the WSPU had become sufficiently confident to declare the perception of suffragettes as frumps all but defeated. An article entitled "The Suffragette and the Dress Problem," published in *Votes for Women* that year, claimed no small degree of success in countering stereotypes. "It was not so very long ago," the piece begins, "that, in the popular mind, the woman who wanted the vote figured as that extremely unpleasant person, a 'frump,'" apparently citing earlier depictions of women, such as that in *Punch*, "in elastic-sided boots and black cotton 'Auntie' gloves."[27] The author of the article goes on to pronounce, "The Suffragette of to-day is dainty and precise in her dress; indeed, she has a feeling that, for the honour of the cause she represents, she must 'live up to' her highest ideals in all respects."

In the course of considering this carefully fashioned image of first-wave feminism, scholars commonly argue that such "costume codes" helped to produce suffrage workers as a corporate or civic body. Along these lines, Katrina Rolley writes that "[t]he WSPU evidently realized that in order to gain an active place *within* society, they had to appear socially acceptable."[28] It is also often pointed out that this uniform image also tended to reinforce normative ideas about gender and class by promoting the ideal suffragette as womanly and respectably middle class. Wendy Parkins is among those who address this difficulty, arguing that the costume codes must be seen as a performative strategy and that "the women conforming to middle-class prescriptions concerning appearance and fashion [need not] be seen . . . as an affirmation of an immanent identity."[29] While these are important considerations, *Votes for Women*'s construction of fashionable suffragettes was more than an attempt to manage a crisis in popular perception, more than a concerted effort to manufacture a uniform civic body for the public to see. Instead, the newspaper was engaged in the active construction of suffragettes as consumers, rather than simply a spectacle for the public to consume. By situating feminists as shoppers, *Votes for Women* began to imagine shopping as a politically efficacious activity for even militant suffragettes to enter into.

This discourse of shopping for the vote becomes apparent in the newspaper as it began to include fashion columns and shopping directories directed to members of the WSPU, who were its main readership. Beginning in 1908, the newspaper offered "Practical Hints" to suffragettes about where to obtain clothing suitable to promote the cause. The fashion columns appeared semiregularly and became more frequent with each year; there were, as Rolley determines in her count, sixteen such fashion columns from July 1908 through November 1911.[30] In the beginning, they would particularly recommend the services of seamstresses who supported suffrage and small West End drapers who were making goods available in approved league colors. The small retail businesses had a profile in the classified section of the newspaper as well, where they placed advertisements to offer such services as seamstressing and millinery.

Although smaller shops and independent milliners, seamstresses, and dressmakers formed early coalitions with the WSPU as suppliers of suffrage-themed clothing and advertisers in *Votes for Women*, larger shops and department stores came to play an increasing role for the paper. Large drapers and department stores such as Derry and Toms, Peter Robinson's, William Owen, and Selfridge's were discovering the extent to which their commercial enterprise could profit from the commodification of suffrage (fig. 5.3). By 1909, the advertisements of the smaller drapers and seamstresses had not been entirely replaced but certainly became less noticeable when department stores and emporia began

5.3. Selfridge's advertisement (*Votes for Women*, March 18, 1910, 398). © British Library Board. All Rights Reserved

to feature large advertisements that occupied a more prominent place, such as a Selfridge's advertisement from March 12 of that year, in which the department store, poised to open officially three days later, declares itself "the newest and most interesting Shopping centre in Europe."[31] Whereas many advertisements from small businesses had formerly appeared at the end of each issue of *Votes for Women* in the classified section, the new advertisements from large retailers sometimes seemed to rival the paper's editorial content for visual dominance.

The phenomenon of more-prominent advertising from bigger retailers coincided with the editorial decision in *Votes for Women* that year to publish the paper in a new format with larger pages and more attention to advertisers to widen circulation. This change not only reflected a growing *Votes for Women* readership but also attested to an increasingly complex relationship between suffrage feminism, advertising, and consumer culture. Whereas the earlier fashion columns (prior to the paper's format change) had arguably been extended advertisements for a handful of carefully selected prosuffrage drapers and seamstresses, the fashion columns that followed the adoption of the new layout seemed far more eager to address details of the seasonal sales and stocks of those department stores that were buying large advertisements in the paper. In addition to fashion columns, the paper also began to include a "Votes for Women" Directory, sometimes called Where to Shop, that acted as an edited version of many of the fashion columns, listing the bootmakers, drapers, furnishers, hairdressers, milliners, restaurants, and so forth, who advertised regularly in the paper and therefore comprised the shops that readers should frequent for all their needs, to the exclusion of others (fig. 5.4). By frequenting only those union-approved shops and department stores that were listed in the directories, suffragettes were shopping for the vote, that is, seeing to it that their consumer activities were in alignment with their politics.

But as Joel H. Kaplan and Sheila Stowell have observed, these alliances were often opportunistic, for the retailers who advertised in *Votes for Women* seemed particularly adept at anticipating the needs of the suffrage movement just before large street demonstrations were to take place.[32] Increasingly, they came to appropriate suffrage as a cause that paid. A case in point is the marketing prior to the procession of 1911, one of the largest of the suffrage street spectacles, a peaceful demonstration to which every suffrage society in the country was invited; it was to boast more than 40,000 participants. The procession is an interesting cultural moment for how it reveals the ways in which suffrage,

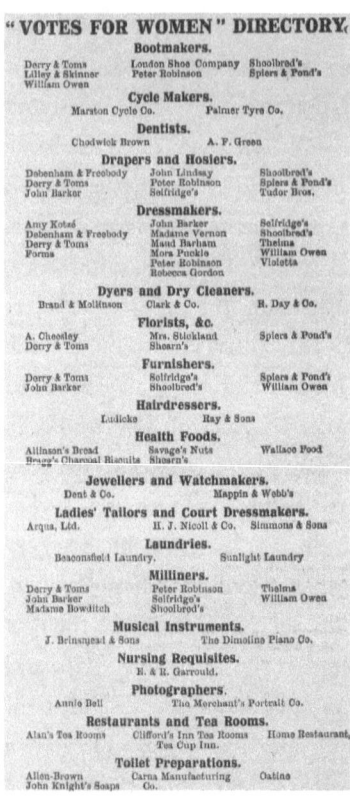

5.4. "Votes for Women" Directory (*Votes for Women*, April 8, 1910, 435). © British Library Board. All Rights Reserved

consumerism, and advertising intersect on the pages of *Votes for Women*. In the weeks leading up to the Great Procession, this suffrage event was an advertising opportunity for shops and department stores. For example, an advertisement placed by Derry and Toms appeared just over a week before the procession, announcing a special stock of "Charming Hats for the June 17 Demonstration. . . . During the next few days we shall be exhibiting in one of our windows hats and toques made in the colours of the various organisations in connection with the Woman Suffrage movement. This should prove to be a unique opportunity for purchasing suitable millinery for the great Procession of June 17" (fig. 5.5).

The editors of *Votes for Women* held no delusions that retailers formed an alliance with them out of convenience, rather than out of political conscience. In a piece called "Whet Your Weapon!" the newspaper reaffirmed the editors' understanding that retailers such as Derry and Toms, William Owen, and Selfridge's were "not philanthropic societies. They are business firms, run on sound business lines. If they find it pays them to advertise in *Votes for Women* they will advertise—if they find it doesn't, they won't. . . . Therefore, let every woman who believes in this cause never enter a shop that does not advertise in *Votes for Women*, and let her deal exclusively with those firms who do, *and inform them why*."[33] In identifying the ways in which the advertisers were the union's partners in politics only so far as it was profitable, the WSPU advocated that its membershoppers remind these allies of the extent to which the retailers relied on the collective purchasing power of a constituency whose decision to buy or not to buy was a matter of political motivation. The article concludes by suggesting a link between retailers' advertising and the union's commitment to militancy: "*Votes for Women* is our most important weapon. . . . [H]elp[ ] to furbish and sharpen

Charming Hats for the June 17 Demonstration. Special Display at
DERRY & TOMS, KENSINGTON HIGH ST., LONDON, W.

During the next few days we shall be exhibiting in one of our windows hats and toques made in the colours of the various organisations in connection with the Woman Suffrage movement.

This should prove to be a unique opportunity for purchasing suitable millinery for the great Procession of June 17.

Very pretty Creation of Ivory Lace, with wreath of Forget-me-nots and Cerise Roses.
18/11
Must be seen to be appreciated.

We have an enormous range of hats in all the fashionable shades, trimmed with ribbon, lace, flowers, etc., at 12s. 9d. to suit every tas'e. A visit of inspection is cordially invited.

Fashionable and becoming Hat, with Underbrim of Black and White Striped Silk, Trimmed with Cornflower and small Cerise Roses.
25/9

Smart Chip Hat, trimmed with Velvet, White Wheat, and Roses.
12/9
Very Effective and Becoming.

The prices range from 12/9, and the quality, style, and value are unsurpassed.

The Hats Illustrated could be made up in the Distinguishing Colours of any Organisation.

5.5. Derry and Toms advertisement (*Votes for Women*, June 9, 1911, 604). © British Library Board. All Rights Reserved

[this] weapon." By shopping at approved shops, WSPU adherents were ultimately ensuring the viability of a commercial endeavor of their own: the newspaper.

Shopping with the WSPU

The WSPU was cognizant that it needed to negotiate carefully its relationship to its advertisers who supplied them with fashionable goods. But it was not unique among suffrage groups in forging alliances with retailers and advertisers and printing shopping guides and fashion columns in its paper. Kaplan and Stowell point out, "Every suffrage paper published 'shopping guides' that were . . . lists of advertisers, as well as recurring reminders to patronize only those establishments."[34] The Women's Freedom League organ, the *Vote*, also carried fashion columns beginning in 1911 that "took the form of shopping excursions."[35] *Common Cause*, the organ of the moderate NUWSS, included shopping directories and urged readers to patronize its advertisers but decided against including fashion columns, which were felt to be too frivolous.[36]

Although many other suffrage groups compiled shopping directories for their newspapers and adopted a costume code, no other group seems to have rivaled the WSPU's incursions into the world of merchandising and retailing. For the WSPU, the business of selling suffrage was never fully conceded or outsourced to establishments such as Derry and Toms, Marshall and Snelgrove, and Selfridge's that, while not hostile, clearly lay outside its organizational ranks. Indeed, *Votes for Women* created merchandise that was offered in a fleet of shops across Great Britain. Through the discursive construction of these shops in the pages of *Votes for Women*, the WSPU created its own practice of shopkeeping, one that assumed the privilege of civic status and insisted on a link between the enterprises of commerce and citizenship.

Even as some retailers were exploiting a demand for suffrage fashions, the WSPU had by 1908 begun to make small wearable items such as badges and scarves available directly from its offices, established in 1907 at Clement's Inn in London. In the 1908 *Votes for Women* article "Popularising the Colours," Pethick-Lawrence went so far as to adopt a discourse of selling suffrage, one that urged members to buy these items to promote suffrage to the public at large. She wrote, "Avail yourselves of the tricolour badge by wearing it always . . . and sell [it] to all your friends. . . . Each one of you can become a subvendor of the colours."[37] Anticipating de Certeau's deconstruction of the conventional opposition between production and consumption, *Votes for Women* constructed suffragettes as not only shoppers but also vendors for the cause. This facet of the WSPU campaign—to use the union's own forms of commerce to sell suffrage—was a political enterprise that went beyond the strategic alliance with retailers and advertisers. An instance of tactical poaching on the sphere of consumption, the WSPU's clever merchandising and shops were a consumable but effective blend of pleasure and propaganda.

In addition to advocating that members use the colors to sell suffrage to those outside its ranks, the WSPU also began to market its own merchandise for consumption by the larger public. In doing so, it found appealing ways to promote the cause through its appropriations of advertising. Perhaps this is nowhere more visible than in the union's marketing of a number of table and card games that were gleefully advertised in *Votes for Women*, becoming particularly popular over the following five years—especially just before Christmas each year. Unlike suffrage colors and a costume code, the games were not concerned specifically with the image of the womanly woman but instead situated ordinary pursuits and entertainment as a tactical opportunity through which the political could be played out. Moreover, they combined the commodity of games with the work of advertising, since the games were designed to advocate subtly for the vote. In 1909, *Votes for Women* advertised one of its popular table games, Pank-A-Squith, a name that playfully conflated "Pankhurst" with "Asquith," the sitting prime minister. In this game, players must make their way from the home of a suffragette to the Houses of Parliament at the center of the board (fig. 5.6)—a game version

5.6. Pank-A-Squith game advertisement (*Votes for Women*, October 8, 1909, 80). © British Library Board. All Rights Reserved

> **'PANK-A-SQUITH'**
>
> *A highly Artistic TABLE GAME that helps to spread the movement*....
>
> *
>
> PUZZLES .
> AMUSES .
> TEASES .
> EXCITES .
> SETS . .
> EVERYBODY
> LAUGHING .
>
> 'PANK-A-SQUITH' concerns the attempt of a "Suffragette" to get from her home to the Houses of Parliament. She has to cross fifty sections and meet with all sorts of opposition. The game is most artistically got up; all are cleverly drawn and reproduced in colours. It consists of a splendid field, six figures of "Suffragettes," witty rules, dice, and clear instructions—all printed in purple, white, and green. . . . . .
>
> *
>
> **'PANK-A-SQUITH'**
> is sold at
> —— 1s. 6d. ——
> in all the shops of the W.S.P.U., at all outdoor meetings, and at
> **THE WOMEN'S PRESS,**
> . . 4, Clements Inn, W.C. . .

The Tactics of Consumption 151

of the actual 1908 suffragettes' attempt to rush the House of Commons. Along the way, players encounter a variety of obstacles, such as glowering prison wardresses and unfriendly policemen. The advertisement promises that the game "helps to spread the movement.... [It] puzzles, amuses, teases, excites, sets everybody laughing."[38] Other games were specially advertised as ways to use humor and fun to recruit new women for the cause. The 1909 advertisement for a card game called "Panko: The Woman's Suffrage Card Game" asked, "Are any of your friends Anti-Suffragists? Then if you begin by amusing them with 'Panko' you can convert them afterwards" (fig. 5.7).[39] Variations on some of these games also included the table games Suffragettes In and Out of Prison, In and Out of Holloway Gaol and Rushing the House. Another, called Suffragette, is described as early as 1907 in a *Votes for Women* notice as a sort of trivia card game. "Although it may be recommended as a novel form of propaganda," the notice read, "let it not be thought that there is no fun in it."[40]

These WSPU games rehearse de Certeau's consideration of what he terms "an entirely different kind of production, called 'consumption' [that is] characterized by its ruses, its fragmentation, ... its tireless but quiet activity ... of using [the products] imposed on it."[41] Taking the conventions of parlor amusements, the WSPU produced versions of popular entertainment but in doing so fundamentally altered them. One does not wish to minimize or flatten the very real, material differences between deploying women to smash windows and engaging women in board or card games. While both endeavors involve forms of risk and ruse, no one was ever imprisoned for playing a suffragette game. What is notable is that the WSPU understood that consumer culture was a field where their militant tactics were at work, and the games they advertised in *Votes for Women* and sold were premised on a discursive link between consumerism and such tactics. In contrast to the spectacle of street pageantry, the games reveal how consumption and militancy alike might be configured as tactical. The games not only materialize de Certeau's concept of consumer tactics but also show how humor and the pleasures of consumption are consistent with political endeavor. By appropriating the typical operations of a table game, the WSPU enacted "cracks and lucky hits in the framework of a system, [for] consumers' ways of operating are the practical equivalent of wit."[42] If suffragettes were shattering shopwindows, they were also cultivating their own consumer culture that shattered the popular view of feminists as dour and humorless.

PANKO
The Woman's Suffrage Card Game.

Drawings by E. T. REED, of "PUNCH."

"PANKO" is a most exciting Card Game, played between supporters and opponents of Woman's Suffrage. The pictures are drawn by the inimitable E. T. Reed, of "Punch," and are exquisitely coloured, half in Red and Black, half in Mauve and Green. They form a portrait gallery of the leading figures in the Movement. Not only is each picture in itself an interesting memento, but the game produces intense excitement without the slightest taint of bitterness.

Are your friends interested in the cause? If so, there is no better way to please them than to buy a pack of "PANKO."

Are any of your friends Anti-Suffragists? Then if you begin by amusing them with "PANKO" you can convert them afterwards.

PANKO can be obtained, Price 2/-

From 4, CLEMENTS INN, and all branches of the W.S.P.U. From all Stationers and Newsagents, and from Peter Gurney Ltd., 2, Breams Buildings, Fetter Lane, E.C.

5.7. Panko game advertisement (*Votes for Women*, December 3, 1909, 157). © *British Library Board. All Rights Reserved*

Along with these novelties, the WSPU also licensed other kinds of merchandise between 1907 and 1913, including such items as jewelry, scarves, purses, belts, ties, brooches, hatpins, games, fountain pen holders, tea, soap, crackers, jams, postcards, cards, notepapers, and calendars, usually in purple, white, and green. These wares were sold at WSPU branch offices, a number of which began to open retail spaces that imitated the look of a conventional shop. The first mention of a WSPU shop in *Votes for Women* appeared in the July 30, 1908, issue of the newspaper in a regular feature, the Campaign throughout the Country, in which the various WSPU branches published a weekly report of their activities. The reporter from Clifton in the west of England, a prominent WSPU member and former mill worker named Annie Kenney, proudly announces that "[t]he shop and committee rooms are open. We have been lucky enough to get a shop in the main street in the best part of the town. There are two front windows. We have a list of all our meetings in one window, and in the other the big photo of Mrs. Pankhurst in the centre.... We show our pamphlets and books, and display our colours and scarves, ties, ribbons, &c., in the big window. Inside we have our banners and our literature beautifully set out on nice shelves round the shop."[43] In the following issue, Kenney follows up to declare that the shop "is the best advertisement we could have for our movement. Scarcely a minute of the day passes but there are people at the window."[44] Reports such as this and ones that followed emphasize the ways in which such shops sought to influence those resistant to women's suffrage by making the argument for the vote through a consumer appeal that was itself appealing.

In the weeks just before Christmas, for example, the WSPU featured seasonal stock that even a hesitant visitor to a suffrage shop might opt to consider. In a short December 1909 feature, "Xmas Gifts at the W.S.P.U. Shops," *Votes for Women* listed special offerings including baked items such as plum pudding and mince pies (made and donated by local members) and manufactured goods such as Christmas crackers and Christmas cards.[45] The shops became so popular that the WSPU went on to open dozens in the years that followed. Over 1909, the weekly Local Notes and the Campaign throughout the Country columns in *Votes for Women* mention shop openings for more than a dozen WSPU branch offices in such places as Kensington, Chelsea, Plymouth, Lewisham, Bradford, Newcastle, Fulham and Putney, and Dundee.[46] At the end of 1910, there were at least thirty such shops.[47] In contrast to the spectacular politics of suffrage street theater, WSPU shopwindows across the country invited onlookers inside, where the shopper browsed for a political affiliation as much as for goods. In creating venues emulating regular shops, the WSPU suggested how the apparatus of retailing could be adopted to persuade the public to buy the suffrage line of thinking.

Another concern evident in *Votes for Women* was that the shops should resemble established commercial enterprises.[48] The July 16, 1909, Campaign throughout the Country column includes a fulsome overview of the ways in which the WSPU shop at Fulham and Putney had come to be organized in a manner that made it "an example of what might be done in other parts of London."[49] Covering details concerning the shop layout and windows, workers and their duties, finances and fund-raising, and schedules and stock, the report suggests how the shops had emerged as centers of activity for the union:

> The shop has been rented from a photographer, and consists of a window and office on the first floor, with a bow window and balcony useful for displays of flags, posters, etc., a kitchen with the necessary fittings, and three rooms above, which are being fitted up as club-room, dressing-room, etc. Two ladies—Miss Lenanton and Mrs. Roberts—are chief shopkeepers, and about twenty of the members take their turn. A timetable of shop assistants has been drawn up. The stock is checked every morning, and the sales are entered in the sales book. The treasurer attends once a week to receive subscriptions, send our receipts, etc., and the Literature Secretary at the same time orders in new stock, and generally overlooks the literature.
>
> The rent, £1 per week (inclusive), is partly raised by weekly subscriptions from 3d. to 1s. from members, and occasional social evenings are held to add to the funds. A collecting-box is also placed in a prominent position for incidental expenses. A lending library is part of the scheme, books relating to woman suffrage, and presented by members, being lent at 1d. per week. It is estimated that the profits on literature, etc., for the first six weeks will amount to 30s. or £2. Jumble sales are resorted to, to add to the funds, and teas are provided at 3d. per head. The advantages of this scheme are obvious. In addition to the sales of colours, postcards, pamphlets, etc., newspaper cuttings, and leaflets . . . are pasted on the window and renewed frequently.[50]

The description continues, relating activities that point to the manner in which the shop not only resembled an actual retail business but was also a tactical operation for the promotion of suffrage politics and the formation of the WSPU's collective identity:

> The shop is a rallying ground for members and a centre of communication, thus effecting a considerable saving of postage. It is also a centre from which speakers and workers go out to open-air meetings, thereby saving much unnecessary waiting about, and it is, in addition, a storage place for banners, temporary platforms, etc. . . . [A] worker having a spare half-hour knows that her help will be welcome at the W.S.P.U. shop. She can call in for copies of VOTES FOR WOMEN, and can take them out to sell, or she can distribute leaflets, advertise special meetings, or address envelopes, etc. It may be added that the shop is a rendezvous for speakers from a distance, where they can be supplied with refreshments, and a room in which to rest after a meeting.[51]

The shops were indeed the locus of a whole host of undertakings. They were the site of weekly members' gatherings to hear guest speakers and outreach meetings to such communities as factory girls, a convenient place to procure tickets for upcoming public suffrage rallies or drop off donated goods for bazaars and jumble sales, and a gathering spot where volunteers could assemble before setting out to sell *Votes for Women* newspapers on the streets or chalk sidewalks to advertise coming events. If a branch of the WSPU decided to open a shop, it became the nerve center of the local campaign.

Once a shop was up and running, the actual profits varied (with some shops doing better than others); profits are difficult to assess apart from the occasional mention in Local Notes and Campaign throughout the Country reports. J. A. Bouvier of the Lewisham shop noted that "[t]he takings at the shop on the first two days . . . amounted to £1 0s. 5d.," but most updates merely state that the shops are doing well.[52] The annual reports, too, make little mention of shop profits, although the 1910–11 report notes that the average takings for the shop at Charing Cross came to twenty pounds a week.[53] The shops do not appear to have been meant to turn a profit, only to sustain themselves insofar as they could. The WSPU was evidently engaged in a form of shopkeeping that observed the outward forms of retailing—emulating the institutional practices associated with a professional enterprise—as part of its tactics of consumption. In light of the fact that the WSPU identified West End shopkeepers as a political constituency in the course of its window-smashing campaign, it is clear that the world of retailing was not separate from the sphere of politics in *Votes for Women*. By setting up shop, the WSPU occupied these intersecting domains and in doing so forged a link between retailing and civics. Insisting on an implicit code of shopkeeping as an undertaking that was premised on fair dealing, the suffragettes' form of shopkeeping operated to authenticate their claim to full civic identity.

Rebel Women Shopkeepers

Votes for Women did not merely report on the successful operations of its shops, for these shops were also a site of considerable discursive construction in the newspaper concerning the idea of professional shopkeeping. In addition to the discussion of shop activities in the newspaper's regular branch reports, *Votes for Women* published a handful of articles featuring WSPU shops at the height of their popularity between 1909 and 1911. In the first of two "Under the Clock" features, published on May 13, 1910, the newspaper focused on a new shop that had opened a week earlier in Charing Cross Road (where the WSPU had moved its main offices when it outgrew the rooms at Clement's Inn). The title of the piece referred to a large "Votes for Women" clock that hung outside above the shop and could be seen from Oxford Street. At the shop-warming on May 6, prominent WSPU member and writer Evelyn Sharp, whose first novel had been published at the Bodley Head, gave a speech that equated fair shopkeeping practices with political justice for women.[54] *Votes for Women* related that Sharp "pointed out that in a nation said to be . . . a nation of shopkeepers, the great thing was to keep shop well, and this was certainly done by the Women's Social and Political Union. The [WSPU] stood for the principle that what was handed across the counter should be that which had been paid for by the purchaser, and it was this principle of straight dealing which the Union demanded from the Government."[55]

Several weeks later, in a second item likewise called "Under the Clock," published on July 1, *Votes for Women* followed up on the success of the new Woman's Press shop at Charing Cross Road. Beginning with an extract from Sharp's shop-warming speech, it similarly links the enterprises of shopkeeping and citizenship: "It is not only the amount of money which is taken over our counter that matters; it is the amount of influence that we hand across that counter that counts for so much."[56] Using Sharp's words to emphasize the parallel between commercial transaction and political assertion, the columnist goes into more detail about the propagandist function of this carefully decorated and well-stocked venue. In a space coded as a commercial interior, the shop was reportedly succeeding in attracting a curious public inside to consider the idea of women's suffrage. Rather than merely inciting the public to take notice of the cause through the spectacle of suffrage and street pageantry, the WSPU hoped to ensure through its shops that idle onlookers would become consumers of suffrage, on suffragist terms. The article observed, "Especially since the great Procession of June 18 callers have been pouring into the shop in an almost continuous stream," inquiring about everything from "the militant methods of the Union . . . [to] elementary instruction in 'Why Women Want the Vote.'" The shop stocked "books, pamphlets, leaflets, not to speak of VOTES FOR WOMEN itself . . . [in which could] be found the answers to these very questions."[57]

After emphasizing the importance of the Charing Cross shop's Information Department, the article goes on to describe the shop's delightful interior and the variety of tricolor merchandise available:

> The shop itself is a blaze of purple, white and green, and the mere enumeration of the pretty and useful things for sale would fill this entire column. Just now the Woman's Press is showing some beautiful motor and other scarves in various shades of purple, as well as white muslin summer blouses, and among the almost unending variety of bags, belts, &c., are noticeable the 'Emmeline' and the 'Christabel' bags, and the 'Pethick' tobacco pouch. In addition to books, pamphlets, and leaflets, stationery, games, blotters, [and] playing cards, . . . almost everything that can be produced in purple, white and green . . . is to be found here.[58]

Pleasure and politics come together in the suffrage shop, where identification of the goods with famous WSPU personages, of commodities with the idea of women's suffrage, was an implicit endorsement of an enterprise that was as civic-minded as it was commercial.[59]

Perhaps the most engaging profile of a WSPU shop in *Votes for Women* is one written by Evelyn Sharp that featured the Kensington shop. In this article,

Sharp observes not only the importance of the shops as effective advertisements for feminism, as the other shop profiles do, but also the pleasures of shopkeeping. Before turning to this article, one should note that even in the brief, weekly Local Notes feature in *Votes for Women*, the Kensington shop was emerging as not simply one of the first but perhaps the most enthusiastic, imaginative, and committed of the many WSPU shop enterprises that were begun that year. Plans to open the Kensington shop appear in Local Notes on January 14, 1909; a few weeks later, after its opening, the Kensington Local Notes reporter, Louise M. Eates, added that "[t]he addition of a counter to our shop has given it a very business-like air" and that "numerous customers" were being "attracted by the display in our windows."[60] Writing on February 26, Eates reports that the shop had acquired a sign for the exterior. In the March 19 Local Notes, the reporter for Chelsea, Charlotte Blacklock, announced that the Chelsea Union had decided to open a shop, having "been inspired by the example of Kensington."[61]

The Chelsea Union's enthusiasm may have been stoked by Evelyn Sharp's account of the Kensington shop, which had appeared a week earlier (March 12) in *Votes for Women*. In "Painting Kensington Purple, White, and Green," Sharp considers the everyday delights of operating a shop where politics need not be separate from pleasure. Sharp even makes a confession of sorts about the shop as an enjoyable enterprise for those women who organized and ran it:

> Nobody said so in committee, but I do not believe a single member of that serious and grown-up group of Kensington Suffragettes was above feeling a secret thrill of glee at the thought of keeping shop at last—real shop, with a counter, and a bell, and a cash-box, and stair-case leading up to a sort of Never-Never Land, where tea is made everyday at five o'clock, and up which you can shout "Shop!" whenever you want to appear particularly professional. It is like raising a humdrum existence to the level of dreams. All the while, though, it is a real business-like shop, with two shop windows; and everything, wherever you look, is glowing in purple, white, and green.[62]

The hard and even dangerous work of political campaigning becomes the delightful task of keeping shop, of selling suffrage. The shop is well stocked with "pamphlets and books," but admittedly the merchandise in union colors filling the windows is what attracts suffrage supporters and nonsupporters alike. This shopfront—a commercial front for militant activities—operates as a tactical space in which suffrage politics are attractively displayed and eminently consumable. "Food for the mind," Sharp writes, "is . . . our aim, and the mind we try to catch is expected to feed just as hungrily on purple, white, and green 'goods' as on pamphlets and books. That is why one of our windows is filled entirely with scarves, hatpins, badges, belts, and anything else we can show in the fighting colours of the Union." "Part of the business of keeping a . . . shop consists, of course," Sharp also admits, "in persuading a coy public that we are not dangerous, and that it is quite safe to come inside." "To this end," she continues, "we place enticing invitations in the window, printed in the colours. This, for instance, . . . 'Do you want an answer to the anti-Suffragist? Do you want to hear why we went to the House of Commons? Then come inside and ask!'"[63] Such invitations did the work of window displays by attracting customers to come in for a closer look at suffrage politics.

Sharp insists that the invitations "have their effect. In ones and twos the public visit us, to offer their services, to buy, to ask for information." The "real effect of our shop," Sharp goes on, "is its moral effect. There it is, a tri-colour evidence to the hundreds of people who pass it every day that the 'Votes for Women' movement is in their midst, whether they like it or not. And, of course, they do like it directly they come in contact with it. They stand round our windows, learning by heart all their contents. They watch our workers in their colours, passing in and out with papers to sell or bills to distribute."[64] In this shop, the public is pleasantly initiated into the WSPU's terms of its argument for the vote. By insinuating itself into the sphere of consumption, including the practice of window display, the WSPU discovers a way to attract converts to the cause by constructing them as customers.

What Sharp's account does more than anything else is admit coyly to the ways in which professional shopkeeping—the practice of running a real shop—is a performative gesture. Sharp's confession, with its recourse to descriptions of the shop as a "Never-Never Land" that "rais[es] a humdrum existence to the level of dreams," is an admission of the acknowledgement made between these suffragettes that they are engaged in the activity of "playing" at shop. In the marketplace of political ideas, the suffragettes are most effective when they are engaged in such forms of play. By observing the outward forms of shopkeeping, they ensure the viability of their version of the marketplace where the public can be sold on the idea of votes for women.

That the Kensington branch of the WSPU may have been a particularly playful and subversive group is suggested by the shop displays it adopted to attract a second look from potential shoppers. The Kensington shop location in Church Street was determined "because the situation at the corner of Edge-street gives the windows great prominence, and they cannot fail to catch the eye of the passers-by."[65] Furthermore, the branch's window dressing was a form of politicized critique that recalls the humorous tactics inscribed through the WSPU game merchandise. One of the early window displays in the Kensington shop parodied the sensationalized images of imprisoned suffragettes that were appearing in the popular press. It was described in *Votes for Women* as "a 'Holloway' corner," which featured "dolls in prison dress and copies of Holloway cutlery."[66] While many of the branch shops made a special effort to display an enticing array of items for sale during the Christmas season, the Kensington WSPU arguably did so with particular energy. In December 1909, *Votes for Women* related that "[e]very preparation is being made at the Kensington shop (143, Church Street) for a purple, white, and green Christmas. A window snow scene, representing 'A Cabinet Minister's Christmas Dream,' will be on view shortly; meanwhile you are invited to try . . . some 'militant jam with stones,' or the 'stoneless variety (stones extracted for other purposes).'"[67] The shop had embraced not only the pleasures of the shop but also the possibilities of satirical political humor. The jam was a product that played upon the WSPU's window-breaking policy, not deflating the importance of this policy for the union so much as reiterating control over it. In the absence of further documentation, we can only suppose that the window display, "A Cabinet Minister's Christmas Dream," was a send-up of the Liberal government's wish that the suffragettes would give up their cause.

In observing the norms of shopping to a certain extent, through advertising campaigns and window dressing, the WSPU shops engaged in an extended parody of the practices and products associated with more-conventional shopping. In her article on the wide-ranging cultural work of the WSPU's Woman's Press, Simone Murray notes "the potentially infinite commercial reproducibility of the suffragette image" that characterized such merchandise as the suffrage postcard.[68] A similar thing can be said about the shops in which the WSPU sold its licensed products. By reproducing the experience of women's middle-class shopping, the suffrage shops were altering the consumer experience. As the Kensington branch threw itself into shop displays and the promotion of specialty products, its energy speaks not only to the pleasures of consumption but also to a rearrangement of the terms of regular shopping. The suffrage retail space was not a neutral one that merely emulated the typical shop; instead, it materialized a whole range of intersecting tactical practices. The WSPU adapted shopwindows and displays to political ends, and women who might hesitate to attend a public meeting of suffragettes might unexpectedly discover their affinity for the cause while shopping. In the disarming space of the shop, the pleasures of a consumer gaze and the roving opportunities of browsing amounted to sizing up and trying on a political identity. One did not have to buy, but one had the option of looking and being gently teased from being a consuming subject into being a politicized one as well.

In other words, the appearance of a network of real shops was an effect of discourse to which the WSPU aspired. The suffrage shops made visible how institutions are, indeed, generated through the work of representation. When *Votes for Women* featured suffrage shops and merchandise, it did so by adopting the guise of professional tradespeople. By assuming the look and feel of actual shops, the union seemed to aspire to ordinary commercial trade, but in reproducing a typical shopping experience, the union also fundamentally reimagined it. The construction of shops in *Votes for Women* suggests how the establishing of these venues was coextensive with, rather than at odds with, the union's more obviously militant activities. The shops were a discursive opportunity in *Votes for Women* to use the language of institutionalized commerce to politically expedient ends.

"Painting Kensington Purple, White, and Green" extols the subversive pleasures of keeping shop, an attitude that is amplified in Sharp's fictional adaptation of this article. Sharp revised her feature on the Kensington shop as a short story, "Votes for Women—Forward!" which first appeared in *Votes for Women* and was later included in *Rebel Women*, a collection of thirteen "fictional sketches" that was published in 1910. Carolyn Christensen Nelson maintains that *Rebel Women* contains the most accomplished short fiction about suffragettes, setting it apart from other collections such as those by Gertrude Colemore and Annie S. Swan.[69] What makes Sharp's stories particularly compelling is her decision to focus on "the daily activities of ordinary suffragettes who . . . find themselves in situations ranging from the serious and frightening to the absurd and comic."[70] The sketches, as Sharp calls them, avoid staging the more dramatic and violent scenes of suffrage, such as imprisonment or forcible feeding, and instead focus on the quotidian experiences of a group of London WSPU suffragettes. Whether the women are portrayed selling newspapers on the street or merely riding the omnibus, Sharp's emphasis is on the "psychological battles" of this group of women.[71] Many of the sketches in *Rebel Women* therefore "demonstrate[ ] the conflicting constructions of femininity imposed upon women when they enter public space."[72] In the ordinary ways in which she represents these suffragettes' attempts to negotiate public and civic identities, Sharp suggests how women's fight for the vote was not limited to spectacular scenes such as processionals and demonstrations but also included the difficulties, awkwardness, and even humor of the workaday world of suffrage agitation.

"Votes for Women—Forward!" is unique among the short stories in *Rebel Women* in its depiction of the challenges and opportunities of running a WSPU shop.[73] As in Sharp's article on the Kensington shop, her fictional version addresses the pleasures of setting up a real shop and the eagerness with which a group of suffragettes extend their politics into the enterprise of shopkeeping. The story also seems to turn to preoccupations that *Votes for Women* had also considered, a concern to appear legitimate in this commercial undertaking as the narrator, an unnamed suffragette begins, "When our local committee determined, in the words of the minutes book, to open a shop and offices in the local main street, 'for the dissemination of suffrage literature,' we made up our minds that we would not be amateur shopkeepers. The success of our venture, we argued solemnly, depended on convincing the neighbourhood that we meant to be taken as seriously as any other tradesman in the street."[74] Despite their glee over running a shop, and the real pleasure this affords them, the women want to appear as competent shopkeepers rather than mere dabblers.

In this instance, this means perfecting a style of saleswomanship that shoppers cannot distinguish from that of established shopkeepers. While the suffragettes resolve to ensure that their enterprise appears thoroughly professional, they discover that they have much to learn about selling. As a consequence of their desire to appear as seasoned shopkeepers, the women realize that they are too earnest and attentive in their treatment of shoppers, hovering over all who enter the shop instead of letting the customers browse. "Naturally," the narrator relates, "we began by taking the customer very seriously. The first one who entered the shop was instantly confronted with three eager shop assistants, who asked breathlessly and in unison what they might have the pleasure of showing him" (92). The customer replies, politely, that he has forgotten what it is he would like to see, having been startled by all of the attention. Two of the saleswomen "beat a wise retreat" (92), but "the militant member of our committee" (93) remains and convinces the customer that he should buy a tie. After this customer leaves, it is clear that he had felt pressure to buy, and so the women on the floor assess their selling technique. They decide that only one of them should serve a customer at a time. If a second customer arrives and there is no one available to wait on him or her, someone is to call "'Shop!' in a professional tone up the spiral staircase" (94) to preserve the aura of a seasoned operation.

As the women learn to observe the casual authority of a real shop and "to sustain [a] professional pose" (97), they also come to realize a fundamental truth about shopkeeping: "It was evident that as shopkeepers we started with a distinct handicap, being ourselves amateurs in selling, whereas no customer is ever an amateur in buying" (93). Even suffragettes, it seems, are on the watch for that category of shopper who comes "not to buy, but to shop" (93). "[W]e found," the narrator relates, "that the majority of [the customers] belonged to those who went out to shop and not to buy. Numbers of them, indeed, seemed to be there on the assumption that if you want to buy something, one shop is as good as another in which to seek it" (94). These suffragettes are able to formulate their selling tactics only when they put themselves in the shoes of their customers, whose dislike of pressure and whose propensity to look and not to buy are commonly ascribed traits of the shopper. In other words, these suffragettes are also shoppers, recalling the ways in which *Votes for Women* doubly inscribed its readers as both consumers and vendors of suffrage. This dual identity characterizes the WSPU's tactics of consumption as a collapsing of the usual boundaries between consumption and production into "the multiform labour of consumption."[75] The result is a fluid form of identity that enabled militant suffragettes to play both sides of the counter simultaneously and, by refusing the terms of fixity, to turn either side to their political advantage.

In the course of refining their selling tactics, one further condition of the WSPU's tactics of consumption also becomes evident. For it is notable that in fiction, as in the *Votes for Women* constructions of the suffrage shop, Sharp's suffragette saleswomen are in the end not as anxious to become professional retailers as to successfully perform the script of shopkeeping. They are not engaged in a moneymaking enterprise but are instead invested in mastering a pose that will confer legitimacy on their status as traders in a marketplace of ideas. Moreover, in the course of constructing the suffrage shop as the scene where feminists play the role of shopkeepers to sell the public on the idea of women's franchise, both Sharp's story and *Votes for Women* inscribe a radical revisioning of the public sphere. In contrast to the bourgeois public sphere that Jürgen Habermas identifies, in which ideas are freely circulated, the WSPU was reimagining the public sphere as a commercial marketplace.[76] Ideas no longer acquired value through, for example, their wit of expression or their status as empirically verifiable; instead, ideas attained value through the fact of their exchange. In this public sphere, ideas (much like commodities) acquire value through their relationships to other ideas. Those political points of view that drive a price, that are deemed desirable or attractive, are those that are considered worthwhile. The world of commerce was one in which the very idea of suffrage was up for sale to a class of middle-class consumers who the WSPU hoped would buy the suffragettes' claim to the vote. As the sketch continues, the truth of this marketplace of ideas is confirmed. In the midst of casual encounters and conversations between the suffragettes and a varied, at times motley, clientele, a "flippant jester" periodically enters the shop. "[A]ttracted by our ingenuous notice inviting people to come in and ask for what they did not see in the window, [he] would sometimes put his head in at the door to ask facetiously for a vote" (96). This jester seems not so much a heckler, for he shares the suffragettes' brand of humor. In this telling moment, he identifies the shop as the performative scene that it is, one where the idea of votes for women is surely what is being sold.

With the fine-tuning of their selling tactics behind them, the suffragettes become excited over the prospect of having their shop photographed. By including this event in the life of the shop in her story, Sharp recalls the WSPU practice of photographing its shops. Indeed, another notable feature of *Votes for Women* is that the newspaper included photographs of exteriors when it profiled a shop. Just as shopwindow displays were a gesture that confirmed the shops as bona fide operations, the practice of photographing the exteriors conferred on them an air of authenticity. The images helped construct the WSPU shops as a viable, going concern of which the organization could be proud. One of the first photographs of a shop accompanied Sharp's 1909

Kensington shop profile. Features such as "Under the Clock" and "Some W.S.P.U. Shops" also included photographs of each of the storefronts that were mentioned.[77] In all, *Votes for Women* published about a dozen of these photographs, most during 1910 and 1911. Occasionally, a small picture of a shop would appear in the pages of the regular branch reports. Although the photographers were not identified, the conventions for the composition of the images were fairly consistent. The pictures framed the exterior of the shop and are composed so that one can see the Votes for Women or WSPU sign that typically hung above. Often, local union members are included in the frame, sometimes a group and sometimes just the local secretary, standing in front of the shop. The dominant feature of the photographs is typically the shopwindow, as in a 1910 picture of the Kilburn shop, and often one can make out details of the displays, including banners and posters that advertised the union, and items for sale, such as pamphlets, leaflets, postcards, and ribbons (fig. 5.8).[78]

Such photographs suggest how the WSPU wished to present itself to the public. This public image was carefully groomed to fulfill politically unaffiliated shoppers' expectations of the middle-class shopping experience, as well as WSPU members' self-image as competent shopkeepers whose business was as viable as their political aims. By including photographs in *Votes for Women*, the WSPU was also ensuring that its members understood the importance of running an operation whose appearance was professional. And, like their fellow shopkeepers who ran productive enterprises, the WSPU suffragettes were staking their claim as an eligible part of the voting public. They wished to position themselves as legitimate and equal players in the public sphere. The concern for an authentic appearance as tradespeople—which is literally framed here as the photographic claim of realism—is thus a concern to appear as players in the civic arena, the concern to project public selves with a self-evident claim to the vote.

The suffragettes in "Votes for Women—Forward!" begin to feel that they are indeed a professional commercial operation when they learn that their shop is to be photographed. However, when a group of bystanders gathers to taunt them, the women do not get the respect they had hoped for. The "glassy eye of the camera" (98) that is meant to authenticate their shop fixes them and renders them unable to reply to the hecklers. The camera, in effect, returns them to the position of being the subject of a gaze. With this loss of agency,

5.8. The N. W. London Union Shop in Kilburn photograph (*Votes for Women*, August 19, 1910, 769). © *British Library Board. All Rights Reserved*

the women are deflated: "'Nobody will ever look upon us as real people in business, after that,' sighed one of our shop assistants when we regained comparative privacy behind the counter" (98–99).

A final episode of this sketch, however, puts the failed photograph into perspective and suggests that the spectacular scenes of suffrage were not finally at the heart of the WSPU's tactics of consumption. Just as the suffragettes are feeling gloomy over their limited success as shopkeepers and, by extension, over their thwarted political aims, an errand boy enters the shop to request change on behalf of the owner of a neighboring shop: "There was no condescension in his tone. . . . He did not ask if we wanted our rights now, or if we would sooner wait till we got them. He did not say he had no wish to see women sitting in *his* Parliament. He just stood there, as shopman to shopman, waiting to effect a trade transaction that raised us, once and for all, beyond the

The Tactics of Consumption 167

level of amateurs" (99). The most "militant member" of the group confidently sees to it that his request is granted, and the sketch concludes, "Henceforth we knew we could count on being treated in the trade as equals" (100). Interestingly, this simple transaction confers legitimacy upon the suffragettes' enterprise where photographic realism does not. Here making a convert to the cause does not matter as much as the simple exchange of money, a service like any other, emptied of its cognitive charge. Ultimately, the barrage of publicly circulated images and mass choreographed processions was not what characterized WSPU consumer culture. Rather, it was the common, even unspoken code of shopkeeping that the WSPU valued, along with the ways in which retail trade suggested a link between commerce and citizenship. In the arena of commerce, the WSPU located a place where anything, including political points of view, might be sold, so far as one assumed the role of willing vendor. Rather than the militant spectacle of street theater, the WSPU's most tactical uses of consumption conflated the political sphere with the commercial marketplace.

By 1913, the WSPU's suffrage shops had begun to decline. An advertisement for the Woman's Press that appears at the very end of the seventh annual report for the year ending February 1913 lists just seventeen shops. As the WSPU came under increased persecution and much of its leadership was driven underground, it scaled back the range of its activities to concentrate its efforts and resources on more-public, more-identifiably militant endeavors. During this time, many shops reverted to branch office activities.[79] The handful of shops that remained (Kensington among them) simplified their operations; although they continued to make printed matter such as books and pamphlets available, other merchandise was no longer promoted or sold. The eighth annual report, for the year ending February 1914, explains that "[t]he Woman's Press [by now located in Lincoln's Inn] has lately been reorganized. . . . The Department has ceased to stock tea, chocolate, cigarettes and the like, and now concentrates upon the sale of literature, badges in the colours, picture postcards and photographs of special interest to suffragists."[80] As Diane Atkinson explains, "[t]he energy and creativity behind the three-colour goods . . . were needed for more urgent political developments[,] [f]or what would be the last 12 months of the suffragette campaign," at which time the WSPU would combine its political actions with its contributions to Britain's war effort.[81]

The WSPU's phasing out of its shops and merchandising in favor of more-obviously militant and propagandist activities is supported by the stated aims found in the annual reports. However, another way of understanding the diminishing nature of the union's consumer culture concerns how the shops and their goods were constituted discursively. The decline of the suffrage shop does not indicate that it was a failure but reaffirms that suffrage consumer culture had been a tactical undertaking to begin with, one that was congruent with the union's early declarations in 1908 that it was to be a militant organization. The shop was a contingent rather than a permanent undertaking. Its trappings of shopwindows and counters did not denote institutional permanency as much as they did the status of a shop front complete with props that could be put up or taken down in response to the particular needs of the suffrage campaigns from moment to moment. The decline of the WSPU's consumer culture does not indicate the abandonment of commercial means of political engagement so much as it attests to the provisional nature of such enterprises in the first place. Tactics are by definition resistant to the forces of institutionalization; they are flexible, mobile, temporary practices that are responsive to the moment, rather than entrenched, universal, or permanent protocols.

The WSPU's invitation to its members and those it sought to convert through shopping for the vote was part of its larger militant incitement to be counted as *inside* the political process. Although the WSPU took to the streets, where it produced such spectacular images as the shopper turned shop vandal, such forms of spectacle had their limitations, subordinated as they often were to capital's propensity to circulate such images to its own homogenizing ends. In fashioning a distinctive consumer culture, one that constructed suffragettes as both shoppers and shopkeepers, *Votes for Women* imagined a richly tactical field for the production of suffrage politics, one in which the very idea of the vote could be sold. The WSPU's invitations to its members and the wider public alike to buy the suffrage line of thinking was part of a militant incitement to be included in the political process. Whether marketing provocatively humorous games or arranging subversive window displays in its own shops, the WSPU was not merely insisting on access into the political sphere but staging and staking a self-evident claim to be recognized within the public sphere already. Its occupation of consumer culture from the inside attested to the ways in which the union was determined to occupy women's right to the franchise. In extolling shopping for the vote as consistent with militant tactics, *Votes for Women* located a way to begin to mediate between insider and outsider status in a commodified public sphere, shattering the divide that had for so long shut women out of the franchise and making transparent the claim that women deserved to have the vote.

Afterword

BECOMING ELIZABETH DALLOWAY

The Future of Shopping

In the course of this study, a shopping excursion of one kind or another has formed the introduction or conclusion to most of the chapters. These anecdotes have ranged from Jane Eyre's anxious deliberations in a silk warehouse to Christina Rossetti's predicament in an artist's studio and have extended to Mary Elizabeth Braddon's and George Eliot's bold forays into the publishing marketplace. They have included Aubrey Beardsley's aesthetic book-browser and Michael Field's art heist and have finally been punctuated by the sound of shattering glass as suffragettes such as Una Blockley applied their hammers to hundreds of West End shopwindows. What these scenes encode ultimately is a shopper who is never fully consolidated but only fleetingly glimpsed from moment to moment, as she turns over the merchandise, as she considers the goods, as she perhaps even enters the marketplace as a writer. In and through such encounters, we briefly catch sight of the shopper in her tactical engagements with the marketplace, never a fixed object of perception but a site of contestation and negotiation between self and world.

These chapters have thus dealt with a series of liminal spaces and practices, with the in-betweens that both divide and join the domestic and public spheres, or the managements of the Angel in the House in *Middlemarch* with the political engagements of suffragettes in *Votes for Women*. They have noted the slide between merely looking at the goods in *Goblin Market* and handling or even secreting them away in *Lady Audley's Secret*. They have also seen the confluence between consumption and production—what links the zeal to consume or acquire for its own sake to the production of literature as commodity, as with Michael Field at the Bodley Head. As women's consumer practices proliferated between the 1860s and the First World War, shopping was not simply being institutionalized for women but being formed equally by them through their incursions into the marketplace. Thus, what made Victorian and Edwardian shopping modern is not that it anticipated a consumer culture still to come in the twentieth century, one that would usher in ever more mass-produced goods, but that it inaugurated forms of identity that were premised on a version of selfhood as that which is always in process, that is always becoming and unbecoming in the same moment.

To these shopping trips we might add one more, that of Elizabeth Dalloway in *Mrs. Dalloway* (1925), for it is in the West End sojourn of Clarissa's daughter that we see Virginia Woolf's articulation of a form of subjectivity that does not produce a fixed subject position so much as imagine identity as practice. With Elizabeth, there is no determinate self as she wanders through London; instead, there is a practice that is never reified into a figure of a singular woman shopper. Whereas Clarissa's shopping trip to Bond Street to "buy the flowers herself" for her party connects her to a sense of the linked possibilities of the past and present, a relationship that guarantees her ongoing sense of the mystery of being in the world, Elizabeth's excursion suggests the future of shopping.[1]

Writing and rewriting the lines of her mother's incursions into the marketplace, Elizabeth's shopping constitutes a most errant form of urban strolling, inscribing a subjectivity of becoming that defies prescribed femininity. Whereas Clarissa's walk is organized around a particular shopping errand, to buy flowers, Elizabeth's journey down the Strand one day in June 1923 is a spontaneous act that follows from her time with Miss Kilman at the Army and Navy Stores. That trip to the stores to help her tutor buy petticoats is the launching point for Elizabeth's formation as an urban subject. Elizabeth, who enjoys but does not feel compelled to buy anything at the stores, seamlessly conflates the pleasures of window-shopping with movement on the streets of the West End.

As those of an urban nomad, Elizabeth's improvised ramblings not only pressure traditional notions of the Baudelairean flaneur's male gaze but also anticipate Gilles Deleuze and Félix Guattari's concepts of the nomadic subject and "becoming-woman" in *A Thousand Plateaus*.[2] Together, these overlapping terms suggest contingent identities that coalesce through the ongoing work of a desire that does not proceed from lack, or the need to fill some void at the heart of being, but is wholly productive. If Michel de Certeau's "consumers produce . . . 'indeterminate trajectories' . . . [that] do not cohere with the constructed, written, and prefabricated space through which they move," the nomad—an "assemblage" that forms through its operations rather than a prior sense of self—suggests how the strolling shopper reconstitutes and thus rewrites the very spaces she traverses. In opposition to what Deleuze and Guattari term the "striated" or regulated spaces of the state, "[t]he life of the nomad is the intermezzo."[3] Privileging flows, flux, and indeterminacy, the "ambulant or nomad science[ ]" dispenses with straight lines and the process of surveying in favor of spiral and vortical movement; rather than "plotting out a closed space for linear and solid things," the nomad ensures the affective condition of "becoming, heterogeneity, [the] infinitesimal, passage to the limit, continuous variation."[4] These smooth spaces, moreover, are "'explor[ed] by legwork.'" Through these itinerant movements, nomads ensure a "process of deterritorialization [that] constitutes and extends the territory itself."[5] Like the nomad, the shopper eschews the need for final goals or fixed routes, roving and gazing her way through the West End and sometimes, as in the case of the shoplifter, even circumventing the rules of the retailing system.[6]

Elisabeth Grosz observes that in the Deleuzian economy, the girl is a "figure of resistance" and "the site of a culture's most intensified disinvestments and recastings of the body."[7] While femininity is synonymous with castration and lack, for example, in the Lacanian schema, the Deleuzian girl is a site through which the male and female binary might be undone. Grosz sees a potential in the forms of material desire that might issue from these conditions, writing that Deleuze and Guattari's "notion of the body as a discontinuous, nontotalizable series of processes, organs, flows, energies, corporeal substances and incorporeal events, speeds and durations, may be of great value to feminists attempting to reconceive bodies outside the binary oppositions imposed on the body by the mind/body, nature/culture, subject/object and interior/exterior oppositions."[8] This discontinuous body of the girl, moreover, accords with forms of desire that, for the shopper, might be negotiated through their wandering acts of consumption. Grosz notes that Deleuzian "desire is an actualization, a series of practices. . . . [It] does not take for itself a particular object whose attainment it requires; rather, it aims at nothing above its own proliferation or self-expansion."[9] Deleuze and Guattari's description of identity as "compositions of desire" thus seems fitting to the roving shopper, whose itinerant movements, or "lines of flight," and pursuit of pleasure ensure her ongoing production as an urban subject.[10]

Happily erring from a sense of plan or obligation, Elizabeth crosses the West End, from the Army and Navy Stores in Victoria Street to the theater district in the Strand on an urban adventure that combines shopping with sightseeing, and walking with public transportation. Having left the Army and Navy, Elizabeth considers how "nice [it is] to be out in the air" (147) as she waits for an omnibus. Here, she begins to narrate her account of being on the streets: "And already, even as she stood there, in her very well-cut clothes, it was beginning . . . People were beginning to compare her to poplar trees, early dawn, hyacinths, fawns, running water, and garden lilies; . . . they would compare her to lilies, and she had to go to parties" (147). But rather than serving as an object of others' gaze, Elizabeth adopts the language of exploration to narrate the terms of her visibility. Her narration is ultimately self-reflexive, since it is she who authors how others may be seeing her. The indirect discourse of "they would compare her to lilies" indicates that the narrative rendered here is not so much the thoughts of others as Elizabeth's interpolating in which she actively constructs herself as a figure of desire and enjoys being the focus of her self-narrativized gaze.

Impulsively, Elizabeth moves into the next leg of her journey as she "[s]uddenly . . . stepped forward and most competently boarded the omnibus, in front of everyone. She took a seat on top" (148). Riding boldly atop the bus, Elizabeth resumes her public visibility and also guarantees her field of vision. The omnibus serves as a means of extending Elizabeth's person, not only by granting her a view and velocity but also by supplementing her body and her status as adventurer: "The impetuous creature—a pirate—started forward, sprang away; she had to hold the rail to steady herself, for a pirate it was, reckless, unscrupulous. . . . And now it was like riding, to be rushing up Whitehall; and to each movement of the omnibus the beautiful body in the fawn-coloured coat responded freely like a rider, like the figure-head of a ship" (148–49). The speed of the bus and the perspectives it offers grant Elizabeth the terms with which to imagine a place in the traditionally male territory of the professions. "[S]he would like to have a profession," Elizabeth thinks. "She would become a doctor, a farmer, possibly go into Parliament if she found it necessary, all because of the Strand" (150). Imagining that the crowds begin to swell with "trivial chatterings" that "compar[ed] women to poplars," she silences them, choosing rather to have "thoughts of ships, of business, of law, of administration, and with it all so stately (she was in the Temple), gay (there was the river), pious (there was the Church), [it] made her quite determined" (150). To Elizabeth, to go from riding the omnibus to participating in other aspects of public life is but a short step; through this act of urban enjoyment, she comes to imagine a future in which women, particularly those of the middle classes, will enjoy vocations that will take them outside of the domestic sphere.

As one who has benefited from the efforts of suffragette agitation a couple of decades earlier, Elizabeth stands as the optimistic future for young women of her class. A modern women, she is at times inscrutable to her Victorian-born mother, who sees Elizabeth as an enigma who "cared not a straw" for gloves (12). Elizabeth is, furthermore, "an Oriental mystery," Clarissa muses. "Was it that some Mongol had been wrecked on the coast of Norfolk . . . [and] had mixed with the Dalloway ladies . . . ?" (134). An adventurer of a different strain, English-born but represented here as racially indeterminate, Elizabeth is not bound to the protocols of the past. A transposition of the goblin men in *Goblin Market* from male to female, from merchant to shopper, Elizabeth (unlike Laura and Lizzie, who must carefully negotiate their pleasures with goblin fruit) is no longer that which is imperiled by the East. In contrast to her mother, for whom the Strand is not a place to loiter, Elizabeth is more free to fashion her relationships to a world whose definition of gendered norms is changing.

Continuing her spontaneous expedition on foot, Elizabeth considers that she has been entering new territory, "walk[ing] just a little way towards St. Paul's, shyly, like some one penetrating on tiptoe. . . . For no Dalloway came down the Strand daily; she was a pioneer, a stray, venturing, trusting" (150–51). The Strand falls outside of Clarissa's beaten path of aristocratic Bond Street and, indeed, is situated along the easterly border of the West End. As a theater district, its carnivalesque streets encode a lively space that begins to push the boundaries of prescribed space for middle-class women's leisure. If Elizabeth's consumption of urban space pressures assumed borders for women of her class, her imagined future also transgresses the traditional limits of women's vocational opportunities, riding along in the omnibus as though moving toward a future of new possibilities for women. Cutting across the urban landscape, consuming the surrounding spectacle and tactically inserting herself within it, Elizabeth is a self-in-the-making whose unfolding horizon includes yet-to-be-written narratives.

Elizabeth exceeds the position of passante, the Baudelairean object of the consuming male gaze, to emerge as an active, mobile subject, one whose perambulations are both occasioned by and ensured through her consumer practices in the West End. Abandoning the implicit recommendations of shopping guides such as *Olivia's Shopping and How She Does It* to keep to a plan and a fixed route when navigating the world of consumption, and refusing distinctions between shop and street, she is poised not only to depart from authorized urban spaces for women but also to take leave from the territorialized versions of femininity that the mass marketplace is predicated on. Elizabeth does not use the West End to consolidate a prior set of assumptions about femininity. Without a prior need, such as for flowers or petticoats (which this marketplace may or may not furnish), or a desire to achieve this or that kind of gendered identity, Elizabeth goes in search of her own versions of pleasure, ones that are not dictated to her but that she improvises through the opportunities that form in the midst of her perambulations. Her consuming practices are ones that come to reimagine the plotted configurations of the West End as smooth spaces, through which she deterritorializes fixed forms of identity.

Fluidly mapping the terms of her formation through her sojourns in the city, the shopper is finally not a totalizable figure but instead a shifting and contingent one whose everyday encounters with the marketplace are the condition of the continuous work of consumption and writing. Moving in and out of our field of vision, she can be spotted only in between her comings and goings. Indeed, the last view of Elizabeth that *Mrs. Dalloway* offers is that of the moment she steps off the omnibus, off the pages of Woolf's novel, and into the future. Instead of one fixed image, what lingers here is a sense of the embodied and ongoing sensations of shopping, the felt pleasures of going to market on your own.

NOTES

Introduction: Danger, Delight, and Victorian Women's Shopping

1. Charlotte Brontë, *Jane Eyre*, ed. Richard Nemesvari (Peterborough, ON: Broadview, 1999), 354. All references in my text are to this edition and will be indicated parenthetically.

2. On the racialized implications of Rochester's "Eastern allusion," see Joyce Zonana, "The Sultan and the Slave: Feminist Orientalism and the Structure of *Jane Eyre*," in *Revising the Word and the World: Essays in Feminist Literary Criticism*, ed. Véve A. Clark, Ruth-Ellen B. Joeres, and Madelon Sprengnether (Chicago: University of Chicago Press, 1993); Reina Lewis, *Gendering Orientalism: Race, Femininity and Representation* (London: Routledge, 1996), especially 158–59.

3. John Ruskin, *Unto This Last*, in *The Works of John Ruskin*, ed. E. T. Cook and Alexander Wedderburn (London: George Allen, 1905), 17:101.

4. Ruskin, "The Nature of Gothic," *The Stones of Venice: Vol. II*, in *The Works of John Ruskin*, ed. E. T. Cook and Alexander Wedderburn (London: George Allen, 1904), 10:197.

5. Nancy Armstrong, "The Occidental Alice," *differences: A Journal of Feminist Cultural Studies* 2, no. 2 (1990): 17. In my study, I favor the term *consumer culture* over *commodity culture*. Jonathan Freedman prefers the latter and writes that it refers to "the supply side, as it were, of the industrial revolution. . . . [A] consumer economy is one whose cultural apparatus . . . has been . . . transformed . . . because it has become an essential part of the process of selling consumer goods." See Freedman, *Professions of Taste: Henry James, British Aestheticism, and Commodity Culture* (Stanford: Stanford University Press, 1990), 266n50. While I agree with Erika Rappaport that neither term should be deployed as though it could "signify a 'coherent' discourse," I suggest that *commodity culture* can refer to the symbolic constitution of objects that are valued for their exchangeability, whereas *consumer culture* refers to a range of cultural practices in which subjects engage and through which they are ideologically produced. See Rappaport, *Shopping for Pleasure: Women in the Making of London's West End* (Princeton, NJ: Princeton University Press, 2000), 12.

6. Jane Austen, *Emma*, ed. James Kinsley (Oxford: Oxford University Press, 2003), 140.

7. Armstrong, "Occidental Alice," 17.

8. Armstrong, "Occidental Alice," 15.

9. These literary studies come in the wake of social history of recent decades, during which consumer culture emerged as an important locus of analysis, one that, far from trivial, constitutes an ideological formation through which cultural values are produced and contested. (See note 12 for this chapter.) The shift from an almost exclusive analysis of models of production to ones that included the sphere of consumption in eighteenth- and nineteenth-century scholarship was prompted by such reassessments of traditional Marxism as Jean Baudrillard's. In *The Mirror of Production*, trans. with an intro. by Mark Poster (St. Louis: Telos, 1975), Baudrillard charges that Marxism works as the mirror of production to dismiss the possibilities of consumption as a space of resistance. Based on the value of human labor, a productivist ideology, he argues, is not sufficient to the task of interpreting the consumption of the sign that characterizes the symbolic economies of late capitalism.

10. Walter Benjamin, "Paris, Capital of the Nineteenth Century," in *Reflections: Essays, Aphorisms, Autobiographical Writings: Walter Benjamin*, ed. Peter Demetz, trans. Edmund Jephcott (New York: Harcourt Brace Jovanovich, 1978), 57.

11. Karl Marx, *Capital: A Critique of Political Economy*, trans. Ben Fowkes, with an intro. by Ernest Mandel (London: Penguin, 1990), 1:178. Originally published in 1867 as *Das Kapital*.

12. Thomas Richards's *Commodity Culture of Victorian England: Advertising and Spectacle, 1851–1914* (Stanford: Stanford University Press, 1990) addresses the Great Exhibition of 1851, along with other historic moments such as the Jubilee, which linked capital to spectacle and produced the public as a new consumer class. Although Richards alludes to "a specifically female consuming subjectivity" (207), his most sustained considerations of women and commodity culture, such as images of the "seaside girl" in popular advertisements, tend to locate women's consumption in the iconic, where it "remains bracketed within male production and consumption as women become the go-betweens mediating men and their particular desires" (246). In *Novels behind Glass: Commodity Culture and Victorian Narrative* (Cambridge: Cambridge University Press, 1995), Andrew H. Miller takes the introduction of new glass-making technologies of the 1830s as his point of departure to consider how "[t]he display windows in this nation of shopkeepers thus served as emblems of an economic dynamic which was also simultaneously libidinal . . . , epistemological . . . , and social" (5). Considering the "impact of this increased exhibition value on the realistic novel" (6), Miller argues that the novel registers the Victorians' "anxiety . . . that their social and moral world was being reduced to a warehouse of goods and commodities" (6) and that the writers of these novels "[a]dopt[ed] a moral stance against the commodification of the world" (7). When Miller ponders women's place within Victorian commodity culture, it tends to emerge as a conflicted one. He writes, for example, that "[i]n *Vanity Fair* and the Great Exhibition, women fluctuate between being objects under the gaze

of men and being agents desiring goods on their own" (11), such that women are "both consumers and things consumed" (195). Christoph Lindner, in his study of the shifting social meanings of the commodity, *Fictions of Commodity Culture: From the Victorian to the Postmodern* (Aldershot, UK: Ashgate, 2003), similarly concludes, in a chapter on Madonna and Trollope, that while a novel such as *The Eustace Diamonds* "challenges, and manipulates commodity culture's economic constructions of the feminine . . . representation of the feminine never radically breaks from—or even negotiates viable alternatives to—the paradigm of capitalist order" (67, 69). Unlike these other studies, Rachel Bowlby's *Just Looking: Consumer Culture in Dreiser, Gissing, and Zola* (London: Methuen, 1985) is devoted to the figure of the female consumer. With particular emphasis on the impulse in naturalist fiction to record the details of modern life, Bowlby considers how the department store in France, Britain, and the United States created new, visual relationships and fantasies that "cross[ed] the boundaries between looking and having" and how the democratization of luxury and the *entrée libre* of these new emporia promised access to luxury goods (4). Identifying the problem of Woman as a paradigmatic embodiment of the commodity, Bowlby attempts to destabilize this identification by considering "woman as ideological sign" and her potential to accede to the status of active subject as "consumers [who] enter into reciprocal relationship with commodities" (27). While Bowlby acknowledges Freud's phallocentrism, with regard to his view of female subjectivity, as castrated, she largely preserves his model for what she sees as its explanatory force in describing "an obvious connection between the figure of the narcissistic woman and the fact of women as consumers. . . . [T]hrough the glass, the woman sees what she wants and what she wants to be" (31 and 32). Although such encounters may offer an "altered self, and one potentially obtainable via the payment of a stipulated price" and also "smash[ ] the illusion that there is a meaningful distinction in modern society between illusion and reality" (34), there is no clarity on how these conditions might fundamentally challenge the persistent analogy between Woman and commodity, which tends to produce women as signs rather than as desiring, historical subjects.

13. Several social historians who have acknowledged consumption as a significant area of inquiry have also argued that a modern consumer culture first emerged in the eighteenth century. See, for example, Neil McKendrick, John Brewer, and John H. Plumb, *The Birth of a Consumer Society: The Commercialization of Eighteenth-Century England* (Bloomington: Indiana University Press, 1982); Grant McCracken, *Culture and Consumption: New Approaches to the Symbolic Character of Consumer Goods and Activities* (Bloomington: Indiana University Press, 1988); John Brewer and Roy Porter, eds., *Consumption and the World of Goods* (London: Routledge, 1993); Ann Bermingham and John Brewer, eds., *The Consumption of Culture, 1600–1800: Image, Object, Text* (London: Routledge, 1995). Numerous other works have focused on the institutionalization of modern retailing between the 1700s and the early decades of the 1900s, often referred to as Britain's first retailing revolution, when fairs, bazaars, peddlers, and the practice of bartering gave

way to the interiorized shop, window displays, and fixed prices. See, for example, W. Hamish Fraser, *The Coming of the Mass Market, 1850–1914* (Hamden, CT: Archon, 1981); John Benson and Gareth Shaw, eds., *The Evolution of Retail Systems, ca. 1800–1914* (Leicester: Leicester University Press, 1992); Carl Gardner and Julie Sheppard, *Consuming Passion: The Rise of Retail Culture* (London: Unwin and Hyman, 1989); Hoh-Cheung Mui and Lorna H. Mui, *Shops and Shopkeeping in Eighteenth-Century England* (Kingston, ON: McGill-Queen's University Press, 1989); Dorothy Davis, *Fairs, Shops, and Supermarkets: A History of English Shopping* (Toronto: University of Toronto Press, 1966).

14. Elizabeth Kowaleski-Wallace, *Consuming Subjects: Women, Shopping, and Business in the Eighteenth Century* (New York: Columbia University Press, 1997), 75, 80.

15. Kowaleski-Wallace, *Consuming Subjects*, 13.

16. Mary Poovey, *Uneven Developments: The Ideological Work of Gender in Mid-Victorian England* (London: Virago, 1989), 3.

17. Brontë, *Jane Eyre*, 356.

18. Lynda Nead, *Victorian Babylon: People, Streets, and Images in Nineteenth-Century London* (New Haven, CT: Yale University Press, 2000), 5.

19. Michel de Certeau, *The Practice of Everyday Life*, trans. Steven Rendall (Berkeley: University of California Press, 1984), xiv.

20. To say that women can operate outside of capitalism is to construct a universal femininity that exists prior to discourse; this statement ignores how subjects are constituted in the midst of economic and social relations. Judith Butler objects to this myth of an origin of female identity: "If sexuality is culturally constructed within existing power relations, then the postulation of a normative sexuality that is 'before,' 'outside,' or 'beyond' power is a cultural impossibility and a politically impracticable dream, one that postpones the concrete and contemporary task of rethinking subversive possibilities for sexuality and identity within the terms of power itself. This critical task presumes, of course, that to operate within the matrix of power is not the same as to replicate uncritically relations of domination." See Butler, *Gender Trouble: Feminism and the Subversion of Identity* (New York: Routledge, 1990), 30.

21. De Certeau, *Practice of Everyday Life*, xii.

22. De Certeau, *Practice of Everyday Life*, xi, xiii. John Fiske's version of cultural studies in "The Culture of Everyday Life" recalls de Certeau's approach. It considers that institutions (including department stores and the sphere of consumption, I would suggest) do not produce subjects; subjects are produced through the practices they deploy within institutions: "The construction, occupation, and ownership of one's own space/setting within their place/arena, the weaving of one's own richly textured life within the constraints of economic deprivation and oppression, are not just ways of controlling some of the conditions of social existence; they are also ways of constructing, and therefore exerting some control over, social identities and social relations. The practices of everyday life within and against the determinate conditions of

the social order construct the identities of difference of the social actors amongst the various formations of the subaltern." In *Cultural Studies*, ed. Lawrence Grossberg, Cary Nelson, and Paula Treichler (New York: Routledge, 1992), 160. Thus, the debate is not about whether women's shopping is an ultimately emancipatory practice or whether women are unwitting victims of consumerism. As Victoria de Grazia has pointed out in her introduction to *The Sex of Things: Gender and Consumption in Historical Perspective* (Berkeley: University of California Press, 1996), rather than debate whether or not consumption is ultimately emancipatory for women, one should consider relationships between consumption, gender, and the work of ideology (7). Carl Gardner and Julie Sheppard have also noted the limits of what they call the "manipulation thesis." See Gardner and Sheppard, *Consuming Passion*, 48.

23. De Certeau, *Practice of Everyday Life*, 36.

24. De Certeau, *Practice of Everyday Life*, xv.

25. Erika Rappaport notes that the author of "The Philosophy of Shopping" is "probably Linton" (Rappaport, *Shopping for Pleasure*, 32). "The Girl of the Period" was published on pages 339–41 of the *Saturday Review* on March 14, 1868.

26. Attributed to Eliza Lynn Linton, "The Philosophy of Shopping," *Saturday Review*, October 16, 1875, 488.

27. Linton, "Philosophy of Shopping," 488–89.

28. Linton, "Philosophy of Shopping," 488.

29. That this woman shopper was typically middle class must always be kept in mind. The pursuit of pleasure was predicated on access to disposable income and available leisure time. The ability to shop for things that one wants, rather than needs, depended on these factors. Moreover, to belong in this sphere of consumption, a woman had to possess the assumption of an entitlement to its pleasures, and the appearance of middle-class respectability was what made her public excursions as a shopper a viable option.

30. Regenia Gagnier, "Productive Bodies, Pleasured Bodies: On Victorian Aesthetics," in *Women and British Aestheticism*, ed. Talia Schaffer and Kathy Alexis Psomiades (Charlottesville: University Press of Virginia, 1997), 271 and 272.

31. De Certeau, *Practice of Everyday Life*, 34.

32. De Certeau, *Practice of Everyday Life*, 36.

33. De Certeau, *Practice of Everyday Life*, 34.

34. In a comparable formulation of female subjectivity, Judith Butler states that "[i]f there is something right in Beauvoir's claim that one is not born, but rather *becomes* a woman, it follows that *woman* itself is a term in process, a becoming, a constructing that cannot rightfully be said to originate or to end. As an ongoing discursive practice, it is open to intervention and resignification." See Butler, *Gender Trouble*, 33.

35. Elizabeth Grosz, *Volatile Bodies: Toward a Corporeal Feminism* (Bloomington: Indiana University Press, 1994), 169.

36. In "God and the Jouissance of ~~The~~ Woman," Jacques Lacan insists that *"The woman can only be written with The crossed through. There is no such thing as The woman, where the definite article stands for the universal. There is no such thing as The woman since of her essence . . . , she is not at all."* In *Feminine Sexuality: Jacques Lacan and the Ecole Freudienne*, ed. Juliet Mitchell and Jacqueline Rose, trans. Jacqueline Rose (New York: W. W. Norton, 1982), 144. In "A Love Letter," Lacan states that "[t]he woman relates to the signifier of this Other, in so far as, being Other, it can only remain always Other" (151).

37. De Certeau, *Practice of Everyday Life*, 34.

38. Michel Foucault, *The Foucault Reader*, ed. Paul Rabinow (New York: Pantheon, 1984), 88.

39. *Olivia's Shopping and How She Does It: A Prejudiced Guide to the London Shops*, illus. Elsa Hahn (London: Gay and Bird, 1906), 8.

40. *Olivia's Shopping*, 7.

Chapter 1: Goblin Markets: Women Shoppers and the East in London's West End

1. See plate 12 in Max Beerbohm, *Rossetti and His Circle* (London: W. Heinemann, 1922). The poem that Dante Gabriel Rossetti alludes to is Christina Rossetti's "A Birthday" (1862), the first line of which reads, "My heart is like a singing bird." See "A Birthday," in *The Complete Poems of Christina Rossetti: A Variorum Edition*, ed. R. W. Crump (Baton Rouge: Louisiana State University Press, 1979), 1:36–37. All references in my text are to this edition.

2. Alison Adburgham, *Liberty's: A Biography of a Shop* (London: George Allen and Unwin, 1975), 19.

3. Dante Gabriel Rossetti, *Letters of Dante Gabriel Rossetti*, ed. Oswald Doughty and John Robert Wahl (Oxford: Clarendon, 1967), 4:1832.

4. Sandra M. Gilbert and Susan Gubar's "aesthetics of renunciation," which privileges the contradictions of Rossetti's writing practices, represents a self-silencing Rossetti who "banquet[ed] on bitterness [to] bury herself alive in a coffin of renunciation" (575). See Gilbert and Gubar, *The Madwoman in the Attic: The Woman Writer and the Nineteenth-Century Literary Imagination* (New Haven, CT: Yale University Press, 1979). More recently, works such as the essays in Mary Arseneau, Antony H. Harrison, and Lorraine Janzen Kooistra, eds., *The Culture of Christina Rossetti: Female Poetics and Victorian Contexts* (Athens: Ohio University Press, 1999) have "demonstrate[d] how the recluse, saint, and renunciatory spinster of former studies was in fact an active participant in Victorian attempts to grapple with new developments in aesthetics, theology, science, economics and politics." See Arseneau, "Introduction," xvi.

5. Elizabeth Campbell has proposed that this fairy tale "asserts the vital socioeconomic function of women despite their marginalization by the Victorian market economy . . . , challeng[ing] the prevailing ideology of production and consumption

by relocating human value in reproduction and motherhood" within a "'female economics'" (394). She notes how Laura and Lizzie's bodies are configured to one another at the end of the poem in a "motherly nourishment" that "reiterat[es] the poem's cyclicality," extending the rhythms of women's domestic space into the masculine linearity that is represented by the goblins' harsh economics (409). Her female economics, however, tend to focus on the sisters' economy rather than the conditions of the goblins' marketplace. See Campbell, "Of Mothers and Merchants: Female Economics in Christina Rossetti's 'Goblin Market,'" *Victorian Studies* 33, no. 3 (1990): 393–410. Whereas Campbell emphasizes a separate female sphere whose economic value is found in reproduction, Terrence Holt accounts for the compulsory capitalism in which the sisters are inscribed. In noting the difficulty of "imagin[ing] a position for women outside systems of power" (51), however, Holt concludes "that utopian fantasies of a separate women's culture are just that" (61) rather than opting to pursue the ways in which women might obtain pleasures within the marketplace. See Holt, "'Men sell not such in any town': Exchange in *Goblin Market*," *Victorian Poetry* 28, no. 1 (1990): 51–67. Elizabeth K. Helsinger's analysis of women in the marketplace also locates women in the marketplace, rather than peripheral to it, by interrogating the ways in which women enter the market under the continual threat of becoming objects of exchange themselves. The poem, she suggests, "sets out to undo this double consumption or erasure of woman" (207). However, Helsinger implies that one effect of the sisters' entrance into the marketplace is a curbing of desire: "Lizzie emerges unscathed with her purchase . . . because she does not bring her desire . . . to market with her" (209). See Helsinger, "Consumer Power and the Utopia of Desire: Christina Rossetti's 'Goblin Market,'" *ELH* 58, no. 4 (1991): 903–33.

Two more recent considerations of *Goblin Market* situate it within material and cultural contexts, but they likewise tend not to emphasize a space for the production of pleasure within the market. Richard Menke, who has produced an illuminating study of fruit as commodity in the poem with close attention to historical specificities, aligns "Rossetti's renunciatory poetics alongside Victorian political economy" (105) to conclude that *Goblin Market* ultimately "rejects consumer desire" (128). See Menke, "The Political Economy of Fruit: *Goblin Market*," in *Culture of Christina Rossetti*, ed. Arseneau, Harrison, and Kooistra. Rebecca F. Stern, in her engaging cultural analysis of Victorian anxieties surrounding food adulteration, acknowledges that "the power of Laura's appetite cannot be ignored" but underscores the ways in which the poem reproduces new forms of consumerist self-regulation that "emphasize the need for Victorian consumers to defend their own interests, and the wisdom of bringing suspicion home" (507 and 499). See Stern, "'Adulterations Detected': Food and Fraud in Christina Rossetti's 'Goblin Market,'" *Nineteenth-Century Literature* 57, no. 4 (2003): 477–511.

6. Although Menke does not focus specifically on the gendering of consumption, one should note that he does consider the goblins' fruit in light of cultural fears surrounding imperial commerce in Victorian England.

7. Mary Wilson Carpenter, "'Eat me, drink me, love me': The Consumable Female Body in Christina Rossetti's *Goblin Market*," *Victorian Poetry* 29, no. 4 (1991): 415.

8. Carpenter, "'Eat me, drink me,'" 425.

9. Christina Rossetti, *The Letters of Christina Rossetti*, ed. Antony H. Harrison (Charlottesville: University Press of Virginia, 1997), 1:76.

10. Rudyard Kipling, *From Sea to Sea: Letters of Travel, Part 1*, in *The Writings in Prose and Verse of Rudyard Kipling* (New York: Charles Scribner's Sons, 1899), 15:335.

11. Kipling, *From Sea to Sea*, 15:339.

12. Adburgham, *Liberty's*, 23.

13. In deploying the term *imperial exhibitionary complex*, I am indebted to Tony Bennett's work in museum culture concerning the exhibitionary complex, *The Birth of the Museum: History, Theory, Politics* (London: Routledge, 1995). To define "exhibitionary complex," Bennett invokes Michel Foucault's notion of the Panopticon, that institution which was "involved in the transfer of objects and bodies from the enclosed and private domains in which they had previously been displayed . . . into more open and public arenas where, through the representations to which they were subjected, they formed vehicles for inscribing and broadcasting messages of power" (60–61). Looking beyond the carceral system, Bennett takes the Great Exhibition of 1851 as the historical moment in which "an ensemble of disciplines and techniques of display . . . translated . . . exhibitionary forms which, in simultaneously ordering objects for public inspection and ordering the public that inspected, were to have a profound . . . influence on the subsequent development of museums, art galleries, expositions, and department stores" (61). The conditions of these "collateral institutions" of the exhibitionary complex, Bennett argues, are more complex than those produced within Foucault's surveillance model, for the exhibitionary complex "perfected a self-monitoring system of looks in which the subject and object positions can be exchanged" (69). While Bennett retains a model that tends to view exhibitionary forms as "instrument[s] of public education" (71), including values of class civility, I want to explore how women shoppers located points of resistance within exhibitionary forms of the imperial marketplace, signaling the failure of empire both to present a coherently commodified vision of the East and to regulate women's consumerist desires and behaviors within these terms.

In my use of the term *imperial exhibitionary complex*, I am also indebted to Timothy Mitchell's observations in "Orientalism and Exhibitionary Order," in *Colonialism and Culture*, ed. Nicholas B. Dirks (Ann Arbor: University of Michigan Press, 1992), 289–317. Prompted by Edward Said's *Orientalism* (New York: Vintage, 1979), Mitchell revisits the notion that "the construction of the colonial order is related to the elaboration of modern forms of representation and knowledge" to add that "the Orient was constructed not just in Oriental studies, romantic novels, and colonial administrations, but in . . . museums and world exhibitions [and even extending] to architecture, schooling, tourism, the fashion industry, and the commodification of everyday life" (289).

14. Judith R. Walkowitz, *City of Dreadful Delight: Narratives of Sexual Danger in Late-Victorian London* (Chicago: University of Chicago Press, 1992), 46–50.

15. Rappaport, *Shopping for Pleasure*, 8.

16. Walkowitz, "Going Public: Shopping, Street Harassment, and Streetwalking in Late Victorian London," *Representations* 62 (1998): 5.

17. Rappaport, *Shopping for Pleasure*, 8.

18. As quoted in Alison Adburgham, *Shopping in Style: London from the Restoration to Edwardian Elegance* (London: Thames and Hudson, 1979), 154.

19. Remy Saisselin, *The Bourgeois and the Bibelot* (New Brunswick, NJ: Rutgers University Press, 1984), 40.

20. Rappaport, *Shopping for Pleasure*, 5.

21. On the history of the department store, see, for example, Gordon Honeycombe, *Selfridges, Seventy-five Years: The Story of the Store, 1909–1984* (London: Park Lane, 1984); Tim Dale, *Harrods: The Store and the Legend* (London: Pan Books, 1981); Adburgham, *Liberty's*; Adburgham, *Shopping in Style*; Adburgham, *Shops and Shopping, 1800–1914: Where and in What Manner the Well-Dressed Englishwoman Bought Her Clothes* (London: George Allen and Unwin, 1964); Susan Porter Benson, *Counter Cultures: Saleswomen, Managers, and Customers in American Department Stores, 1890–1940* (Urbana: University of Illinois Press, 1986); Simon J. Bronner, ed., *Consuming Visions: Accumulation and Display of Goods in America, 1880–1920* (New York: W. W. Norton, 1989); John William Ferry, *A History of the Department Store* (New York: Macmillan, 1960); William Lancaster, *The Department Store: A Social History* (London: Leicester University Press, 1995); Geoffrey Crossick and Serge Jaumain, eds., *Cathedrals of Consumption: The European Department Store, 1850–1939* (Aldershot, UK: Ashgate, 1999); Richard Wightman Fox and T. J. Jackson Lears, eds., *The Culture of Consumption: Critical Essays in American History, 1880–1980* (New York: Pantheon, 1983); Michael B. Miller, *The Bon Marché: Bourgeois Culture and the Department Store, 1869–1920* (Princeton, NJ: Princeton University Press, 1981).

22. Richards, *Commodity Culture*, 17.

23. Richards, *Commodity Culture*, 4, 17.

24. Henry Cole, *Miscellanies* (London: Richard Bentley and Sons, 1875), 207.

25. Thomas James Wise and John Alexander Symington, eds., *The Brontës: Their Lives, Friendships and Correspondence* (Oxford: Blackwell, 1980), 3:243.

26. George Augustus Sala, *Twice Round the Clock, or the Hours of the Day and Night in London* (1858; New York: Leicester University Press, 1971), 155.

27. Sala, *Twice Round the Clock*, 157.

28. Adburgham, *Liberty's*, 42.

29. For more on the popularity of these shawls, see Nupur Chaudhuri, "Shawls, Jewelry, Curry, and Rice in Victorian Britain," in *Western Women and Imperialism: Complicity and Resistance*, ed. Nupur Chaudhuri and Margaret Strobel (Bloomington: Indiana University Press, 1992), 231–46.

30. Fashion News, *Ladies Gazette of Fashion*, December 1879, 329. By the mid-nineteenth century, these shawls had become thoroughly commodified, dropping in price because of their availability and because imitations from mills in northern England were available in shops in Regent Street, New Bond Street, and Fleet Street. See Adburgham, *Shopping in Style*, 110–11.

31. Fashion in London, *Ladies Gazette of Fashion*, April 1879, 100.

32. Fashion in London, *Ladies Gazette of Fashion*, January 1880, 33. The house jacket appears in the *Ladies Gazette of Fashion*, February 1880, 33. The same issue features an ad for Liberty's Indian silks on the back cover, as does the back of the March issue.

33. Fashion and Gossip in Paris, *Ladies Gazette of Fashion*, April 1880, 85.

34. *Olivia's Shopping*, 69.

35. *Olivia's Shopping*, 69.

36. Said, *Orientalism*, 3.

37. E. W. Godwin, *Architect*, December 23, 1876, as quoted in Adburgham, *Liberty's*, 21.

38. Armstrong, "Occidental Alice," 27–28.

39. Rita Felski, *The Gender of Modernity* (Cambridge, MA: Harvard University Press, 1995), 70. In this sense, the displays of East India House were like another imperial technology alongside those discussed by Benedict Anderson: "Interlinked with one another . . . the census, the map and the museum illuminate the late colonial state's style of thinking about its domain. The 'warp' of this thinking was a totalizing classifactory grid, which could be applied with endless flexibility to anything under the state's real or contemplated control. . . . The effect of the grid was always to be able to say of anything that it was this, not that; it belonged here, not there. It was bounded, determinate, and therefore—in principle—countable. . . . The 'weft' was what one could call serialization: the assumption that the world was made up of replicable plurals" (184). See Anderson, *Imagined Communities: Reflections on the Origin and Spread of Nationalism* (London: Verso, 1991). Anderson's comments could also apply to the displays of oriental bazaars in Britain, where the fruits of empire were itemized and commodified.

40. See Bennett, *Birth of the Museum*, 59–69.

41. For example, while Liberty's did not sell opium, it naturalized the scene of opium consumption with its smoking-room furniture displays. Opium, which came to be associated with the dangers of the East, stands as an unstable commodity among the more benign foreign imports, as their dark correlative and as a visible reminder of Britain's culpability in the opium wars. Barry Milligan has shown how the spectre of addiction and fears of racial invasion were meanings that circulated around opium, particularly around women and opium. See Milligan, *Pleasures and Pains: Opium and the Orient in Nineteenth-Century British Culture* (Charlottesville: University Press of Virginia, 1995). Liberty's "Saracenic Smoking Room," as it was envisioned in the 1889 *Liberty Handbook of Sketches*, domesticated opium consumption by resituating it within

the bourgeois home, as though to reconstruct therein the forbidden delights of an Eastern divan.

42. Said, *Orientalism*, 57.
43. Bennett, *Birth of the Museum*, 81.
44. As quoted in Adburgham, *Liberty's*, 43.
45. The commodity persists when its representational value is repeated endlessly, and the misrecognition of the object's use value enables this mystification—that is to say, as Marx notes, when exchange value exceeds use value. The goods of Liberty's oriental bazaar are thus a realization of Marx's discussion of the mystical nature of commodities. Marx writes of how, under capitalism, "[a] commodity appears . . . [a] trivial thing" at first. "But," he continues, "its analysis brings out that it is a very strange thing, abounding in metaphysical subtleties and theological niceties. So far as it is a use-value, there is nothing mysterious about it" (*Capital*, 1:163). The oriental goods available to women shoppers were such fantasy objects that, acquiring a racialized otherness, stood in for an exotic East. The work of commodification resembles that of the racial othering implicit in orientalism, since both depend on the mystifying or othering of objects. This mystifying or othering is obtained through an ordering of signification, violent yokings that assign an object pure exchange or representational value under the constraints of imperial capitalism. In other words, commodification and imperialism are homologous terrains that are ideologically laden: both present apparently naturalized fields that nonetheless depend on mimetic forms of representation produced through the discursive violence of othering.

Marx also likens the commodity to a fetish (*Capital*, 1:163). Anne McClintock notes that a fetish need not be a phallic substitute (184) and that Marx's use of the term predates Freud's appropriation of it into the discourse of sexuality (181) in her efforts to determine how the fetish operates within the discourse of imperialism. She also points out that the fetish is always a contradictory image: "[A]ll fetishes . . . visibly express[ ] a crisis in value but cannot resolve it. [A fetish] can only embody the contradiction, frozen as commodity spectacle, luring the spectator deeper and deeper into consumerism" (218). See McClintock, *Imperial Leather: Race, Gender and Sexuality in the Colonial Conquest* (New York: Routledge, 1995). Fetishism thus depends both on an object's being visible and on a gazer. The women who beheld the consumer spectacle at Liberty's Eastern bazaar did so embodying a productive contradiction: even as women were associated with the goods held in display, they exercised the privilege of gaze as agents in the imperial marketplace. In doing so, they enacted a crisis of capitalism in which woman could indeed go to market on her own, rather than entering it as identical to the commodity. If, as McClintock puts it, "[t]he fetish marks a crisis in social meaning" (184), then the presence of women in the marketplace can be seen to trouble the phallic organization of social relations under capitalism. But while these bodies may have occluded colonial others, women's presence as consumers within imperial consumer culture disrupted the imperial visual field to expose the extent to which it was a manufactured space.

46. On this point, see Bennett's reworking of Foucault in *Birth of the Museum*, 63. On the Great Exhibition's "exhibitionary complex" and "exhibitionary architecture," see 61–73 and 101.

47. "Shopping without Money," *Leisure Hour*, February 18, 1865, 110.

48. "Shopping without Money," 110.

49. "Shopping in London," *Living Age* 4 (June 1844): 250.

50. Lady M. Jeune, "The Ethics of Shopping," *Fortnightly Review* 57 (January 1895): 127.

51. *Olivia's Shopping*, 42.

52. May Isabel Fisk, "A Woman in a Shoe Shop," in *The Monologue Series*, no. 39 (New York: Harper and Bros., 1903), 5.

53. *Warehouseman and Draper's Trade Journal*, March 1, 1873, 111, as quoted in Rappaport, "'The Halls of Temptation': Gender, Politics, and the Construction of the Department Store in Late Victorian London," *Journal of British Studies* 35, no. 1 (1996): 76.

54. My use of the term *shopper's gaze* was prompted by Anne Friedberg's observation that "with the new mobilities produced by changes in transportation, architecture and urban planning, photography brought with it a virtual gaze. . . . At the beginnings of consumer culture, this gaze became imbued with the power of choice and incorporation: the shopper's gaze" (4). See Friedberg, *Window Shopping: Cinema and the Postmodern* (Berkeley: University of California Press, 1993). Rachel Bowlby's "just looking" should not be confused with the shopper's gaze. The look Bowlby describes is similar to that of Mary Ann Doane's idea of self-commodifying narcissism. See Doane, "Film and the Masquerade: Theorizing the Female Spectator," *Screen* 23, nos. 3–4 (1982): 74–87. Bowlby writes, "Consumer culture transforms the narcissistic mirror into a shop window, the *glass* which reflects an idealized image of the woman . . . who stands before it, in the form of the model she could buy or become" (*Just Looking*, 32). This Lacanian formative moment, however, sees desire as reflective rather than potentially disruptive. My exploration of the shopper's gaze follows through on Reina Lewis's intervention into debates about the female gaze that revisits the female gaze "as part of a critical movement that has undercut the potentially unified, and paradigmatically male, colonial subject outlined in Said's *Orientalism*" (Lewis, *Gendering Orientalism*, 3). Lewis constructs an active female viewership in contrast to Laura Mulvey's passive woman object in "Visual Pleasure and Narrative Cinema," *Screen* 16, no. 3 (1975): 6–18. Lewis argues "that women's differential, gendered access to the positionalities of imperial discourse produced a gaze on the Orient and the Orientalized 'other' that registered difference less pejoratively and less absolutely than was implied by Said's original formulation" (4) or, I would add, gazes through which women shoppers produced positionalities and identities that were in excess of those prescribed by an imperial marketplace.

55. Armstrong, "Occidental Alice," 20. The italics are Armstrong's emphasis.

56. Carpenter, "'Eat me, drink me,'" 415–16.
57. Carpenter, "'Eat me, drink me,'" 416.
58. Herbert F. Tucker, "Rossetti's Goblin Marketing: Sweet to Tongue and Sound to Eye," *Representations* 82, no. 1 (2003): 120.
59. Tucker, "Rossetti's Goblin Marketing," 121.
60. Christina Rossetti, *Goblin Market*, in *The Complete Poems of Christina Rossetti: A Variorum Edition*, ed. R. W. Crump (Baton Rouge: Louisiana State University Press, 1979), 1:11–26. All references in my text are to this edition; line numbers will be cited parenthetically.
61. McClintock, *Imperial Leather*, 215.
62. McClintock, *Imperial Leather*, 216.
63. Henry Mayhew, *London Labour and the London Poor* (New York: Dover, 1968), 1:159, 1:195. *London Labour and the London Poor*, first published as a series of articles in the *Morning Chronicle* in 1849–50, later appeared as four volumes over 1861–62.
64. Mayhew, *London Labour*, 1:195, 1:197.
65. Mayhew, *London Labour*, 1:196.
66. *Daily Telegraph*, April 2, 1858, 5, as quoted in Nead, *Victorian Babylon*, 86–87.
67. Mayhew, *London Labour*, 1:206.
68. Mayhew, *London Labour*, 1:206.
69. De Certeau, *Practice of Everyday Life*, xii.
70. De Certeau, *Practice of Everyday Life*, xii.
71. Butler, *Gender Trouble*, 30. See also note 20 of the introduction.

Chapter 2: Lady Audley's Shopping Disorders

1. Henry Mansel, "Sensation Novels," *Quarterly Review* 113 (1863): 483.
2. Mansel, "Sensation Novels," 489.
3. Mansel, "Sensation Novels," 482.
4. "Our Female Sensation Novelists," *Christian Remembrancer* 46 (1863): 211.
5. Mansel, "Sensation Novels," 483.
6. Margaret Oliphant, "Sensation Novels," *Blackwoods* 91 (May 1862): 568.
7. Mansel, "Sensation Novels," 483, 484–85.
8. Mansel, "Sensation Novels," 484.
9. See Katherine Montwieler, "Marketing Sensation: *Lady Audley's Secret* and Consumer Culture," in *Beyond Sensation: Mary Elizabeth Braddon in Context*, ed. Marlene Tromp, Pamela K. Gilbert, and Aeron Haynie (Albany: State University of New York, 2000), 44. See Winifred Hughes, *The Maniac in the Cellar: Sensation Novels of the 1860s* (Princeton, NJ: Princeton University Press, 1980), 267. In his 1862 review of *Lady Audley's Secret*, Eneas Sweetland Dallas declared that "[t]his is the age of lady novelists," whose heroines are "high-strung women, full of passion, purpose, and movement—very liable to error" (*Times*, November 18, 1862, 4). As Lyn Pykett has shown, critics of the

period also tended to characterize the affects of sensation fiction as a feminizing influence. See *The "Improper" Feminine: The Women's Sensation Novel and the New Woman Writing* (London: Routledge, 1992), 32. Deborah Wynne's *Sensation Novel and the Victorian Family Magazine* (Houndmills, UK: Palgrave, 2001) and Jennifer Phegley's *Educating the Proper Woman Reader: Victorian Family Literary Magazines and the Cultural Health of the Nation* (Columbus: Ohio State University Press, 2004) are recent works that include assessments of how the serialization of sensation did not necessarily reproduce the stereotype of the diseased woman reader but instead constructed women as capable, discerning readers.

10. Susan David Bernstein, "Dirty Reading: Sensation Fiction, Women, and Primitivism," *Criticism* 36, no. 2 (1994): 217.

11. Mansel, "Sensation Novels," 488–89.

12. Julia McNair Wright, *The Complete Home: An Encyclopedia of Domestic Life and Affairs* (Philadelphia: Bradley, Garretson, 1879), 466.

13. Ann Cvetkovich, *Mixed Feelings: Feminism, Mass Culture, and Victorian Sensationalism* (New Brunswick, NJ: Rutgers University Press, 1992), 204, 201. Many recent studies of sensation fiction, such as Jane Wood's, have considered how the genre was associated in the 1860s with the nervous disorders of a diseased mind and body at a time when theories of delirium cast doubt on "the psychological stability of the self" and "the reliability of the impressions which secure individuals' sense of their own place in an interpretable external world." See Wood, *Passion and Pathology in Victorian Fiction* (Oxford: Oxford University Press, 2001), 114. On disease and somatic effects (such as nervousness and delirium) associated with sensation fiction, see also the following: Sally Shuttleworth, "'Preaching to the Nerves': Psychological Disorder in Sensation Fiction," in *A Question of Identity: Women, Science, and Literature*, ed. Marina Benjamin (New Brunswick, NJ: Rutgers University Press, 1993), 192–222; Pamela K. Gilbert, *Disease, Desire, and the Body in Victorian Women's Popular Novels* (Cambridge: Cambridge University Press, 1997); D. A. Miller, "*Cage aux folles*: Sensation and Gender in Wilkie Collins's *The Woman in White*," in *The Making of the Modern Body: Sexuality and Society in the Nineteenth Century*, ed. Catherine Gallagher and Thomas Laqueur (Berkeley: University of California Press, 1987), 107–36. I would suggest that the somatic effects of sensation were not only a matter of pathology but were also being materialized in the world of consumerism.

14. Nor does the novel rehearse the usual terms of object-relations theory, in which "an object that is not recognized as a person . . . [is] there only to satisfy libidinal needs." See Howard A. Bacal and Kenneth M. Newman, *Theories of Object Relations: Bridges to Self Psychology* (New York: Columbia University Press, 1990), 58. Whereas the model of commodified identity that I am suggesting celebrates a mobile, fluid, and contiguous affiliation with objects, the self in object-relations tends to be posited as one that is projected on objects as part of a fantasy to possess or master them.

15. Jean-Christophe Agnew, "A House of Fiction: Domestic Interiors and the Commodity Aesthetic," in *Consuming Visions: Accumulation and Display of Goods in America, 1880–1920*, ed. Simon J. Bronner (New York: Norton, 1989), 135.

16. Susanne Scholz and Martina Strange argue that by the 1890s, a shift had occurred in the ways in which people used objects. "If Osborne's possessions signify himself [in *Vanity Fair*], they do so as part of a social structure.... Wilde uses things, however, to signify himself." See Scholz and Strange, "Framed Subjects—Displayed Objects: Mantelpiece Decoration in Nineteenth-Century English Literature," *Journal for the Study of British Cultures* 8, no. 2 (2001): 172. Late-Victorian consumer practices might be distinguished from those earlier in the century in the sense that mass-produced objects were multiplying, rather than fixing, the options of the sort of face that one could present to the world.

17. Linton, "Philosophy of Shopping," 488.

18. Lady M. Jeune, "Ethics of Shopping," 124. For a full-length study of the construction of the shopgirl in late-Victorian and Edwardian literature and culture, see Lise Shapiro Sanders, *Consuming Fantasies: Labor, Leisure, and the London Shopgirl, 1880–1920* (Columbus: Ohio State University Press, 2006).

19. Jeune, "Ethics of Shopping," 123–24.

20. Jeune, "Ethics of Shopping," 124.

21. Jeune, "Ethics of Shopping," 124, 125.

22. Walkowitz, "Going Public," 5.

23. Eliza Lynn Linton, "Out Walking," *Temple Bar* 5 (July 1862): 132–33. Lynda Nead also addresses Linton's *Temple Bar* article in "Shopping and Seduction," *Tate* 18 (1999): 54–58.

24. Linton, "Out Walking," 133. See "Answers to Correspondents" in *Girl's Own Paper*, 1881, as quoted in Walkowitz, "Going Public," 7.

25. See Marianna Valverde, "The Love of Finery: Fashion and the Fallen Woman in Nineteenth-Century Social Discourse," *Victorian Studies* 32, no. 2 (1989): 168–88.

26. Nead, "Shopping and Seduction," 58.

27. "Shop Rovers and Shop Prowlers," *Drapers' Record*, October 3, 1899, 661, as quoted in Rappaport, *Shopping for Pleasure*, 206.

28. Adrian Ross and Percy Greenbank, *Our Miss Gibbs* (London: Chappell, 1909), 5. The joke is quoted in Brent Shannon, "ReFashioning Men: Fashion, Masculinity, and the Cultivation of the Male Consumer in Britain, 1860–1914," *Victorian Studies* 46, no. 4 (2004): 601.

29. "Shopping," *Queen*, April 2, 1892, 520. Also quoted in Walkowitz, "Going Public," 6.

30. Jeune, "Ethics of Shopping," 128.

31. *Draper*, July 25, 1903, 992, as quoted in Shannon, "ReFashioning Men," 600.

32. Walkowitz, "Going Public," 6. Rachel Bowlby, *Shopping with Freud* (London: Routledge, 1993), 99.

33. "Business Habits," *Queen*, October 12, 1889, 506.

34. "Shop Rovers and Shop Prowlers," *Drapers' Record*, October 3, 1899, 661.

35. Elaine S. Abelson, *When Ladies Go A-Thieving: Middle-Class Shoplifters in the Victorian Department Store* (New York: Oxford University Press, 1989), 4.

36. For a social history of consumer crime in the early nineteenth century (before the appearance of the department store), see Tammy C. Whitlock, *Crime, Gender and Consumer Culture in Nineteenth-Century England* (Aldershot, UK: Ashgate, 2005). The middle-class female shoplifter was a product of cultural anxieties and of the retail practices and spaces that were specific to Victorian consumer culture, distinguishing her from her seventeenth- and eighteenth-century counterparts: the genteel shop-thief and the working-class "common" thief who worked the shops. Although the verb *to shop* would not appear until 1764, the expression *shop-lift* was in currency as early as the 1670s and could apply to men or women. See Kowaleski-Wallace, *Consuming Subjects*. On shoplifting in the early nineteenth century, including the severity of punishments for working-class versus genteel shop-thieves, see Adela Pinch, "Stealing Happiness: Shoplifting in Early Nineteenth-Century England," in *Border Fetishisms: Material Objects in Unstable Places*, ed. Patricia Spyer (New York: Routledge, 1998), 122–49. A highly placed woman stood a better chance of legal absolution than did a working-class woman, who was far more likely to be criminalized for the same crime. See, for example, the 1828 case of a London "Carriage Lady," which Henry Goddard relates in *Memoirs of a Bow Street Runner* (London: Museum Press, 1956). In this case, a wealthy young woman is caught stealing ribbons from the shop of a Regent Street silk mercer and haberdasher. She is taken to appear before a magistrate, but before she can appear, a well-placed friend of her family (who is a peer and a magistrate) hears of her predicament and intervenes. He quietly arranges for her case to be dismissed so as not to bring public shame to her distinguished family.

37. As quoted in Abelson, *When Ladies Go A-Thieving*, 2.

38. Following the first theorizations of a "stealing mania" by a Swiss doctor, André Matthey, in 1816, the first case of kleptomania was diagnosed in France by C. C. Marc in 1840. See Pinch, "Stealing Happiness," 124, and Abelson, *When Ladies Go A-Thieving*, 183. The *Oxford English Dictionary* records the first English use of *kleptomania* in Britain in 1830, and by the latter part of the nineteenth century, the medical community had begun to actively formulate the terms of this form of mania as a medical disorder.

39. Abelson, *When Ladies Go A-Thieving*, 183.

40. Dr. Orpheus Everts, head of a Cincinnati sanitarium, gave his cautious endorsement of kleptomania as a valid form of mental disease, suggesting that a woman's persistent compulsion to steal might in some cases be symptomatic of a more pervasive illness and that a woman's "natural desire to accumulate" could be "exaggerated by disease." See Everts, "Are Dipsomania, Kleptomania, Pyromania, etc., Valid Forms of Mental Disease?" *American Journal of Insanity* 44 (July 1887): 56. Following the physical examination of a shoplifter, Dr. S. Weir Mitchell reported that the woman suffered from abnormalities to her uterus and cervix, all of which were indications of "very positive and long-neglected uterine and rectal disease [that] had much to do with the disorder of the mind [i.e., kleptomania] from which she suffered." See Mitchell,

"Nervous Disorders (Especially Kleptomania) in Women and Pelvic Disease," *American Journal of Insanity* 53 (April 1897): 605–6. Abelson also discusses Everts and Mitchell in *When Ladies Go A-Thieving* (173–74, 178, 186, 195).

41. Patricia O'Brien summarizes the findings of French case studies following 1880: "[M]ost of the diagnosed kleptomaniacs [almost exclusively women] were not guilty merely of isolated acts but appear to have stolen over long periods of time. . . . Most of the individuals . . . described themselves as in some way 'driven' or 'compelled' to steal. Common explanations included: 'It was stronger than I'; 'I didn't know what I was doing'; . . . Most kleptomaniacs also appear to have acted as packrats, amassing quantities of goods, often of little value, and hiding them.'" See O'Brien, "The Kleptomania Diagnosis: Bourgeois Women and Theft in Late Nineteenth-Century France," *Journal of Social History* 17, no. 1 (Fall 1983): 67.

42. On April 12, 1855, the *Times* printed the sensational details of one shoplifter's exploits, "The Case of Ramsbotham," a case that illustrates the ways in which kleptomania was emerging in the popular imagination, as well as in medical and legal communities, as a shopping disorder to which respectable women were deemed vulnerable. With the jury unable to decide whether Mrs. Ramsbotham was guilty or the victim of a "mania" and "a morbid sensation," the judge threw the case out (10). Mrs. Ramsbotham's hung jury marks a historical moment at which vexing questions of women's shopping disorders and criminal insanity were becoming linked. By 1896, the link had been well established, and the *Law Times* noted "the change which has come over the spirit in which English criminal law in regard to the responsibility of the insane is now administered." See "Kleptomania," *Law Times* 102 (November 14, 1896): 28. Whereas shoplifters in decades past "would unquestionably have been . . . convicted" (28), the institutionalization of criminal insanity meant that judges had to weigh such cases in a way that accounted for "scientific conclusions" (28). I am indebted to Abelson's work for the *Law Times* source.

43. Abelson, *When Ladies Go A-Thieving*, 7.

44. John Bucknill, "Kleptomania," *Journal of Mental Science* 8, no. 24 (1863): 265–66. I am indebted to Pinch's "Stealing Happiness" for the Bucknill source.

45. Bucknill, "Kleptomania," 266.

46. Pinch, "Stealing Happiness," 122.

47. Leslie Camhi, "Stealing Femininity: Department Store Kleptomania as Sexual Disorder," *differences: A Journal of Feminist Critical Studies* 5, no. 1 (1993): 39.

48. Camhi, "Stealing Femininity," 38.

49. Joan Rivière, "Womanliness as Masquerade," in *Formations of Fantasy*, ed. Victor Burgin, James Donald, and Cora Kaplan (London: Methuen, 1986), 38.

50. Camhi, "Stealing Femininity," 39.

51. As Louise J. Kaplan points out in *Female Perversions: The Temptations of Emma Bovary* (New York: Doubleday, 1991), a conventional psychoanalytic view of female kleptomania situates it in the context of fetishism and penis envy: "[T]he kleptomaniac

feels a vengeful envy and experiences the stolen goods as phallic trophies" (287). Kaplan revises this model somewhat, arguing that the kleptomaniac "[u]ses commodity fetishes as substitutes for human relationships" (297). By contrast, I am arguing that the shoplifter does not steal out of a fundamental lack. Shoplifting is not so much a form of fetishism that enacts visible substitutions when a woman steals as it is a cultural practice that rehearses both the fraudulent nature of gendered identity (a fraud that both sexual and capitalist exchanges perpetuate) and the ways in which the modern consuming subject is bound up in goods rather than existing prior to them.

52. Armstrong, "Occidental Alice," 18, 19.

53. Cvetkovich, *Mixed Feelings*, 46.

54. Mary Elizabeth Braddon, *Lady Audley's Secret*, ed. Natalie M. Houston (Peterborough, ON: Broadview, 2003), 170. All references in my text are to this edition and will be cited parenthetically.

55. See Naomi Schor, *Reading in Detail: Aesthetics and the Feminine* (New York: Methuen, 1987).

56. Montwieler, "Marketing Sensation," 44, 57.

57. Jill L. Matus, *Unstable Bodies: Victorian Representations of Sexuality and Maternity* (Manchester: Manchester University Press, 1995), 192–93.

58. Bernstein, "Dirty Reading," 219.

59. Rudi Laermans, "Learning to Consume: Early Department Stores and the Shaping of Modern Consumer Culture (1860–1914)," *Theory, Culture and Society* 10, no. 4 (1993): 97.

60. Natalie M. Houston, introduction to Braddon, *Lady Audley's Secret*, 24. Similarly, Montwieler writes that Lucy's "self-production" is part of "an elaborate theatrical performance" through which she affects gentility. See Montwieler, "Marketing Sensation," 51.

61. Cvetkovich, *Mixed Feelings*, 49.

62. Pykett, *"Improper" Feminine*, 90.

63. Pykett, *"Improper" Feminine*, 102. For Helena Michie, the "duplicity, this multiplicity of identity" can point to "an anxiety about the sexual and class doubleness that might potentially inhabit all women." See Michie, *Sororophobia: Differences among Women in Literature and Culture* (New York: Oxford University Press, 1992), 59, 62.

64. Bernstein elaborates on the ideological implications of Lucy's angelic disguise: "I conjecture that sensation novels expose . . . inherent contradictions of bourgeois ideology, split between the conflicting needs of the marketplace and the home, and attempt to resolve these competing claims on women: the sensation heroine cultivates the *appearance* of the domestic angel of modest appetites as a screen for her more intensely acquisitive diet. Once her angelic cover is blown, her lust for commodities emerges full force." See Bernstein, "Dirty Reading," 219.

65. Kimberley Reynolds and Nicola Humble, *Victorian Heroines: Representations of Femininity in Nineteenth-Century Literature and Art* (New York: New York University Press, 1993), 110.

66. Eliza Lynn Linton, "Little Women," *Saturday Review*, April 25, 1868, 545.

67. Interestingly, Clair Hughes argues in *Dressed in Fiction* (Oxford: Berg, 2006) that Lady Audley's elaborate dress constitutes a "colour" version, or rewriting, of Wilkie Collins's *Woman in White* and that her clothing can be read as forms of protest against the restrictions of mid-Victorian society.

68. Walter Benjamin, "The Work of Art in the Age of Mechanical Reproduction," *Illuminations*, ed. and with an intro. by Hannah Arendt, trans. Harry Zohn (New York: Schocken, 1988), 221.

69. On the connections between Victorian advertising and domestic ideology, see Lori Anne Loeb, *Consuming Angels: Advertising and Victorian Women* (New York: Oxford University Press, 1994); Ellen Gruber Garvey, *The Adman in the Parlour: Magazines and the Gendering of Consumer Culture, 1880s to 1910s* (New York: Oxford University Press, 1996).

70. Mrs. H. R. [Mary Eliza] Haweis, *The Art of Decoration* (London: Chatto and Windus, 1881), 17.

71. George Eliot, *Middlemarch*, ed. W. J. Harvey (London: Penguin, 1985). All references in my text are to this edition and will appear parenthetically.

72. "The Boudoir," *Queen*, June 6, 1863, 269.

73. Charles Eastlake, *Hints on Household Taste* (London: Longmans, Green, 1872), 7.

74. Eastlake, *Hints on Household Taste*, 11.

75. Eastlake, *Hints on Household Taste*, 162.

76. Eastlake, *Hints on Household Taste*, 201.

77. Eastlake, *Hints on Household Taste*, 207.

78. Lady [Mary Anne] Barker, *The Bedroom and Boudoir* (London: Macmillan, 1878), 84.

79. Thad Logan, *The Victorian Parlour: A Cultural Study* (Cambridge: Cambridge University Press, 2001), xiii.

80. Logan considers that "[i]t is the appearance of 'excessive' ornamental detail that declares the home to be liberated from an economy driven by necessity—to participate, instead, in a new economy of desire." See Logan, *Victorian Parlour*, 205.

81. Another important moment in Robert's investigation occurs when he reads Helen Talboy's inscription to her husband, George Talboys, in a literary annual. Robert realizes that the handwriting matches Lucy's and thus that they are the same woman. The scene is another instance of reading the surfaces of a commodity object, in this case a feminized, commercial form of literature that Robert has a real aversion to: he considers the annual a "mild production[ ]" and finds the costumed figures in the volume's engravings "grotesque and outlandish" (184).

82. On Victorian men's active engagements with consumer culture, see, for example, Brent Shannon, *The Cut of His Coat: Men, Dress, and Consumer Culture in Britain, 1860–1914* (Athens: Ohio University Press, 2006); Christopher Breward, *The Hidden Consumer: Masculinities, Fashion and City Life, 1860–1914* (Manchester: Manchester University Press, 1999).

83. On homosocial desire in the novel, see Richard Nemesvari, "Robert Audley's Secret: Male Homosocial Desire in *Lady Audley's Secret*," *Studies in the Novel* 27, no. 4 (1995): 515–28; Ann Cvetkovich, *Mixed Feelings*, 56–65. As with the marriage market and the laws of patrimony, the novel makes visible the ways in which capital depends on homosocial desire.

84. Eastlake, *Hints on Household Taste*, 206.

85. As Brent Shannon explains, the phrase "Great Masculine Renunciation" was "coined in 1930 by J. C. Flugel" to describe "a [Victorian] reserved and muted middle-class sartorial aesthetic." See Shannon, "ReFashioning Men," 626n2. Shannon productively questions the monolithic way in which this term has been applied. Although Robert's repudiation of consumerism might seem to suggest a monolithic instance of the so-called Great Renunciation, I am suggesting that Robert's obsessive concern to cast off consumer practices reveals the work of commodities in the production of bourgeois subjectivity.

86. Patrick Brantlinger, "Household Taste: Industrial Art, Consumerism, and Pre-Raphaelitism," *Journal of Pre-Raphaelite Studies* 9 (2000): 90.

87. "The sensation novel, be it mere trash or something worse, is usually a tale of our own times. . . . It is necessary to be near a mine to be blown up by its explosion; and a tale which aims at electrifying the nerves of the readers is never thoroughly effective unless the scene be laid in our own days and among the people we are in the habit of meeting"; Mansel, "Sensation Novels," 488–89.

Chapter 3: Middlemarch *and the Extravagant Domestic Spender: Managing an Epic Life*

1. For a more detailed account, see N. N. Feltes, *Modes of Production of Victorian Novels* (Chicago: University of Chicago Press, 1986); Frederick R. Karl, *George Eliot, Voice of a Century: A Biography* (New York: W. W. Norton, 1995); Jerome Beaty, *Middlemarch from Notebook to Novel* (Urbana: University of Illinois Press, 1960); Carol A. Martin, *George Eliot's Serial Fiction* (Columbus: Ohio State University Press, 1994); Guinivere L. Griest, *Mudie's Circulating Library and the Victorian Novel* (Bloomington: Indiana University Press, 1970).

2. Lewes letter included in *The George Eliot Letters*, ed. Gordon S. Haight (New Haven, CT: Yale University Press, 1954–78), 5:145–46.

3. David Carroll, introduction to *Middlemarch*, by George Eliot (Oxford: Clarendon, 1986), xxxiii.

4. Carroll, introduction to *Middlemarch*, xxxiii. Carroll also notes that the price of new fiction in the 1860s was about 10s. 6d. per volume (xxxiv). The aim apparently was not to entirely circumvent the lending libraries, but to mute their influence. Although Mudie's initially "threatened to boycott" *Middlemarch*, it bought 1,500 copies of the first book. W. H. Smith received "a 10 percent discount from Blackwood," and bought up to 1,000 copies (lviii).

5. In a letter on September 11, 1866, to Blackwood, Eliot expresses her frustration over the underdistribution of *Felix Holt* (*George Eliot Letters*, 4:309).

6. Eliot, *George Eliot Letters*, 2:431.

7. Eliot, *George Eliot Letters*, 4:49.

8. George Eliot, "Silly Novels by Lady Novelists," *Westminster Review* 66 (July 1856): 442. George Henry Lewes, "Of Vision in Art," in *The Principles of Success in Literature*, ed. with an intro. and notes by Fred N. Scott (Boston: Allyn and Bacon, 1891), 84, 83.

9. See, for example, Gillian Beer, "Circulatory Systems: Money and Gossip in *Middlemarch*," in *Studies in George Eliot* 26, ed. J. C. Amalric (Montpellier, France: Centre d'Études et de Recherches Victoriennes et Édouardiennes, 1987), 49; Richard D. Altick, *The Presence of the Present: Topics of the Day in the Victorian Novel* (Columbus: Ohio State University Press, 1991), 654.

10. See Barbara Weiss, *The Hell of the English: Bankruptcy and the Victorian Novel* (Lewisburg, PA: Bucknell University Press, 1986), 14 and 27; Altick, *Presence of the Past*, 651. The *London Gazette* regularly published bankruptcy lists, a testament to the regularity with which many small businesses failed during the nineteenth century, a phenomenon that had been less frequent during the previous century. A significant number of these bankruptcies were small retailers or business owners, such as drapers and shoe dealers. See V. Markham Lester, *Victorian Insolvency: Bankruptcy, Imprisonment for Debt, and Company Winding-up in Nineteenth-Century England* (Oxford: Clarendon, 1995), 251. Anticipating this growing crisis, a tradesman named Thomas Foster wrote to Earl Grey in 1831 to express his fear that the crippling effects of debt, speculation, and flawed bankruptcy law were wreaking havoc on Britain's economic situation, creating a burden that "is now become more, in its amount, than the interest of the National Debt" (as quoted in Weiss, *Hell of the English*, 28).

11. Gillian Beer has observed that *Middlemarch* is "in touch with the issues being debated in the women's movement of the 1850s and 1860s, and how thoroughly it entered the debates." See Beer, *George Eliot* (Brighton, UK: Harvester, 1986), 148.

12. Under the centuries-old common law, coverture subsumed a married woman's legal status under that of her husband's. She was "covered" by her husband, who legally represented her, since a married couple's interests were assumed to be identical. See Mary Poovey, *Uneven Developments: The Ideological Work of Gender in Mid-Victorian England* (Chicago: University of Chicago Press, 1988), 51. Because married women possessed no legal status of their own under the law, husbands were held responsible for debts incurred by their wives either before or during marriage. The 1857 Matrimonial Causes Act, prompted by a women's petition to reform the Married Women's Property Bill, did little to enhance women's access to their own property following marriage, and still found husbands liable for their wives' debts. One year after the abolishment of imprisonment for debtors, the Married Women's Property Bill (1870) allowed married women to own their own separate estate, which previously under common law had been owned and controlled by their husbands. See Dorothy M. Stetson,

A Woman's Issue: The Politics of Family Law Reform in England (Westport, CT: Greenwood, 1982), 8. The Married Women's Property Bill was therefore hailed as a great advance for women's legal reform. In practice, however, the legislation still placed limits on the uses to which women could put their property; moreover, loopholes remained by which women debtors were not required to pay their creditors if their separate estates did not constitute security in the eyes of the law. The 1882 Married Women's Property Act addressed both the restrictions placed on women's property rights in 1870 and the loopholes by which women were not required to repay debt that the 1870 act had only partially closed. One significant loophole remained, however. If a woman's debt exceeded the value of her separate estate, a plaintiff had the option of suing the husband and wife jointly to collect the balance of the outstanding debt from the husband. See Lee Holcombe, *Wives and Property: Reform of the Married Women's Property Law in Nineteenth-Century England* (Toronto: University of Toronto Press, 1983), 223. Not until the Law Reform (Married Women and Tortfeasors) Act of 1935 did women become fully liable for contracts, being granted the same economic and legal status as single women and men, including equal responsibilities regarding debt.

13. Together, these books constructed a specific ideology of gender that, as Nancy Armstrong has shown, cast "the female character and that of the home [as] one and the same as she translated her husband's income into the objects and personnel comprising his household." See Armstrong, *Desire and Domestic Fiction: A Political History of the Novel* (Oxford: Oxford University Press, 1987), 83. For further discussion of Victorian domestic economy, see, for example, Elizabeth Langland, *Nobody's Angels: Middle-Class Women and Domestic Ideology in Victorian Culture* (Ithaca, NY: Cornell University Press, 1995); Bronwyn Rivers, *Women at Work in the Victorian Novel: The Question of Middle-Class Women's Employment, 1840–1870* (Lewiston, NY: Edwin Mellen, 2005).

14. Anne Cobbett, *The English Housekeeper; or, Manual of Domestic Management, the Whole Being Intended for the Use of Young Ladies Who Undertake the Superintendence of Their Own Housekeeping* (London: W. J. Sears, 1835); Sarah Stickney Ellis, *The Women of England: Their Social Duties and Domestic Habits* (London: Fisher, Son, 1839); Mrs. [Isabella Mary] Beeton, *The Book of Household Management* (London: S. O. Beeton, 1859–1861); Samuel Smiles, *Thrift* (New York: Harper, 1875).

15. Hughes, *Dressed in Fiction*, 89.

16. *Cassell's Household Guide: Being a Complete Encyclopedia of Domestic and Social Economy* (London: Cassell, Petter, and Galpin, 1869), 1:1.

17. Mary Jewry, *Warne's Model Cookery and Housekeeping Book: A New Edition* (London: Frederick Warne, 1871), 5.

18. Smiles, *Thrift*, 187–88.

19. J. H. Walsh, *A Manual of Domestic Economy: Suited to Families Spending from £100 to £1000 a Year* (London: G. Routledge, 1856).

20. The manual goes on to delineate the most economic ways to take on a host of domestic tasks. It strives for an encyclopedic account of the home, beginning with

ways of procuring a house: by purchase, renting, or building. Next, it discusses how best to furnish a home and employ servants. There is a detailed section on obtaining household supplies, primarily food, followed by directions on cooking. The manual finally moves on to briefer topics such as hygiene and nursery management, and social duties and etiquette. Each main section is pursued with four different income levels in mind. The first income level corresponds to a household budget of 1000 pounds per year, the second to 500, the third to 250, and the fourth to 100. In the section on selecting furniture, for example, a lengthy chart organizes required furniture according to room and includes estimates for each piece. Those in the top income bracket may obtain expensive stair carpeting, for example, while those in the lowest must do without. The highest income bracket allows for the employment of a butler, a coachman or groom, one or two housemaids, a cook, and perhaps a lady's-maid. The lower stratum is not allotted any servants and permits in its household budget only the most basic necessities of food, shelter, and clothing (Walsh, *Manual of Domestic Economy*, 192–212).

21. Walsh, *Manual of Domestic Economy*, 1.
22. Walsh, *Manual of Domestic Economy*, 1.
23. Ellis, *Women of England*, 131.
24. Walsh, *Manual of Domestic Economy*, 131.
25. Rivers, *Women at Work*, 50.
26. Mrs. [Eliza] Warren, *How I Managed My House on Two Hundred Pounds a Year* (London: Houlston and Wright, 1864), iii.
27. See Margot Finn, "Women, Consumption and Coverture in England, c. 1760–1860," *Historical Journal* 39, no. 3 (1996): 707.
28. Rappaport, *Shopping for Pleasure*, 50–51. These necessities, as Rappaport argues, were socially constructed.
29. "Observations on Credit," *Pamphleteer* 13 (1819): 363.
30. Jeune, "Ethics of Shopping," 126.
31. Smiles, *Thrift*, 260–61.
32. Rappaport, *Shopping for Pleasure*, 52.
33. Armstrong, *Desire and Domestic Fiction*, 81.
34. Armstrong, *Desire and Domestic Fiction*, 95.
35. Armstrong, *Desire and Domestic Fiction*, 77.
36. Langland, *Nobody's Angels*, 208.
37. *The Family Exchequer Book, or, Housekeeping and General Expenditure Book* (London: Hector M'Lean, 1839), B.
38. Walsh's chart is organized according to the four income levels. Housekeeping items constitute the largest household expense once totaled, with meat costs ranking high for each income level. Rent, although a significant item for all four subclasses, is noticeably lower than the combined housekeeping expenses, attesting to the need for proper management of the latter, since it constituted such a significant part of the overall budget. The housewife was tasked with making the proper calculations for her

situation and was to further subdivide to determine weekly costs. "The great thing," Walsh advises, "is *to make the calculation on paper, and when that is done, to determine to adhere to it somehow or other.* But without this weekly estimate, it is scarcely possible to check the expenditure, until it has gone so far as to trench severely upon the whole sum to be laid out in the year" (*Manual of Domestic Economy*, 607). Beeton gives similar advice: "A housekeeping account-book should invariably be kept, and kept punctually and precisely" (*Book of Household Management*, 6).

39. Walsh, *Manual of Domestic Economy*, 211.

40. Langland, *Nobody's Angels*, 144.

41. Sandra M. Gilbert and Susan Gubar argue that Rosamond is more than "a vindictive portrait... of pretty women" and point out that Rosamond "has worked 'for' the female community by entangling the representatives of patriarchal culture—Casaubon, Bulstrode, Featherstone, and Lydgate—and by calling into question their authority." See Gilbert and Gubar, *Madwoman in the Attic*, 520, 524.

42. Miller, *Novels behind Glass*, 192.

43. Miller, *Novels behind Glass*, 13.

44. Ellen Moers, *Literary Women* (Garden City, NY: Doubleday, 1976), 195.

45. *Etiquette for the Ladies: Eighty Maxims on Dress, Manners, and Accomplishments* (London: Charles Tilt, 1837), 9.

46. Beeton, *Book of Household Management*, 10. *Etiquette for Ladies and Gentlemen* (London: Frederick Warne, 1876), 13–14.

47. Beeton, *Book of Household Management*, 5.

48. Hughes, *Dressed in Fiction*, 93.

49. Hughes, *Dressed in Fiction*, 93.

50. Hughes calls Dorothea's mourning "a cover, even penance, for an absence of grief" (*Dressed in Fiction*, 106).

51. Jeff Nunokawa, *The Afterlife of Property: Domestic Security and the Victorian Novel* (Princeton, NJ: Princeton University Press, 1994), 117.

52. Romans 8:18, KJV: "For I reckon that the sufferings of this present time are not worthy to be compared with the glory which shall be revealed in us."

53. Even Dorothea's ambitious charity schemes, as J. Jeffrey Franklin points out, are forms of speculation that are "infiltrated by the discourse of gambling." See Franklin, "The Victorian Discourse of Gambling: Speculations on *Middlemarch* and *The Duke's Children*," *ELH* 61, no. 4 (1994): 916.

54. Tim Dolin, *Mistress of the House: Women of Property in the Victorian Novel* (Aldershot, UK: Ashgate, 1997), 9.

55. Beer, "Circulatory Systems," 61. For Beer, this expenditure is about "the cost of individual experience."

56. Alfred Tennyson, *In Memoriam A. H. H.* (1850), in *The Poems of Tennyson in Three Volumes*, ed. Christopher Ricks, 2nd ed. (Harlow: Longman, 1987), 315–458. The quotation is from stanza 1, line 8 (2:318).

57. Eliot, *George Eliot Letters*, 5:348–49, 6:10.

58. Eliot, *George Eliot Letters*, 5:353, 5:268. It was not until a one-volume edition was issued in 1874 that 10,000 copies of *Middlemarch* were sold. Eliot was delighted, describing the sales as "wonderful out of all whooping" (*George Eliot Letters*, 6:75).

Chapter 4: To Those Who Love Them Best: The Erotics of Connoisseurship in Michael Field's Sight and Song

1. James G. Nelson, *Elkin Mathews: Publisher to Yeats, Joyce, Pound* (Madison: University of Wisconsin Press, 1989), 251n23. In September 1894, after the first volume of *The Yellow Book* had appeared in April of that year, Bodley Head founders Elkin Mathews and John Lane dissolved their partnership over differences of personality and business practice. Mathews stayed on at the Vigo Street shop, while Lane moved his business to Albany Street, where he continued to publish using the Bodley Head name.

2. James G. Nelson, "The Bodley Head," in *The 1890s: An Encyclopedia of British Literature, Art, and Culture*, ed. G. A. Cevasco (New York: Garland, 1993), 67.

3. Bridget Elliot sees the woman as an "advanced" or "new" woman, dressed in the modern clothes of the 1890s. See Elliot, "New and Not So 'New Women' on the London Stage: Aubrey Beardsley's *Yellow Book* Images of Mrs Patrick Campbell and Réjane," *Victorian Studies* 31, no. 1 (1987): 40–42.

4. Sally Ledger, "Wilde Women and *The Yellow Book:* The Sexual Politics of Aestheticism and Decadence," *English Literature in Transition* 50, no. 1 (2007): 16.

5. An interest in cultural production as well as consumption characterizes recent Michael Field criticism and studies of women's aestheticism in general. Critics writing during the initial stages of the Michael Field revival often focused on production—especially conditions of authorship in *Long Ago* (1889), *Underneath the Bough: A Book of Verses* (1893), and *Wild Honey from Various Thyme* (1908). See, for example, Holly Laird, "Contradictory Legacies: Michael Field and Feminist Restoration," *Victorian Poetry* 33, no. 1 (1995): 111–28; Angela Leighton, *Victorian Women Poets: Writing against the Heart* (New York: Harvester Wheatsheaf, 1992), 202–43; Chris White, "'Poets and Lovers Evermore': Interpreting Female Love in the Poetry and Journals of Michael Field," *Textual Practice* 4, no. 2 (1990): 197–212. In doing so, they often noted Michael Field's challenge to singular authorship in lyric poetry and the coauthors' deployment of the figure of Sappho in the formation of lesbian desire. More recently, critics have turned to the cultural conditions of the poetry. In *Victorian Sappho*, for example, Yopie Prins examines Michael Field's work in light of the discourse of Hellenism to consider how the deployment of Greek eros was not solely the province of homoerotic exchanges between men but also occurred between women. See Prins, *Victorian Sappho* (Princeton, NJ: Princeton University Press, 1999). Talia Schaffer's book, *The Forgotten Female Aesthetes: Literary Culture in Late-Victorian England* (Charlottesville: University Press

of Virginia, 2000), is indicative of a larger trend toward studies of the culture of women's aestheticism. It, along with Schaffer and Kathy Alexis Psomiades's jointly edited *Women and British Aestheticism* (Charlottesville: University Press of Virginia, 1997), continues the work of examining the importance of connoisseurship, mass culture, and consumerism to an understanding of the literary production of women's aestheticism.

6. Regenia Gagnier, *Idylls of the Marketplace: Oscar Wilde and the Victorian Public* (Stanford: Stanford University Press, 1986), 5. See also Gagnier, "Productive Bodies, Pleasured Bodies," 272.

7. Freedman, *Professions of Taste*, xix–xx.

8. Felski, *Gender of Modernity*, 99.

9. Kathy Alexis Psomiades, *Beauty's Body: Femininity and Representation in British Aestheticism* (Stanford: Stanford University Press, 1997). See, for example, 198–202.

10. De Certeau, *Practice of Everyday Life*, xi.

11. The Bodley Head also published three other Michael Field works: *Stephania*, a "trialogue" verse drama (1892); *A Question of Memory: A Play* (1893); and another verse drama, *Attila, My Attila* (1896).

12. Matthew Arnold, "The Function of Criticism at the Present Time" (1864), in *Poetry and Criticism of Matthew Arnold*, ed. A. Dwight Culler (Boston: Houghton Mifflin, 1961), 237.

13. Ana Parejo Vadillo, *Women Poets and Urban Aestheticism: Passengers of Modernity* (Houndmills, UK: Palgrave, 2005), 167–68.

14. T. Sturge Moore and D. C. Sturge Moore, editors' preface to Michael Field, *Works and Days: From the Journal of Michael Field* (London: John Murray, 1933), xvii–xviii.

15. Emma Donoghue, *We Are Michael Field* (Bath, UK: Absolute, 1998), 106–7; as quoted in 107.

16. Donoghue, *We Are Michael Field*, 112.

17. Vadillo, *Women Poets*, 172.

18. Mary Sturgeon, *Michael Field* (London: George G. Harrap, 1922), 45–46.

19. Quoted in Sturgeon, *Michael Field*, 46.

20. Percy H. Muir, *Minding My Own Business: An Autobiography* (London: Chatto and Windus, 1956), 6.

21. James G. Nelson, *The Early Nineties: A View from the Bodley Head* (Cambridge, MA: Harvard University Press, 1971), 77.

22. Nelson, *Early Nineties*, 79.

23. Nelson, *Early Nineties*, 77.

24. Margaret Diane Stetz, "Sex, Lies, and Printed Cloth: Bookselling at the Bodley Head in the Eighteen-Nineties," *Victorian Studies* 35, no. 1 (1991): 74.

25. Nelson, *Early Nineties*, 80–81.

26. Stetz, "Sex, Lies, and Printed Cloth," 74.

27. Nelson, *Early Nineties*, 81.

28. Stetz, "Sex, Lies, and Printed Cloth," 74.
29. Stetz, "Sex, Lies, and Printed Cloth," 76.
30. Stetz, "Sex, Lies, and Printed Cloth," 82.
31. Stetz, "Sex, Lies, and Printed Cloth," 79–80.
32. Stetz, "Sex, Lies, and Printed Cloth," 80.
33. Donoghue, *We Are Michael Field*, 68.
34. Nelson, *Early Nineties*, 87.
35. Nelson, *Early Nineties*, 63.
36. Nelson, *Early Nineties*, 318–19. In *A Checklist of Early Bodley Head Books: 1889–1894*, revised and enlarged (High Wycombe, UK: Rivendale, 1999), Nelson records the price as 5 shillings (34).
37. "Announcement for the Season," *Publisher's Circle* 55, no. 1340 (March 5, 1892): 271. (See Nelson, *Early Nineties*, 35.) Nelson also notes, "It was standard practice at the Bodley Head to issue a prospectus of 1,000 copies two or three months before a book was to be published" (*Early Nineties*, 107). These pamphlets would describe the book and provide the price (and perhaps a lower prepublication price for subscribers), as well as an order form.
38. Donoghue, *We Are Michael Field*, 69.
39. Stetz, "Sex, Lies, and Printed Cloth," 81.
40. These reviews are found on the back of Le Gallienne's *Religion of a Literary Man* (1894). See Stetz, "Sex, Lies, and Printed Cloth," 83.
41. Stetz, "Sex, Lies, and Printed Cloth," 82.
42. Nicholas Frankel, "The Concrete Poetics of Michael Field's *Sight and Song*," in *Michael Field and Their World*, ed. Margaret D. Stetz and Cheryl A. Wilson (High Wycombe, UK: Rivendale, 2007), 221n8.
43. Walter Pater, *The Renaissance: Studies in Art and Poetry: The 1893 Text*, ed. Donald L. Hill (Berkeley: University of California Press, 1980), xix–xx, 43. Originally published in 1873 as *Studies in the History of the Renaissance*.
44. Pater, *Renaissance*, 187–88.
45. Michael Field, *Sight and Song* (London: Elkin Mathews and John Lane, 1892), v. All references in my text are to this edition and will be referred to parenthetically.
46. Julia F. Saville, "The Poetic Imaging of Michael Field," in *The Fin-de-Siècle Poem: English Literary Culture and the 1890s*, ed. Joseph Bristow (Athens: Ohio University Press, 2005), 180.
47. Walter Pater, "Prosper Mérimée," *Miscellaneous Studies: A Series of Essays* (London: Macmillan, 1899), 23. Saville, "Poetic Imaging," 179.
48. Vadillo, *Women Poets*, 195. In another analysis of *Sight and Song*, Jill Ehnenn also considers the "model of visuality" in *Sight and Song*, but she departs from a phenomenological reading of the poems "that assumes the stable essence of an object" (216, 214). Instead, Ehnenn "posits *Sight and Song* as a series of resistant readings that critique Victorian ideologies regarding sex, gender, and aesthetics from what today might

be called feminist and queer perspectives" (214). While Ehnenn's focus is not so much concerned with the poems in light of economic discourse, she is interested in how "the picture-poems . . . reclaim[ ] previously objectified female images" (214). See Ehnenn, "Looking Strategically: Feminist and Queer Aesthetics in Michael Field's *Sight and Song*," *Victorian Poetry* 42, no. 3 (2004): 213–59.

49. Freedman observes that "the transforming encounter between self and art object is a central—perhaps *the* central—topos of the aesthetic imagination in England. . . . [T]he encounter between an alert, interrogating consciousness and a work of visual art has been a sustaining, even a defining, staple of the aesthetic movement—perhaps one of its very few characteristics that enable us to define it as an 'aesthetic' movement at all." See Freedman, *Professions of Taste*, 211.

50. Carpenter, "'Eat me, drink me,'" 425.

51. Frankel, "Concrete Poetics," 212.

52. On the possibilities for the queering of images of boys and of men (such as the versions of the martyrdom of Saint Sebastian) in *Sight and Song*, see Ehnenn's "Looking Strategically." Like Saville, I look to the volume's ekphrasis of women, where we often "perceive agency in an apparently passive female figure." See Saville, "Poetic Imaging," 185.

53. Logan Pearsall Smith apparently later acquired Pater's copy of *Sight and Song*, inscribing it, "From the library of Walter Pater." In May 1892, Pater thanked Bradley and Cooper for the volume, writing, "Sincere thanks for the gift of it, and for the kind expressions in your letter; which, however, I feel I don't deserve. I read almost no contemporary poetry; have, alas! almost no time to do so." See Margaret D. Stetz and Mark Samuels Lasner, eds., *England in the 1890s: Literary Publishing at the Bodley Head* (Washington, DC: Georgetown University Press, 1990), 19.

54. Pater, *Renaissance*, 97–99.

55. Psomiades, *Beauty's Body*, 198–99.

56. Marx, *Capital*, 1:163.

57. Michael Field, "La Gioconda," in *Sight and Song*, 8.

58. Psomiades, *Beauty's Body*, 202.

59. Michael Field, "A Portrait," in *Sight and Song*, 27–30.

60. Chris White, "Flesh and Roses: Michael Field's Metaphors of Pleasure and Desire," *Women's Writing* 3, no. 1 (1996): 52–53.

61. Michael Field, "The Birth of Venus," in *Sight and Song*, 13–15.

62. Donoghue, *We Are Michael Field*, 68.

63. Michael Field, "The Sleeping Venus," in *Sight and Song*, 98–105.

64. As quoted in Donoghue, *We Are Michael Field*, 62.

65. Hilary Fraser, "A Visual Field: Michael Field and the Gaze," *Victorian Literature and Culture* 34, no. 2 (2006): 554.

66. Michael Field, *Works and Days*, 48.

67. Frankel, "Concrete Poetics," 217.

68. Michael Field, "A Pen-Drawing of Leda," in *Sight and Song*, 81.

69. Luce Irigaray, "Commodities among Themselves," *This Sex Which Is Not One*, trans. Catherine Porter (Ithaca, NY: Cornell University Press, 1985), 196–97.

70. Michael Field, "L'Embarquement Pour Cythère," in *Sight and Song*, 117–25.

71. Vadillo, *Women Poets*, 194.

72. Kenneth Grahame, "Non Libri Sed Liberi," in *Pagan Papers* (London: John Lane, 1898), 32–33. First published in 1894.

73. As quoted in Donoghue, *We Are Michael Field*, 116.

Chapter 5: Votes for Women *and the Tactics of Consumption*

1. W. L. [William Leonard] Courtney, "The Soul of a Suffragette," in *Literature of the Women's Suffrage Campaign in England*, ed. Carolyn Christensen Nelson (Peterborough, ON: Broadview, 2004), 316–17.

2. Emmeline Pankhurst, *My Own Story* (New York: Hearst's International Library Co., 1914), 216.

3. *Draper and Drapery Times*, March 9, 1912, pp. 331–32, as quoted in Rappaport, *Shopping for Pleasure*, 216.

4. *Votes for Women* (hereafter *VFW*), March 8, 1912, 352.

5. The *Times* and the *Pall Mall Gazette* are among those newspapers that reported damages in this amount. Numbers on the arrests vary; whereas the two aforementioned papers recorded that 124 women were arrested (March 4, 1912, 4; March 2, 1912, 2), the WSPU's seventh annual report, for February 1912–February 1913, states that there were 267 arrested (*The Suffragette Fellowship Collection from the Museum of London* [Brighton, UK: Harvester Microform, 1985], 13:11). The WSPU figures, however, may also include women who were arrested at a simultaneous demonstration in Downing Street.

6. In a letter to the *Daily News*, Millicent Fawcett, the NUWSS leader, distanced herself from the militant tactics of those who "are attempting to grasp by violence what should be yielded to the growing conviction that our demand is based on justice and common sense." *Daily News*, March 9, 1912, as quoted in Joyce Marlow, ed., *Votes for Women: The Virago Book of Suffragettes* (London: Virago, 2000), 164.

7. *Standard*, March 4, 1912, 12, as quoted in Rappaport, *Shopping for Pleasure*, 215.

8. Quoted in *VFW*, March 8, 1912, 352. *VFW* provided this account as one of several "taken from the Press" over "the last few days" from papers such as the *Daily Telegraph*.

9. Quoted in Pankhurst, *My Own Story*, 217.

10. Of the dozens of turn-of-the-century suffrage organizations in Britain, the three most dominant were the National Union of Women's Suffrage Societies, a "constitutional" or moderate group founded in 1897 and led by Millicent Garrett Fawcett; the Women's Social and Political Union; and the Women's Freedom League, a group that formed when it separated from the Women's Social and Political Union in 1907. For social and cultural histories of the WSPU and other suffrage groups, see,

for instance, Roger Fulford, *Votes for Women: The Story of a Struggle* (London: Faber and Faber, 1957); Andrew Rosen, *Rise Up Women! The Militant Campaign of the Women's Social and Political Union, 1903–1914* (London: Routledge and Kegan Paul, 1974); Jill Liddington and Jill Norris, *One Hand Tied behind Us: The Rise of the Women's Suffrage Movement* (London: Virago, 1985); Sandra Stanley Holton, *Feminism and Democracy: Women's Suffrage and Reform Politics in Britain, 1900–1918* (Cambridge: Cambridge University Press, 1987); June Purvis and Sandra Stanley Holton, eds., *Votes for Women* (London: Routledge, 2000); Laura E. Nym Mayhall, *The Militant Suffrage Movement: Citizenship and Resistance in Britain, 1860–1930* (Oxford: Oxford University Press, 2003).

11. As quoted in Jane Marcus, ed., *Suffrage and the Pankhursts* (London: Routledge and Kegan Paul, 1987), 119.

12. Several recent collections of essays have reassessed the suffrage movement in Britain, showing the wide-ranging nature of cultural activities associated with suffrage and the diverse nature of suffrage material production, including but not limited to print culture. See, for example, Claire Eustance, Joan Ryan, and Laura Ugolini, eds., *A Suffrage Reader: Charting Directions in British Suffrage History* (London: Leicester University Press, 2000); Purvis and Holton, *Votes for Women*; Maroula Joannou and June Purvis, eds., *The Women's Suffrage Movement: New Feminist Perspectives* (Manchester: Manchester University Press, 1998).

13. Marcus, *Suffrage and the Pankhursts*, 183.

14. In her important study of suffrage iconography, *The Spectacle of Women: Imagery of the Suffrage Campaign, 1907–14* (Chicago: University of Chicago Press, 1988), Lisa Tickner shows how suffragists manipulated public images of femininity "with great skill and ingenuity. They were indeed part of the spectacle, but they also produced and controlled it" (81). With particular emphasis on the WSPU, Barbara Green's *Spectacular Confessions: Autobiography, Performative Activism, and the Sites of Suffrage, 1905–1938* (New York: St. Martin's, 1997) examines "the display of the spectacular woman in the public sphere [as] a feminist strategy" (2) and the "spectacular confessions" of suffrage autobiography that politicized displays of and testimonials about the body, including those of prisoners. But Green also constitutes an important departure from Tickner, whose work has tended to emphasize a distinction between an earlier phase of the suffrage campaigns (from about 1905 to 1911) that is characterized by street pageantry, and a later militant phase following 1911. By contrast, Green works against this "tendency to separate [later] militant activism from the theatrical performances of the first half of the [suffrage] campaign ... [for this] misses the complexity of the relationship" between the two (Green, *Spectacular Confessions*, 72). While my own emphasis is on consumer discourse rather than street spectacle, I follow Green in my consideration of how the WSPU's consumer culture formed in conjunction with its growing militancy rather than as a precursor to it. By examining militancy and consumerism as mutual, rather than sequential, I hope to avoid this periodization and show how the two were often simultaneous and mutually constitutive.

15. Guy Debord, *The Society of the Spectacle* (Detroit: Black and Red, 1977), 36.

16. Debord, *Society of the Spectacle*, 12.

17. De Certeau, *Practice of Everyday Life*, xvii.

18. De Certeau, *Practice of Everyday Life*, xix.

19. The paper began its run in October 1907 under the coeditorship of Frederick W. and Emmeline Pethick-Lawrence. It continued this way until October 1912, when the WSPU adopted a new organ, *The Suffragette*, which was edited by Christabel Pankhurst. After disagreements over the militant policy and friction over Emmeline Pankhurst's perceived autocratic leadership style, many suffragists left the WSPU and formed the United Suffragists. Among those to defect were the Pethick-Lawrences, who took *Votes for Women* with them and continued to edit it until 1918. Meanwhile, the WSPU published the first issue of its new paper, *The Suffragette*, on October 18, 1912. After October 8, 1915, *The Suffragette* adopted a new name, *Britannia*, a title that reflected the WSPU's patriotic view of Britain during wartime. Following the war in 1918, the WSPU, along with other suffrage groups, joined the Women's Party. For more on WSPU publication during the war, see Angela K. Smith, "The Pankhursts and the War: Suffrage Magazines and First World War Propaganda," *Women's History Review* 12, no. 1 (2003): 103–18.

20. Maria DiCenzo, "Gutter Politics: Women Newsies and the Suffrage Press," *Women's History Review* 12, no. 1 (2003): 15–33. Simone Murray, "'Deeds *and* Words': The Woman's Press and the Politics of Print," *Women: A Cultural Review* 11, no. 3 (2000): 197–222.

21. *VFW*, November 1907, 13.

22. In "'Deeds, not words': Daily Life in the Women's Social and Political Union in Edwardian Britain," in *Votes for Women*, ed. June Purvis and Sandra Stanley Holton (London: Routledge, 2000), Purvis is among those who have recently begun to show how various groups that made up the suffrage movement were by no means monolithic in their leadership, organization, and practices. Not only a middle-class movement, the campaigns also attracted far more diverse groups of women. WSPU working-class campaigner Annie Kenney made some public appearances clothed in her mill worker's garb, one instance that suggests that there were other images available to women besides those of the fashionable and affluent middle-class suffragette. See Jane Marcus, "The Asylums of Antaeus: Women, War, and Madness—Is There a Feminist Fetishism?" in *The New Historicism*, ed. H. Aram Veeser (New York: Routledge, 1989), for her suggestion "that the suffrage movement deliberately created multiple new images of women as a political act, unsettling female identity in the process" (148). In addition to the fashionable middle-class woman, Rita Felski points out that the suffragettes also adopted historical images of women such as "Boadicea, Athena, and above all Joan of Arc . . . as idealized symbols of feminine heroic power." See Felski, *Gender of Modernity*, 166.

23. Third Annual Report for the year ending February 1909, in *Suffragette Fellowship Collection*, 13:6.

24. The colors of the National Union of Women's Suffrage Societies were red and white, and later, green as well. The Women's Freedom League scheme was green, white, and gold. At least eight other smaller groups had colors as well. See Tickner, *Spectacle of Women*, 265. The colors of the Artists' Suffrage League were blue and silver, and the Writers' Suffrage League were black, white, and gold.

25. Emmeline Pethick-Lawrence, "Popularising the Colours," *VFW*, June 18, 1908, 249.

26. Christabel Pankhurst, "The Political Importance of the Colours," *VFW*, May 7, 1909, 632.

27. "The Suffragette and the Dress Problem," *VFW*, July 30, 1908, 348.

28. Katrina Rolley, "Fashion, Femininity and the Fight for the Vote," *Art History* 13, no. 1 (1990): 56.

29. Wendy Parkins, "What to Wear to a Protest March: Identity Politics and Fashion in the Suffragette Movement," *Southern Review: Literary and Interdisciplinary Essays* 28, no. 1 (1995): 75.

30. Rolley, "Fashion, Femininity," 52.

31. *VFW*, March 12, 1909, 437.

32. Joel H. Kaplan and Sheila Stowell, *Theatre and Fashion: Oscar Wilde to the Suffragettes* (Cambridge: Cambridge University Press, 1994), 173. Retailers did this not only for the WSPU but also for other suffrage societies.

33. "Whet Your Weapon!" *VFW*, June 2, 1911, 579.

34. Kaplan and Stowell, *Theatre and Fashion*, 172.

35. Kaplan and Stowell, *Theatre and Fashion*, 171.

36. Kaplan and Stowell, *Theatre and Fashion*, 180.

37. Pethick-Lawrence, "Popularizing the Colours," *VFW*, June 18, 1908, 249.

38. *VFW*, October 8, 1909, 30.

39. *VFW*, December 3, 1909, 157.

40. *VFW*, November 1907, 28. Diane Atkinson includes photographs of some of these games in *The Purple, White and Green: Suffragettes in London, 1906–14* (London: Museum of London, 1992), 30, 38, 43.

41. De Certeau, *Practice of Everyday Life*, 31.

42. De Certeau, *Practice of Everyday Life*, 38.

43. The Campaign throughout the Country, *VFW*, July 30, 1908, 350.

44. The Campaign throughout the Country, *VFW*, August 6, 1908, 366. The constitutional (i.e., moderate) NUWSS also appears to have had a handful of "committee rooms," but these do not seem to have emerged as fully elaborated shops. Tickner records that "[t]hree London branches of the NUWSS rented premises together in 1908 and filled the windows with banners and posters for the three weeks preceding the demonstration of 13 June" (Tickner, *Spectacle of Women*, 47). The militant Women's Freedom League had a few shops. Its newspaper, the *Vote*, occasionally alludes to a handful of shops in Manchester, Glasgow, and Edinburgh. The Saturday, December

10, 1910, issue of the *Vote* contains a brief profile of the Glasgow Centre, including its shop. The WFL's annual report for 1910 announces that "[s]uffrage shops have been started as propaganda centres" and mentions shops in Battersea, southwestern London, and Hackney, plus plans for another in Croydon (*Suffragette Fellowship Collection*, 13:15). After October 1912, *Votes for Women*, by then the organ of the United Suffragists, alludes to a handful of suffrage shops, but these appear to be continuations of some of the enterprises that had been founded earlier under WSPU auspices. Each of the major suffrage societies seems to have supplied regalia in their official colors from their offices or shops. At the end of the first issue (October 30, 1909) of the WFL's *Vote*, for example, an advertisement for the WFL main offices lists items for sale such as scarves, ties, badges, and brooches. Although most of the larger societies sold such regalia, and some (such as the WFL) also had some shops, the WSPU commercial enterprise seems to have been more extensive. Furthermore, no other suffrage paper seems to have duplicated the range or frequency of *Votes for Women*'s discursive investments in suffrage consumer culture in inscribing shopping and shopkeeping as an extension of militant tactics.

45. "Xmas Gifts at the W.S.P.U. Shops," *VFW*, December 10, 1909, 170.

46. Although many of the first shops sprang up in 1909, there appears to have been another surge of shop openings the following year. John Mercer attributes the 1910 growth of shops to the "committee rooms" set up by a number of branches that year in response to the general election. The WSPU used these committee rooms to campaign against the reigning Liberal Party, which had been resistant to the suffrage cause. After the election, which saw the Liberals reinstated, many of the committee rooms that had sold suffrage merchandise and printed materials before the election remained intact following it because they had been so successful. The fact that some of the shops began as committee rooms for the election inscribes their origins as political and attests to the ways in which the WSPU conducted its politics through commercial enterprise. See Mercer, "Commercial Places, Public Spaces: Suffragette Shops and the Public Sphere," *Journal of Contemporary History* 7 (2004): 3.

47. The WSPU's fourth annual report, for the year ending February 1910, includes an advertisement for the Woman's Press for that year, which lists the locations and addresses of "Branch Shops in London and Suburbs" (Chelsea, Croydon, Fulham and Putney, Hammersmith, Hampstead, Kensington, Kilburn, Lewisham, Paddington, Sydenham, Wandsworth, Wimbledon) and "Branch Shops in the Provinces" (Bath, Bexhill-on-Sea, Birmingham, Bradford, Brighton, Bristol, Dundee, Edinburgh, Glasgow, Ipswich, Leicester, Newcastle, Newport, Nottingham, Rayleigh, Reading, Redhill, Scarborough, Sheffield) (Suffragette Fellowship Collection, 13: no page).

48. *Votes for Women* also includes other accounts of how the WSPU shops approached the day-to-day management and realities of shopkeeping. Each shop was autonomous, and the decision to open a shop at all lay with the members of each local branch. Many of the shops appear to have initially paid their rent, or at least a portion of it,

by establishing a shop fund or subscription to which members were encouraged to make donations. For example, the Kensington WSPU hoped to help finance its enterprise through a portion of the guaranteed annual donations from several of its members. "Already three ladies have each guaranteed the sum of £10 per annum," wrote Kensington reporter Louise M. Eates, who went on to encourage members to make "more offers of this nature," adding that "[t]he shop should, of course, earn a certain amount of money by the sale of literature, &c" (Local Notes, *VFW,* January 14, 1909, 269). Later that year, Charlotte Blacklock made a similar appeal for members who would be willing to pay the rent for a shop to be opened at the Chelsea WSPU branch (Local Notes, *VFW,* March 19, 1909, 460). As shops were established, *Votes for Women* included regular appeals for donations of furniture and linoleum to furbish the shop interiors. Each shop was overseen by a shop secretary (who was sometimes the local branch secretary), and she was assisted by other WSPU members, who volunteered their time as shop assistants. Branch reports between 1909 and 1912 regularly include calls for such volunteers. A 1909 announcement from Lewisham is representative of these appeals: "A strong appeal is made to all members of our Union to volunteer as assistants in the shop—i.e., on one or more afternoons regularly. Mrs. Bouvier will attend to the shop every day from 10.30 till 2 or 2.30 p.m. The afternoon could be divided between two members, but they must attend regularly" (J. A. Bouvier, Local Notes, *VFW,* June 4, 1909, 764).

49. The Campaign throughout the Country, *VFW,* July 16, 1909, 954.
50. The Campaign throughout the Country, *VFW,* July 16, 1909, 954.
51. The Campaign throughout the Country, *VFW,* July 16, 1909, 954.
52. Local Notes, *VFW,* June 4, 1909, 764.
53. Fifth Annual Report, for the year ending February 1911, *Suffragette Fellowship Collection,* 13:7.
54. Evelyn Sharp was part of the local Kensington committee, which decided to open a shop in Church Street early in 1909. Sharp (1869–1955) was born in London and made her living as a writer, both in journalism and in fiction. Between 1918 and 1923, she was on the staff of the *Daily Herald,* but as early as 1903 she was writing for several other newspapers as well, including the *Manchester Guardian.* As a fiction writer, she contributed six short stories to the *Yellow Book;* her first novel, *At the Relton Arms,* was published in 1895 in John Lane's Keynote Series at the Bodley Head. Lane also published her novella, *The Making of a Schoolgirl* (1897). In all, she published about twenty-six volumes of fiction and essays throughout her life. Sharp was an active member of the WSPU and was imprisoned twice for her suffrage involvements. She was also a member of the Women Writer's Suffrage League. Sharp was among those who left the WSPU to found the United Suffragists and was also one of the founders of the Women's League for Peace and Freedom. She became the new editor of *Votes for Women* after the Pethick-Lawrences left the WSPU. In 1933 she married Henry Nevison, who had long been her companion. For more on Sharp's significance as a suffrage writer,

see Wendell Harris, "H.W. Nevison, Margaret Nevison, Evelyn Sharp: Little Known Writers and Crusaders," *English Literature in Transition* 45, no. 3 (2002): 280–305; Angela V. John, "'Behind the Locked Door': Evelyn Sharp, Suffragette and Rebel Journalist," *Women's History Review* 12, no. 1 (2003): 5–13; and Sharp's autobiography, *Unfinished Adventure: Selected Reminiscences from an Englishwoman's Life* (London: John Lane, 1933).

55. "Under the Clock," *VFW,* May 13, 1910, 533.

56. "Under the Clock," *VFW,* July 1, 1910, 651.

57. "Under the Clock," *VFW,* July 1, 1910, 651.

58. "Under the Clock," *VFW,* July 1, 1910, 651.

59. *Votes for Women* also published two features in September 1911 and October 1911 that reported on the work of shops in Croydon, Edinburgh, Scarborough, Clacton, and Bath that had opened between late 1909 and early 1911. The discussion of each shop typically opened with the date the shop opened, named the local secretary, and often commented on the successes of each shop, particularly on brisk sales of *Votes for Women* and a shop's ability to attract the attention of customers through window displays. The October piece reaffirmed the important outreach work of the shops for the WSPU: "No one can gauge the value or the extent of the propagandist work carried on from the many centres throughout the country where the magic words 'Votes for Women' are seen over an attractively dressed shop window! In the window itself are displayed VOTES FOR WOMEN . . . , books and pamphlets, brooches, scarves, and all kinds of other pretty things in the colours, photographs of the leaders of the Women's Social and Political Union, and many other attractive and saleable articles" (*VFW,* October 6, 1911, 7).

60. Local Notes, *VFW,* February 11, 1909, 342.

61. Local Notes, *VFW,* March 19, 1909, 460.

62. Evelyn Sharp, "Painting Kensington Purple, White, and Green," *VFW,* March 12, 1909, 422.

63. Sharp, "Painting Kensington Purple, White, and Green," *VFW,* March 12, 1909, 422.

64. Sharp, "Painting Kensington Purple, White, and Green," *VFW,* March 12, 1909, 422.

65. Local Notes, *VFW,* January 14, 1909, 269.

66. Local Notes, *VFW,* March 5, 1909, 414. The Bradford shop, on at least one occasion, was "devoted . . . to the subject of forcible feeding," a provocative display campaign that used the conventions of commercial display to bring attention to the mistreatment of suffragette prisoners (The Campaign throughout the Country, *VFW,* November 12, 1909, 103).

67. "Xmas Gifts at the W.S.P.U. Shops," *VFW,* December 10, 1909, 170.

68. Murray, "Deeds *and* Words," 207.

69. I use the term *suffrage fiction* much as Sowon R. Park does (see citation below) to denote fiction written with a political motivation rather than works, such as Virginia

Woolf's *Night and Day* (1919), that might peripherally represent aspects of the suffrage movement. In addition to *Rebel Women*, there are at least two other collections of stories about suffragettes that have been of recent interest to scholars of suffrage fiction. Gertrude Colemore's *Mr. Jones and the Governess and Other Stories* (1913) first appeared in a variety of periodicals before being collected and published in London by the Women's Freedom League, of which Colemore was an early member. Another collection of short fiction is Annie S. Swan's *Margaret Holroyd, or The Pioneers* (1910). Among the best known of the suffrage novels are Gertrude Colemore's *Suffragette Sally* (1911), Elizabeth Robins's *Convert* (a 1907 novelization of the play *Votes for Women!* produced at the London Court Theatre earlier that same year), and Constance Maud's *No Surrender* (1912). On suffrage fiction, see Jane Eldridge Miller, *Rebel Women: Feminism, Modernism and the Edwardian Novel* (London: Virago, 1994); Joannou and Purvis, *Women's Suffrage Movement*; Sowon R. Park, "Suffrage Fiction: A Political Discourse in the Marketplace," *English Literature in Transition* 39, no. 4 (1996): 450–61; Shirley Peterson, "The Politics of a Moral Crusade: Gertrude Colmore's *Suffragette Sally*," in *Rediscovering Forgotten Radicals: British Women Writers, 1889–1939*, ed. Angela Ingram and Daphne Patai (Chapel Hill: University of North Carolina Press, 1993), 101–17; Kabi Hartman, "'What Made Me a Suffragette': The New Woman and the New (?) Conversion Narrative," *Women's History Review* 12, no. 1 (2003): 35–50.

70. Carolyn Christensen Nelson, introduction to *Literature of the Women's Suffrage Campaign in England* (Peterborough, ON: Broadview, 2004), 293.

71. Miller, *Rebel Women*, 141.

72. Glenda Norquay, ed., *Voices and Votes: A Literary Anthology of the Women's Suffrage Campaign* (Manchester: Manchester University Press, 1995), 224.

73. One other sketch from *Rebel Women* also appeared in an earlier form as a journalistic piece in *Votes for Women*. Originally called "Between Two Boards" (*VFW*, April 9, 1909, 526), it was adapted into a fictional sketch entitled "Patrolling the Gutter." It features a group of suffragettes who briefly gather in a shop, then go out on the streets in sandwich boards to advertise an upcoming meeting.

74. Evelyn Sharp, "Votes for Women—Forward!" in *Rebel Women* (London: A. C. Fifield, 1910), 92. All references in my text are from this edition and will be referred to parenthetically.

75. De Certeau, *Practice of Everyday Life*, 30.

76. Jürgen Habermas, *The Structural Transformation of the Public Sphere: An Inquiry into a Category of Bourgeois Society*, trans. Thomas Burger (Cambridge, MA: MIT Press, 1989).

77. Photographs of shop interiors were less common. An interior of the Woman's Press shop at Charing Cross Road appeared in the September 15, 1911, issue and shows two shop assistants behind a counter and three women shoppers browsing for literature and other merchandise (792).

78. In her illuminating reading of selected photographs from the Museum of London's Suffragette Fellowship Collection, Diane Atkinson considers one photograph

of a suffrage shop, a 1910 image of the Putney and Fulham shop, with particular reference to the variety of goods displayed in the shop window. See Atkinson, "Six Suffragette Photographs," in *Women's Suffrage Movement*, ed. Joannou and Purvis, 89–100.

79. Mercer, "Commercial Places, Public Spaces," 8.

80. Eighth Annual Report, for February 1913–February 1914, in *Suffragette Fellowship Collection*, 13:10–11. The Kensington shop was among the few that continued after the decline of WSPU shops in 1913. Its activities, though scaled back such that the shop seems to have functioned more as a meeting place and office during that time, are occasionally reported on in the pages of the WSPU's new organ, *Suffragette*, until May 1914, when the war became the focus of the paper.

81. Atkinson, *Purple, White, and Green*, 48.

Afterword: Becoming Elizabeth Dalloway: The Future of Shopping

1. Virginia Woolf, *Mrs. Dalloway*, ed. Stella McNichol (London: Penguin, 1992), 3. All references in my text are to this edition and will be indicated parenthetically. In *Mrs. Dalloway*, Clarissa continuously draws the parts of herself together to produce the sense of coherence that the novel will celebrate as her triumph in its final words: "For there she was" (213). These acts of self-production occur through the punctuations of her walk as she consumes the urban spectacle from her Westminster home, from Victoria Street to St. James Park, Arlington, and Piccadilly, before reaching the flower shop in Bond Street. While Clarissa's path is knowable to an extent, the walk is not entirely reproducible. The sounds of Big Ben and the nuances of the urban "bellow and the uproar" on that day suggest a walk that is particular to "this moment of June" (4). We are not told Clarissa's origins—the exact location of her home—nor does the narrative track her return. It is through the act of walking about that Clarissa is reconciled to the contingent nature of subjectivity, to the mystery of consciousness as it forms from moment to moment: "[S]omehow in the streets of London, on the ebb and flow of things, here, there, she survived" (9). It is by wandering that Clarissa is so often struck by the contingent nature of identity: "She would not say on any one in the world now that they were this or were that. She felt very young; at the same time unspeakably aged. She sliced like a knife through everything; at the same time was outside, looking on. She had a perpetual sense, as she watched the taxi cabs, of being out, out, far out to sea and alone; she always had the feeling that it was very, very dangerous to live even one day.... [S]he would not say of herself, I am this, I am that" (8–9). Such is Clarissa's cycle of expansion and contraction, set into motion by a stream of consciousness text that is as peripatetic as she is.

2. For a well-known precedent of the urban female as *passante* or object of the male gaze, see Charles Baudelaire's 1861 poem, "À une passante" ("To a Passing Woman"), *Les fleurs du mal*, in *Oeuvres complètes*, intro. by Claude Roy, ed. Michel Jamet (Paris: Laffont, 1980). On the problematics of the female *flâneuse* and/or walking as narrative

practice in *Mrs. Dalloway* and elsewhere, see, for example, Janet Wolff, "The Invisible Flâneuse: Women and the Literature of Modernity," *Theory, Culture and Society* 2, no. 3 (1985): 37–46; Rachel Bowlby, "Walking, Women and Writing: Virginia Woolf as *Flâneuse*," in *New Feminist Discourses: Critical Essays on Theories and Texts*, ed. Isobel Armstrong (London: Routledge, 1992), 26–47; Laura Marcus, *Virginia Woolf* (Plymouth, UK: Northcote, 1997); Deborah L. Parsons, *Streetwalking the Metropolis: Women, the City, and Modernity* (Oxford: Oxford University Press, 2000); Deborah Epstein Nord, *Walking the Victorian Streets: Women, Representation, and the City* (Ithaca, NY: Cornell University Press, 1995).

3. De Certeau, *Practice of Everyday Life*, 34. Gilles Deleuze and Félix Guattari, *A Thousand Plateaus: Capitalism and Schizophrenia*, trans. with a foreword by Brian Massumi (Minneapolis: University of Minnesota Press, 1987), 361, 380.

4. Deleuze and Guattari, *Thousand Plateaus*, 373, 361, 363.

5. Deleuze and Guattari, *Thousand Plateaus*, 373, 372.

6. Elizabeth Grosz and Alice Jardine are among those feminist critics who have considered how a Deleuzian approach can usefully position female subjectivity as a form of potential or future becoming, one that might wrest female identity from the burden of cultural scripts. They point, for example, to Deleuze and Guattari's description of the "girl" as a way to imagine a form of identity that is unencumbered by a pre-history or origins. Here, it is also interesting that the name of Virginia Woolf is invoked: "The girl is not defined by virginity; she is defined by a relation of movement and rest, speed and slowness, by a combination of atoms, an emission of particles: haecceity. She never ceases to roam upon a body without organs. She is an abstract line, or a line of flight. Thus girls do not belong to an age group, sex, order, or kingdom: they slip in everywhere, between orders, acts, ages, sexes; they produce n molecular sexes on the line of flight in relation to the dualism machines they cross through. The only way to get outside the dualisms is to be-between, to pass between, the intermezzo—that is what Virginia Woolf lived with all her energies, in all of her work, never ceasing to become. The girl is like the block of becoming that remains contemporaneous to each opposable term, man, woman, child, adult" (Deleuze and Guattari, *Thousand Plateaus*, 276–77). Nevertheless, Jardine remains cautious about Deleuzian subjectivity, particularly about the way "that all becomings begin with and pass through becoming-woman" (*Thousand Plateaus*, 277). Does this, Jardine asks, deem women merely a "spatial surface necessary only for *His* metamorphosis?" See Alice Jardine, *Gynesis: Configurations of Woman and Modernity* (Ithaca, NY: Cornell University Press, 1985), 217.

7. Grosz, *Volatile Bodies*, 175.

8. Grosz, *Volatile Bodies*, 164.

9. Grosz, *Volatile Bodies*, 165.

10. Deleuze and Guattari, *Thousand Plateaus*, 399, 282.

BIBLIOGRAPHY

Abelson, Elaine S. *When Ladies Go A-Thieving: Middle-Class Shoplifters in the Victorian Department Store.* New York: Oxford University Press, 1989.

Adburgham, Alison. *Liberty's: A Biography of a Shop.* London: George Allen and Unwin, 1975.

———. *Shopping in Style: London from the Restoration to Edwardian Elegance.* London: Thames and Hudson, 1979.

———. *Shops and Shopping, 1800–1914: Where, and In What Manner the Well-Dressed Englishwoman Bought Her Clothes.* London: George Allen and Unwin, 1964.

Agnew, Jean-Christophe. "A House of Fiction: Domestic Interiors and the Commodity Aesthetic." In *Consuming Visions: Accumulation and Display of Goods in America, 1880–1920,* edited by Simon J. Bronner, 133–55. New York: Norton, 1989.

Altick, Richard D. *The Presence of the Present: Topics of the Day in the Victorian Novel.* Columbus: Ohio State University Press, 1991.

"Always Make Room for a Lady." Postcard. London: Archibald English and Edward Wise, ca. 1910.

Anderson, Benedict. *Imagined Communities: Reflections on the Origin and Spread of Nationalism.* London: Verso, 1991.

Armstrong, Nancy. *Desire and Domestic Fiction: A Political History of the Novel.* Oxford: Oxford University Press, 1987.

———. "The Occidental Alice." *differences: A Journal of Feminist Cultural Studies* 2, no. 2 (1990): 3–40.

Arnold, Matthew. "The Function of Criticism at the Present Time." In *Poetry and Criticism of Matthew Arnold,* edited by A. Dwight Culler, 237–58. Boston: Houghton Mifflin, 1961.

Arseneau, Mary, Antony H. Harrison, and Lorraine Janzen Kooistra, eds. *The Culture of Christina Rossetti: Female Poetics and Victorian Contexts.* Athens: Ohio University Press, 1999.

Atkinson, Diane. *The Purple, White and Green: Suffragettes in London, 1906–14.* London: Museum of London, 1992.

———. "Six Suffragette Photographs." In *The Women's Suffrage Movement: New Feminist Perspectives,* edited by Maroula Joannou and June Purvis, 89–100. Manchester: Manchester University Press, 1998.

Austen, Jane. *Emma*. Edited by James Kinsley, with an introduction and notes by Adela Pinch. Oxford: Oxford University Press, 2003.

Bacal, Howard A., and Kenneth M. Newman. *Theories of Object Relations: Bridges to Self Psychology*. New York: Columbia University Press, 1990.

Barker, Lady (Mary Anne). *The Bedroom and Boudoir*. London: Macmillan, 1878.

Baudelaire, Charles. *Les fleurs du mal*. In *Oeuvres complètes*. Introduction by Claude Roy, edited by Michel Jamet. Paris: Laffont, 1980.

Baudrillard, Jean. *The Mirror of Production*. Translated with an introduction by Mark Poster. St. Louis: Telos, 1975.

Beardsley, Aubrey. Cover design for the prospectus for vol. 1 (April 1894) of *The Yellow Book*. London: Bodley Head, 1894.

Beaty, Jerome. *Middlemarch from Notebook to Novel: A Study of George Eliot's Creative Method*. Urbana: University of Illinois Press, 1960.

Beer, Gillian. "Circulatory Systems: Money and Gossip in *Middlemarch*." In *Studies in George Eliot* no. 26, edited by J. C. Amalric, 47–62. Montpellier, France: Centre d'Études et de Recherches Victoriennes et Édouardiennes, 1987.

———. *George Eliot*. Brighton, UK: Harvester, 1986.

Beerbohm, Max. *Rossetti and His Circle*. London: W. Heinemann, 1922.

Beeton, Mrs. (Isabella Mary). *The Book of Household Management*. London: S.O. Beeton, 1861.

Benjamin, Walter. "Paris, Capital of the Nineteenth Century." In *Reflections: Essays, Aphorisms, Autobiographical Writings: Walter Benjamin*, edited with an introduction by Peter Demetz, translated by Edmund Jephcott, 146–62. New York: Harcourt Brace Jovanovich, 1978.

———. "The Work of Art in the Age of Mechanical Reproduction." In *Illuminations*, edited and with an introduction by Hannah Arendt, translated by Harry Zohn, 217–51. New York: Schocken, 1988.

Bennett, Tony. *The Birth of the Museum: History, Theory, Politics*. London: Routledge, 1995.

Benson, John, and Gareth Shaw, eds. *The Evolution of Retail Systems, ca. 1800–1914*. Leicester: Leicester University Press, 1992.

Benson, Susan Porter. *Counter Cultures: Saleswomen, Managers, and Customers in American Department Stores, 1890–1940*. Urbana: University of Illinois Press, 1986.

Bermingham, Ann, and John Brewer, eds. *The Consumption of Culture, 1600–1800: Image, Object, Text*. London: Routledge, 1995.

Bernstein, Susan David. "Dirty Reading: Sensation Fiction, Women, and Primitivism." *Criticism* 36, no. 2 (1994): 213–41.

Bowlby, Rachel. *Just Looking: Consumer Culture in Dreiser, Gissing, and Zola*. London: Methuen, 1985.

———. *Shopping with Freud*. London: Routledge, 1993.

———. "Walking, Women and Writing: Virginia Woolf as *Flâneuse*." In *New Feminist Discourses: Critical Essays on Theories and Texts*, edited by Isobel Armstrong, 26–47. London: Routledge, 1992.

Braddon, Mary Elizabeth. *Lady Audley's Secret.* Edited by Natalie M. Houston. Peterborough, ON: Broadview, 2003.

Brantlinger, Patrick. "Household Taste: Industrial Art, Consumerism, and Pre-Raphaelitism." *Journal of Pre-Raphaelite Studies* 9 (2000): 83–100.

Breward, Christopher. *The Hidden Consumer: Masculinities, Fashion and City Life, 1860–1914.* Manchester: Manchester University Press, 1999.

Brewer, John, and Roy Porter, eds. *Consumption and the World of Goods.* London: Routledge, 1993.

Bronner, Simon J., ed. *Consuming Visions: Accumulation and Display of Goods in America, 1880–1920.* New York: W. W. Norton, 1989.

Brontë, Charlotte. *Jane Eyre.* Edited by Richard Nemesvari. Peterborough, ON: Broadview, 1999.

Bucknill, John. "Kleptomania." *Journal of Mental Science* 8, no. 24 (1863): 262–75.

Butler, Judith. *Gender Trouble: Feminism and the Subversion of Identity.* New York: Routledge, 1990.

Camhi, Leslie. "Stealing Femininity: Department Store Kleptomania as Sexual Disorder." *differences: A Journal of Feminist Critical Studies* 5, no. 1 (1993): 26–50.

Campbell, Elizabeth. "Of Mothers and Merchants: Female Economics in Christina Rossetti's 'Goblin Market.'" *Victorian Studies* 33, no. 3 (1990): 393–410.

Carpenter, Mary Wilson. "'Eat me, drink me, love me': The Consumable Female Body in Christina Rossetti's *Goblin Market.*" *Victorian Poetry* 29, no. 4 (1991): 415–34.

Carroll, David. Introduction to *Middlemarch,* by George Eliot, edited by David Carroll, xiii–lxxxv. Oxford: Clarendon, 1986

Cassell's Household Guide: Being a Complete Encyclopedia of Domestic and Social Economy. London: Cassell, Petter, and Galpin, 1869.

Chaudhuri, Nupur. "Shawls, Jewelry, Curry, and Rice in Victorian Britain." In *Western Women and Imperialism: Complicity and Resistance,* edited by Nupur Chaudhuri and Margaret Strobel, 231–46. Bloomington: Indiana University Press, 1992.

Cobbett, Anne. *The English Housekeeper; or, Manual of Domestic Management, the Whole Being Intended for the Use of Young Ladies Who Undertake the Superintendence of Their Own Housekeeping.* London: W. J. Sears, 1835.

Cole, Henry. *Miscellanies.* London: Richard Bentley and Sons, 1875.

Courtney, W. L. (William Leonard). "The Soul of a Suffragette." In *Literature of the Women's Suffrage Campaign in England,* edited by Carolyn Christensen Nelson. Peterborough, ON: Broadview, 2004.

Crossick, Geoffrey, and Serge Jaumain, eds. *Cathedrals of Consumption: The European Department Store, 1850–1939.* Aldershot, UK: Ashgate, 1999.

Cvetkovich, Ann. *Mixed Feelings: Feminism, Mass Culture, and Victorian Sensationalism.* New Brunswick, NJ: Rutgers University Press, 1992.

Dale, Tim. *Harrods: The Store and the Legend.* London: Pan Books, 1981.

Dallas, Eneas Sweetland. "*Lady Audley's Secret.*" *Times*, November 18, 1862, 4.

Davis, Dorothy. *Fairs, Shops, and Supermarkets: A History of English Shopping.* Toronto: University of Toronto Press, 1966.

Debord, Guy. *Society of the Spectacle.* Revised edition. Detroit: Black and Red, 1977.

De Certeau, Michel. *The Practice of Everyday Life.* Translated by Steven Rendall. Berkeley: University of California Press, 1984.

De Grazia, Victoria, ed. *The Sex of Things: Gender and Consumption in Historical Perspective.* Berkeley: University of California Press, 1996.

Deleuze, Gilles, and Félix Guattari. *A Thousand Plateaus: Capitalism and Schizophrenia.* Translated with a foreword by Brian Massumi. Minneapolis: University of Minnesota Press, 1987.

Derry and Toms hat advertisement. *Votes for Women*, June 9, 1911, 604.

DiCenzo, Maria. "Gutter Politics: Women Newsies and the Suffrage Press." *Women's History Review* 12, no. 1 (2003): 15–33.

Doane, Mary Ann. "Film and the Masquerade: Theorizing the Female Spectator." *Screen* 23, nos. 3–4 (1982): 74–87.

Dolin, Tim. *Mistress of the House: Women of Property in the Victorian Novel.* Aldershot, UK: Ashgate, 1997.

Donoghue, Emma. *We Are Michael Field.* Bath, UK: Absolute, 1998.

Eastern Antiquities Catalogue. London: Liberty, 1897–1900.

Eastlake, Charles. *Hints on Household Taste.* London: Longmans, Green, 1872.

Ehnenn, Jill. "Looking Strategically: Feminist and Queer Aesthetics in Michael Field's *Sight and Song.*" *Victorian Poetry* 42, no. 3 (2004): 213–59.

Eliot, George. *The George Eliot Letters.* Edited by Gordon S. Haight. 9 vols. New Haven, CT: Yale University Press, 1954–78.

———. *Middlemarch.* Edited by W. J. Harvey. London: Penguin, 1985.

———. "Silly Novels by Lady Novelists." *Westminster Review* 66 (July 1856): 442–61.

Elliot, Bridget. "New and Not So 'New Women' on the London Stage: Aubrey Beardsley's *Yellow Book* Images of Mrs Patrick Campbell and Réjane." *Victorian Studies* 31, no. 1 (1987): 33–57.

Ellis, Sarah Stickney. *The Women of England: Their Social Duties and Domestic Habits.* London: Fisher, Son, 1839.

Etiquette for Ladies and Gentlemen. London: Frederick Warne, 1876.

Etiquette for the Ladies: Eighty Maxims on Dress, Manners, and Accomplishments. London: Charles Tilt, 1837.

Eustance, Claire, Joan Ryan, and Laura Ugolini, eds. *A Suffrage Reader: Charting Directions in British Suffrage History.* London: Leicester University Press, 2000.

Everts, Orpheus. "Are Dipsomania, Kleptomania, Pyromania, etc., Valid Forms of Mental Disease?" *American Journal of Insanity* 44 (July 1887): 52–59.

Family Exchequer Book, or, Housekeeping and General Expenditure Book, The. London: Hector M'Lean, 1839.

Felski, Rita. *The Gender of Modernity*. Cambridge, MA: Harvard University Press, 1995.
Feltes, N. N. *Modes of Production of Victorian Novels*. Chicago: University of Chicago Press, 1986.
Ferry, John William. *A History of the Department Store*. New York: Macmillan, 1960.
Field, Michael. *Sight and Song*. London: Elkin Mathews and John Lane, 1892.
———. *Works and Days: From the Journal of Michael Field*. Edited by T. Sturge Moore and D. C. Sturge Moore, with an introduction by Sir William Rothenstein. London: John Murray, 1933.
Finn, Margot. "Women, Consumption and Coverture in England, c. 1760–1860." *Historical Journal* 39, no. 3 (1996): 703–22.
Fisk, May Isabel. "A Woman in a Shoe Shop." In *The Monologue Series* no. 39, 5–8. New York: Harper and Bros., 1903.
Fiske, John. "The Culture of Everyday Life." In *Cultural Studies*, edited by Lawrence Grossberg, Cary Nelson, and Paula Treichler, 154–73. New York: Routledge, 1992.
Foucault, Michel. *Discipline and Punish: The Birth of the Prison*. Translated by Alan Sheridan. New York: Pantheon, 1977.
———. *The Foucault Reader*. Edited by Paul Rabinow. New York: Pantheon, 1984.
Fox, Richard Wightman, and T. J. Jackson Lears, eds. *The Culture of Consumption: Critical Essays in American History, 1880–1980*. New York: Pantheon, 1983.
Frankel, Nicholas. "The Concrete Poetics of Michael Field's *Sight and Song*." In *Michael Field and Their World*, edited by Margaret D. Stetz and Cheryl A. Wilson, 211–21. High Wycombe, UK: Rivendale, 2007.
Franklin, J. Jeffrey. "The Victorian Discourse of Gambling: Speculations on *Middlemarch* and *The Duke's Children*." *ELH: English Literary History* 61, no. 4 (1994): 899–921.
Fraser, Hilary. "A Visual Field: Michael Field and the Gaze." *Victorian Literature and Culture* 34, no. 2 (2006): 553–71.
Fraser, W. Hamish. *The Coming of the Mass Market, 1850–1914*. Hamden, CT: Archon, 1981.
Freedman, Jonathan. *Professions of Taste: Henry James, British Aestheticism, and Commodity Culture*. Stanford: Stanford University Press, 1990.
Friedberg, Anne. *Window Shopping: Cinema and the Postmodern*. Berkeley: University of California Press, 1993.
Fulford, Roger. *Votes for Women: The Story of a Struggle*. London: Faber and Faber, 1957.
Gagnier, Regenia. *Idylls of the Marketplace: Oscar Wilde and the Victorian Public*. Stanford: Stanford University Press, 1986.
———. "Production, Reproduction, and Pleasure in Victorian Aesthetics and Economics." In *Victorian Sexual Dissidence*, edited by Richard Dellamora, 127–46. Chicago: University of Chicago Press, 1999.
———. "Productive Bodies, Pleasured Bodies: On Victorian Aesthetics." In *Women and British Aestheticism*, edited by Talia Schaffer and Kathy Alexis Psomiades, 270–89. Charlottesville: University Press of Virginia, 1999.

Gardner, Carl, and Julie Sheppard. *Consuming Passion: The Rise of Retail Culture.* London: Unwin and Hyman, 1989.

Garvey, Ellen Gruber. *The Adman in the Parlour: Magazines and the Gendering of Consumer Culture, 1880s to 1910s.* New York: Oxford University Press, 1996.

Gilbert, Pamela K. *Disease, Desire, and the Body in Victorian Women's Popular Novels.* Cambridge: Cambridge University Press, 1997.

Gilbert, Sandra M., and Susan Gubar. *The Madwoman in the Attic: The Woman Writer and the Nineteenth-Century Literary Imagination.* New Haven, CT: Yale University Press, 1979.

Goddard, Henry. *Memoirs of a Bow Street Runner.* London: Museum Press, 1956.

Grahame, Kenneth. "Non Libri Sed Liberti." In *Pagan Papers,* 31–39. London: John Lane, 1898.

Green, Barbara. *Spectacular Confessions: Autobiography, Performative Activism, and the Sites of Suffrage, 1905–1938.* New York: St. Martin's, 1997.

Griest, Guinivere L. *Mudie's Circulating Library and the Victorian Novel.* Bloomington: Indiana University Press, 1970.

Grosz, Elizabeth. *Volatile Bodies: Toward a Corporeal Feminism.* Bloomington: Indiana University Press, 1994.

Habermas, Jürgen. *The Structural Transformation of the Public Sphere: An Inquiry into a Category of Bourgeois Society.* Translated by Thomas Burger with the assistance of Frederick Lawrence. Cambridge, MA: MIT Press, 1989.

Harris, Wendell. "H. W. Nevison, Margaret Nevison, Evelyn Sharp: Little Known Writers and Crusaders." *English Literature in Transition* 45, no. 3 (2002): 280–305.

Hartman, Kabi. "'What Made Me a Suffragette': The New Woman and the New (?) Conversion Narrative." *Women's History Review* 12, no. 1 (2003): 35–50.

Haweis, Mrs. H. R. (Mary Eliza). *The Art of Decoration.* London: Chatto and Windus, 1881.

Helsinger, Elizabeth K. "Consumer Power and the Utopia of Desire: Christina Rossetti's 'Goblin Market.'" *ELH: English Literary History* 58, no. 4 (1991): 903–33.

Holcombe, Lee. *Wives and Property: Reform of the Married Women's Property Law in Nineteenth-Century England.* Toronto: University of Toronto Press, 1983.

Holt, Terrence. "'Men sell not such in any town': Exchange in *Goblin Market.*" *Victorian Poetry* 28, no. 1 (1990): 51–67.

Holton, Sandra Stanley. *Feminism and Democracy: Women's Suffrage and Reform Politics in Britain, 1900–1918.* Cambridge: Cambridge University Press, 1987.

Honeycombe, Gordon. *Selfridges, Seventy-Five Years: The Story of the Store, 1909–1984.* London: Park Lane, 1984.

Hughes, Clair. *Dressed in Fiction.* Oxford: Berg, 2006.

Hughes, Winifred. *The Maniac in the Cellar: Sensation Novels of the 1860s.* Princeton, NJ: Princeton University Press, 1980.

Irigaray, Luce. "Commodities among Themselves." In *This Sex Which Is Not One,* translated by Catherine Porter with Carolyn Burke, 192–97. Ithaca, NY: Cornell University Press, 1985.

Jardine, Alice. *Gynesis: Configurations of Woman and Modernity.* Ithaca, NY: Cornell University Press, 1985.
Jeune, Lady M. "The Ethics of Shopping." *Fortnightly Review* 57 (January 1895): 123–32.
Jewry, Mary. *Warne's Model Cookery and Housekeeping Book: A New Edition.* London: Frederick Warne, 1871.
Joannou, Maroula, and June Purvis, eds. *The Women's Suffrage Movement: New Feminist Perspectives.* Manchester: Manchester University Press, 1998.
John, Angela V. "'Behind the Locked Door': Evelyn Sharp, Suffragette and Rebel Journalist." *Women's History Review* 12, no. 1 (2003): 5–13.
Kaplan, Joel H., and Sheila Stowell. *Theatre and Fashion: Oscar Wilde to the Suffragettes.* Cambridge: Cambridge University Press, 1994.
Kaplan, Louise J. *Female Perversions: The Temptations of Emma Bovary.* New York: Doubleday, 1991.
Karl, Frederick R. *George Eliot, Voice of a Century: A Biography.* New York: Norton, 1995.
Kipling, Rudyard. *From Sea to Sea: Letters of Travel, Part 1.* In vol. 15 of *The Writings in Prose and Verse of Rudyard Kipling.* New York: Charles Scribner's Sons, 1899.
Kowaleski-Wallace, Elizabeth. *Consuming Subjects: Women, Shopping, and Business in the Eighteenth Century.* New York: Columbia University Press, 1997.
Lacan, Jacques. "God and the Jouissance of T̶h̶e̶ Woman." In *Feminine Sexuality: Jacques Lacan and the Ecole Freudienne,* edited by Juliet Mitchell and Jacqueline Rose, translated by Jacqueline Rose, 137–48. New York: W. W. Norton, 1982.
———. "A Love Letter." In *Feminine Sexuality: Jacques Lacan and the Ecole Freudienne,* edited by Juliet Mitchell and Jacqueline Rose, translated by Jacqueline Rose, 149–61. New York: W. W. Norton, 1982.
Ladies Gazette of Fashion, Fashion and Gossip in Paris, April 1880, 85.
———, Fashion in London, January 1880, 33; April 1879, 100.
———, Fashion News, December 1879, 329.
Laermans, Rudi. "Learning to Consume: Early Department Stores and the Shaping of Modern Consumer Culture (1860–1914)." *Theory, Culture and Society* 10, no. 4 (1993): 79–102.
Laird, Holly. "Contradictory Legacies: Michael Field and Feminist Restoration." *Victorian Poetry* 33, no. 1 (1995): 111–28.
Lancaster, William. *The Department Store: A Social History.* London: Leicester University Press, 1995.
Langland, Elizabeth. *Nobody's Angels: Middle-Class Women and Domestic Ideology in Victorian Culture.* Ithaca, NY: Cornell University Press, 1995.
Law Times, "Kleptomania," November 14, 1896, 28.
Ledger, Sally. "Wilde Women and *The Yellow Book:* The Sexual Politics of Aestheticism and Decadence." *English Literature in Transition* 50, no. 1 (2007): 5–26.
Leighton, Angela. *Victorian Women Poets: Writing against the Heart.* New York: Harvester Wheatsheaf, 1992.

Leisure Hour, "Shopping without Money," February 18, 1865, 110–12.

Lester, V. Markham. *Victorian Insolvency: Bankruptcy, Imprisonment for Debt, and Company Winding-up in Nineteenth-Century England.* Oxford: Clarendon, 1995.

Lewes, George Henry. "Of Vision in Art." In *The Principles of Success in Literature*, edited with introduction and notes by Fred N. Scott, 57–85. Boston: Allyn and Bacon, 1891.

Lewis, Reina. *Gendering Orientalism: Race, Femininity and Representation.* London: Routledge, 1996.

Liberty advertisement. London: Liberty, ca. 1880.

Liberty Carpet Catalogue. London: Liberty, 1887.

Liberty Handbook of Sketches. London: Liberty, 1889.

Liddington, Jill, and Jill Norris. *One Hand Tied behind Us: The Rise of the Women's Suffrage Movement.* London: Virago, 1985.

Lindner, Christoph. *Fictions of Commodity Culture: From the Victorian to the Postmodern.* Aldershot, UK: Ashgate, 2003.

Linton, Eliza Lynn. "The Girl of the Period." *Saturday Review*, March 14, 1868, 339–41.

———. "Little Women." *Saturday Review*, April 25, 1868, 545–47.

———. "Out Walking." *Temple Bar* 5 (July 1862): 132–39.

———. "The Philosophy of Shopping." *Saturday Review*, October 10, 1875, 488–89.

Loeb, Lori Anne. *Consuming Angels: Advertising and Victorian Women.* New York: Oxford University Press, 1994.

Logan, Thad. *The Victorian Parlour: A Cultural Study.* Cambridge: Cambridge University Press, 2001.

Mansel, Henry. "Sensation Novels." *Quarterly Review* 113 (1863): 481–514.

Marcus, Jane. "The Asylums of Antaeus: Women, War, and Madness—Is There a Feminist Fetishism?" In *The New Historicism*, edited by H. Aram Veeser, 132–51. New York: Routledge, 1989.

———, ed. *Suffrage and the Pankhursts.* London: Routledge and Kegan Paul, 1987.

Marcus, Laura. *Virginia Woolf.* Plymouth, UK: Northcote, 1997.

Marlow, Joyce, ed. *Votes for Women: The Virago Book of Suffragettes.* London: Virago, 2000.

Martin, Carol A. *George Eliot's Serial Fiction.* Columbus: Ohio State University Press, 1994.

Marx, Karl. *Capital: A Critique of Political Economy.* Translated by Ben Fowkes, with an introduction by Ernest Mandel. 3 vols. London: Penguin, 1990.

Matus, Jill L. *Unstable Bodies: Victorian Representations of Sexuality and Maternity.* Manchester: Manchester University Press, 1995.

Mayhall, Laura E. Nym. *The Militant Suffrage Movement: Citizenship and Resistance in Britain, 1860–1930.* Oxford: Oxford University Press, 2003.

Mayhew, Henry. *London Labour and the London Poor.* 4 vols. New York: Dover, 1968.

McClintock, Anne. *Imperial Leather: Race, Gender and Sexuality in the Colonial Conquest.* New York: Routledge, 1995.

McCracken, Grant. *Culture and Consumption: New Approaches to the Symbolic Character of Consumer Goods and Activities.* Bloomington: Indiana University Press, 1988.

McKendrick, Neil, John Brewer, and John H. Plumb. *The Birth of a Consumer Society: The Commercialization of Eighteenth-Century England.* Bloomington: Indiana University Press, 1982.

Menke, Richard. "The Political Economy of Fruit: *Goblin Market.*" In *The Culture of Christina Rossetti: Female Poetics and Victorian Contexts*, edited by Mary Arseneau, Antony H. Harrison, and Lorraine Janzen Kooistra, 105–36. Athens: Ohio University Press, 1999.

Mercer, John. "Commercial Places, Public Spaces: Suffragette Shops and the Public Sphere." *Journal of Contemporary History* 7 (2004): 1–10.

Michie, Helena. *Sororophobia: Differences among Women in Literature and Culture.* New York: Oxford University Press, 1992.

Miller, Andrew H. *Novels Behind Glass: Commodity Culture and Victorian Narrative.* Cambridge: Cambridge University Press, 1995.

Miller, D. A. "*Cage aux folles:* Sensation and Gender in Wilkie Collins's *The Woman in White.*" In *The Making of the Modern Body: Sexuality and Society in the Nineteenth Century*, edited by Catherine Gallagher and Thomas Laqueur, 107–36. Berkeley: University of California Press, 1987.

Miller, Jane Elridge. *Rebel Women: Feminism, Modernism and the Edwardian Novel.* London: Virago, 1994.

Miller, Michael B. *The Bon Marché: Bourgeois Culture and the Department Store, 1869–1920.* Princeton, NJ: Princeton University Press, 1981.

Milligan, Barry. *Pleasures and Pains: Opium and the Orient in Nineteenth-Century British Culture.* Charlottesville: University Press of Virginia, 1995.

Mitchell, S. Weir. "Nervous Disorders (Especially Kleptomania) in Women and Pelvic Disease." *American Journal of Insanity* 53 (April 1897): 605–6.

Mitchell, Timothy. "Orientalism and Exhibitionary Order." In *Colonialism and Culture*, edited by Nicholas B. Dirks, 289–317. Ann Arbor: University of Michigan Press, 1992.

Moers, Ellen. *Literary Women.* Garden City, NY: Doubleday, 1976.

Montwieler, Katherine. "Marketing Sensation: *Lady Audley's Secret* and Consumer Culture." In *Beyond Sensation: Mary Elizabeth Braddon in Context*, edited by Marlene Tromp, Pamela K. Gilbert, and Aeron Haynie, 43–61. Albany: State University of New York, 2000.

Moore, T. Sturge, and D. C. Sturge Moore. Editors' preface to Michael Field, *Works and Days: From the Journal of Michael Field.* London: John Murray, 1933.

Mui, Hoh-Cheung, and Lorna H. Mui. *Shops and Shopkeeping in Eighteenth-Century England.* Kingston, ON: McGill-Queen's University Press, 1989.

Muir, Percy H. *Minding My Own Business: An Autobiography.* London: Chatto and Windus, 1956.

Mulvey, Laura. "Visual Pleasure and Narrative Cinema." *Screen* 16, no. 3 (1975): 6–18.

Murray, Simone. "'Deeds *and* Words': The Woman's Press and the Politics of Print." *Women: A Cultural Review* 11, no. 3 (2000): 197–222.

Nead, Lynda. "Shopping and Seduction." *Tate* 18 (1999): 54–58.

———. *Victorian Babylon: People, Streets, and Images in Nineteenth-Century London.* New Haven, CT: Yale University Press, 2000.

Nelson, Carolyn Christensen, ed. *Literature of the Women's Suffrage Campaign in England.* Peterborough, ON: Broadview, 2004.

Nelson, James G. "The Bodley Head." In *The 1890s: An Encyclopedia of British Literature, Art, and Culture,* edited by G. A. Cevasco, 67–69. New York: Garland, 1993.

———. *A Checklist of Early Bodley Head Books: 1889–1894.* Revised and enlarged. High Wycombe, UK: Rivendale, 1999.

———. *The Early Nineties: A View from the Bodley Head.* Cambridge, MA: Harvard University Press, 1971.

———. *Elkin Mathews: Publisher to Yeats, Joyce, Pound.* Madison: University of Wisconsin Press, 1989.

Nemesvari, Richard. "Robert Audley's Secret: Male Homosocial Desire in *Lady Audley's Secret.*" *Studies in the Novel* 27, no. 4 (1995): 515–28.

Nord, Deborah Epstein. *Walking the Victorian Streets: Women, Representation, and the City.* Ithaca, NY: Cornell University Press, 1995.

Norquay, Glenda, ed. *Voices and Votes: A Literary Anthology of the Women's Suffrage Campaign.* Manchester: Manchester University Press, 1995.

Nunokawa, Jeff. *The Afterlife of Property: Domestic Security and the Victorian Novel.* Princeton, NJ: Princeton University Press, 1994.

N. W. London Union Shop in Kilburn. *Votes for Women,* August 19, 1910, 769.

O'Brien, Patricia. "The Kleptomania Diagnosis: Bourgeois Women and Theft in Late Nineteenth-Century France." *Journal of Social History* 17, no. 1 (Fall 1983): 65–77.

"Observations on Credit." *Pamphleteer* 13 (1819): 360–67.

Oliphant, Margaret. "Sensation Novels." *Blackwoods* 91 (May 1862): 564–84.

Olivia's Shopping and How She Does It: A Prejudiced Guide to the London Shops. Illustrated by Elsa Hahn. London: Gay and Bird, 1906.

"Our Female Sensation Novelists." *Christian Remembrancer* 46 (1863): 209–11, 230–34.

Pank-A-Squith advertisement. *Votes for Women,* October 8, 1909, 30.

Pankhurst, Christabel. "The Political Importance of the Colours." *Votes for Women,* May 7, 1909, 632.

Pankhurst, Emmeline. *My Own Story.* New York: Hearst's International Library, 1914.

Panko advertisement. *Votes for Women,* December 3, 1909, 157.

Park, Sowon R. "Suffrage Fiction: A Political Discourse in the Marketplace." *English Literature in Transition* 39, no. 4 (1996): 450–61.

Parkins, Wendy. "What to Wear to a Protest March: Identity Politics and Fashion in the Suffragette Movement." *Southern Review: Literary and Interdisciplinary Essays* 28, no. 1 (1995): 69–82.

Parsons, Deborah L. *Streetwalking the Metropolis: Women, the City, and Modernity.* Oxford: Oxford University Press, 2000.

Partridge, Bernard. "The Shrieking Sister." *Punch,* January 17, 1907, 39.

Pater, Walter. "Prosper Mérimée." In *Miscellaneous Studies,* 1–25. London: Macmillan, 1899.

———. *The Renaissance: Studies in Art and Poetry: The 1893 Text.* Edited by Donald L. Hill. Berkeley: University of California Press, 1980.

Peterson, Shirley. "The Politics of a Moral Crusade: Gertrude Colmore's *Suffragette Sally.*" In *Rediscovering Forgotten Radicals: British Women Writers, 1889–1939,* edited by Angela Ingram and Daphne Patai, 101–17. Chapel Hill: University of North Carolina Press, 1993.

Pethick-Lawrence, Emmeline. "Popularizing the Colours." *Votes for Women,* July 18, 1908, 249.

Phegley, Jennifer. *Educating the Proper Woman Reader: Victorian Family Literary Magazines and the Cultural Health of the Nation.* Columbus: Ohio State University Press, 2004.

Pinch, Adela. "Stealing Happiness: Shoplifting in Early Nineteenth-Century England." In *Border Fetishisms: Material Objects in Unstable Spaces,* edited by Patricia Spyer, 122–49. New York: Routledge, 1998.

Poovey, Mary. *Uneven Developments: The Ideological Work of Gender in Mid-Victorian England.* Chicago: University of Chicago Press, 1988.

Prins, Yopie. *Victorian Sappho.* Princeton, NJ: Princeton University Press, 1999.

Psomiades, Kathy Alexis. *Beauty's Body: Femininity and Representation in British Aestheticism.* Stanford: Stanford University Press, 1997.

Publisher's Circle, "Announcement for the Season," March 5, 1892, 271.

Purvis, June. "'Deeds, not words': Daily Life in the Women's Social and Political Union in Edwardian Britain." In *Votes for Women,* edited by June Purvis and Sandra Stanley Holton, 135–58. London: Routledge, 2000.

———, and Sandra Stanley Holton, eds. *Votes for Women.* London: Routledge, 2000.

Pykett, Lyn. *The "Improper" Feminine: The Women's Sensation Novel and the New Woman Writing.* London: Routledge, 1992.

———. *The Sensation Novel: From "The Woman in White" to "The Moonstone."* Plymouth, UK: Northcote House in association with the British Council, 1994.

Queen, "The Boudoir," June 6, 1863, 269–70.

———, "Business Habits," October 12, 1889, 506.

———, "Shopping," April 2, 1892, 520.

Rappaport, Erika Diane. "'The Halls of Temptation': Gender, Politics, and the Construction of the Department Store in Late Victorian London." *Journal of British Studies* 35, no. 1 (1996): 58–83.

———. *Shopping for Pleasure: Women in the Making of London's West End.* Princeton, NJ: Princeton University Press, 2000.

Reynolds, Kimberley, and Nicola Humble. *Victorian Heroines: Representations of Femininity in Nineteenth-Century Literature and Art.* New York: New York University Press, 1993.

Richards, Thomas. *The Commodity Culture of Victorian England: Advertising and Spectacle, 1851–1914.* Stanford: Stanford University Press, 1990.

Rivers, Bronwyn. *Women at Work in the Victorian Novel: The Question of Middle-Class Women's Employment, 1840–1870.* Lewiston, NY: Edwin Mellen, 2005.

Rivière, Joan. "Womanliness as Masquerade." In *Formations of Fantasy,* edited by Victor Burgin, James Donald, and Cora Kaplan, 35–44. London: Methuen, 1986.

Rolley, Katrina. "Fashion, Femininity and the Fight for the Vote." *Art History* 13, no. 1 (1990): 45–71.

Rosen, Andrew. *Rise Up Women! The Militant Campaign of the Women's Social and Political Union, 1903–1914.* London: Routledge and Kegan Paul, 1974.

Ross, Adrian, and Percy Greenbank. *Our Miss Gibbs.* London: Chappell, 1909.

Rossetti, Christina. "Goblin Market." In *The Complete Poems of Christina Rossetti: A Variorum Edition,* edited by R. W. Crump, 1:11–26. Baton Rouge: Louisiana State University Press, 1979.

———. *The Letters of Christina Rossetti.* Edited by Antony H. Harrison. 4 vols. Charlottesville: University Press of Virginia, 1997.

Rossetti, Dante Gabriel. *Letters of Dante Gabriel Rossetti.* Edited by Oswald Doughty and John Robert Wahl. 4 vols. Oxford: Clarendon, 1967.

Ruskin, John. "The Nature of Gothic." In *The Stones of Venice,* vol. 2; *The Works of John Ruskin,* edited by E. T. Cook and Alexander Wedderburn, 10:180–269. London: George Allen, 1904.

———. *Unto This Last.* In *The Works of John Ruskin,* edited by E. T. Cook and Alexander Wedderburn, 17:25–114. London: George Allen, 1905.

Said, Edward. *Orientalism.* New York: Vintage, 1979.

Saisselin, Remy. *The Bourgeois and the Bibelot.* New Brunswick, NJ: Rutgers University Press, 1984.

Sala, George Augustus. *Twice Round the Clock, or the Hours of the Day and Night in London.* New York: Leicester University Press, 1971.

Sanders, Lisa Shapiro. *Consuming Fantasies: Labor, Leisure, and the London Shopgirl, 1880–1920.* Columbus: Ohio State University Press, 2006.

Saville, Julia F. "The Poetic Imaging of Michael Field." In *The Fin-de-Siècle Poem: English Literary Culture of the 1890s,* edited by Joseph Bristow, 178–206. Athens: Ohio University Press, 2005.

Schaffer, Talia. *The Forgotten Female Aesthetes: Literary Culture in Late-Victorian England.* Charlottesville: University Press of Virginia, 2000.

———, and Kathy Alexis Psomiades, eds. *Women and British Aestheticism.* Charlottesville: University Press of Virginia, 1999.

Scholz, Susanne, and Martina Strange. "Framed Subjects—Displayed Objects: Mantelpiece Decoration in Nineteenth-Century English Literature." *Journal for the Study of British Cultures* 8, no. 2 (2001): 157–74.

Schor, Naomi. *Reading in Detail: Aesthetics and the Feminine.* New York: Methuen, 1987.

Selfridge's advertisement. *Votes for Women*, March 18, 1910, 398.

Shannon, Brent. *The Cut of His Coat: Men, Dress, and Consumer Culture in Britain, 1860–1914.* Athens: Ohio University Press, 2006.

———. "ReFashioning Men: Fashion, Masculinity, and the Cultivation of the Male Consumer in Britain, 1860–1914." *Victorian Studies* 46, no. 4 (2004): 597–630.

Sharp, Evelyn. *At the Relton Arms.* London: John Lane, 1895.

———. *The Making of a Schoolgirl.* London: John Lane, 1897.

———. "Painting Kensington Purple, White, and Green." *Votes for Women*, March 12, 1909, 422.

———. *Rebel Women.* London: A. C. Fifield, 1910.

———. *Unfinished Adventure: Selected Reminiscences from an Englishwoman's Life.* London: John Lane, 1933.

"Shopping in London." *Living Age* 4 (June 1844): 250–52.

Shuttleworth, Sally. "'Preaching to the Nerves': Psychological Disorder in Sensation Fiction." In *A Question of Identity: Women, Science, and Literature*, edited by Marina Benjamin, 192–222. New Brunswick, NJ: Rutgers University Press, 1993.

Smiles, Samuel. *Thrift.* New York: Harper, 1875.

Smith, Angela K. "The Pankhursts and the War: Suffrage Magazines and First World War Propaganda." *Women's History Review* 12, no. 1 (2003): 103–18.

Stern, Rebecca F. "'Adulterations Detected': Food and Fraud in Christina Rossetti's 'Goblin Market.'" *Nineteenth-Century Literature* 57, no. 4 (2003): 477–511.

Stetson, Dorothy M. *A Woman's Issue: The Politics of Family Law Reform in England.* Westport, CT: Greenwood, 1982.

Stetz, Margaret Diane. "Sex, Lies, and Printed Cloth: Bookselling at the Bodley Head in the Eighteen-Nineties." *Victorian Studies* 35, no. 1 (1991): 71–86.

———, and Mark Samuels Lasner, eds. *England in the 1890s: Literary Publishing at the Bodley Head.* Washington, DC: Georgetown University Press, 1990.

Sturgeon, Mary. *Michael Field.* London: George G. Harrap, 1922.

Suffragette Fellowship Collection from the Museum of London, The. Reel 13. Brighton, UK: Harvester Microform, 1985.

Tennyson, Alfred. *In Memoriam A. H. H.* In *The Poems of Tennyson in Three Volumes*, edited by Christopher Ricks, 2nd ed., 2:315–458. Harlow: Longman, 1987.

Tickner, Lisa. *The Spectacle of Women: Imagery of the Suffrage Campaign, 1907–14.* Chicago: University of Chicago Press, 1988.

Times, "The Case of Ramsbotham," April 12, 1855, 10.

Tucker, Herbert F. "Rossetti's Goblin Marketing: Sweet to Tongue and Sound to Eye." *Representations* 82, no. 1 (2003): 117–33.

Under the Clock. *Votes for Women*, May 13, 1910, 533.

———. *Votes for Women*, July 1, 1910, 651.

Vadillo, Ana Parejo. "Sight and Song: Transparent Translations and a Manifesto for the Observer." *Victorian Poetry* 38, no. 1 (2000): 15–34.

———. *Women Poets and Urban Aestheticism: Passengers of Modernity.* Houndmills, UK: Palgrave, 2005.
Valverde, Marianna. "The Love of Finery: Fashion and the Fallen Woman in Nineteenth-Century Social Discourse." *Victorian Studies* 32, no. 2 (1989): 168–88.
"Votes for Women" shopping directory. *Votes for Women*, April 8, 1910, 435.
Walkowitz, Judith R. *City of Dreadful Delight: Narratives of Sexual Danger in Late-Victorian London.* Chicago: University of Chicago Press, 1992.
———. "Going Public: Shopping, Street Harassment, and Streetwalking in Late Victorian London." *Representations* 62 (1998): 1–30.
Walsh, J. H. *A Manual of Domestic Economy: Suited to Families Spending from £100 to £1000 a Year.* London: G. Routledge, 1856.
Warren, Mrs. (Eliza). *How I Managed My House on Two Hundred Pounds a Year.* London: Houlston and Wright, 1864.
Weiss, Barbara. *The Hell of the English: Bankruptcy and the Victorian Novel.* Lewisburg, PA: Bucknell University Press, 1986.
"Whet Your Weapon!" *Votes for Women*, June 2, 1911, 579.
White, Chris. "Flesh and Roses: Michael Field's Metaphors of Pleasure and Desire." *Women's Writing* 3, no. 1 (1996): 47–62.
———. "'Poets and Lovers Evermore': Interpreting Female Love in the Poetry and Journals of Michael Field." *Textual Practice* 4, no. 2 (1990): 197–212.
Whitlock, Tammy C. *Crime, Gender and Consumer Culture in Nineteenth Century England.* Aldershot, UK: Ashgate, 2005.
Wise, Thomas James, and John Alexander Symington, eds. *The Brontës: Their Lives, Friendships and Correspondence.* 4 vols. Oxford: Blackwell, 1980.
Wolff, Janet. "The Invisible Flâneuse: Women and the Literature of Modernity." *Theory, Culture and Society* 2, no. 3 (1985): 37–46.
Wood, Jane. *Passion and Pathology in Victorian Fiction.* Oxford: Oxford University Press, 2001.
Woolf, Virginia. *Mrs. Dalloway.* Edited by Stella McNichol, with an introduction and notes by Elaine Showalter. London: Penguin, 1992.
Wright, Julia McNair. *The Complete Home: An Encyclopedia of Domestic Life and Affairs.* Philadelphia: Bradley, Garretson, 1879.
Wynne, Deborah. *The Sensation Novel and the Victorian Family Magazine.* Houndmills, UK: Palgrave, 2001.
Zonana, Joyce. "The Sultan and the Slave: Feminist Orientalism and the Structure of *Jane Eyre.*" In *Revising the Word and the World: Essays in Feminist Literary Criticism,* edited by Vévé A. Clark, Ruth-Ellen B. Joeres, and Madelon Sprengnether, 592–617. Chicago: University of Chicago Press, 1993.

INDEX

A.B.C. restaurants, 20
Abelson, Elaine S., 53, 55
Academy, 116, 119
Adburgham, Alison, 187n21
Addington, John, 112
advertisements, 13, 18, 24, 25, 30–33, 35, 37, 41, 66, 116, 117, 146, 147, 149, 151
advertising, 6, 30–33, 119, 145, 148, 150
advice literature. *See* domestic economy: manuals; etiquette manuals
aestheticism, 8, 12, 13, 116, 121
    relation to consumerism, 111, 112, 113, 117, 119, 125
    relation to the feminine, 112, 123, 124, 130, 134
Agnew, Jean-Christophe, 48
Alice's Adventures in Wonderland (L. Carroll), 4
Altick, Richard D., 199n9, 199n10
"Always Make Room for a Lady" (postcard), 142, 143
Anderson, Benedict, 188n39
antidiscipline, 8
"Arab" Tea Room, 24–25
Armstrong, Nancy, 3, 17, 26, 29, 89, 200n13
Army and Navy, 172–73, 174
Arnold, Matthew, 113, 121
Arseneau, Mary, 184n4
Art of Decoration, The (Haweis), 66
Asquith, H. H., 151
Athenaeum, 116
Atkinson, Diane, 168
Austen, Jane, 3

Bacal, Howard A., 192n14
bankruptcy, 83, 88, 199n10
Barker, Lady, 69
Baudelaire, Charles, 173, 176, 215n2
Baudrillard, Jean, 180n9

Beardsley, Aubrey, 109, 110, 116, 135, 171
Beaty, Jerome, 198n1
becoming, 11, 12, 173
Bedroom and Boudoir, The (Barker), 69
Beer, Gillian, 107, 199n9, 199n11
Beerbohm, Max, 15, 16, 17, 19, 24
Beeton, Isabella, 84, 99, 202n38
Benjamin, Walter, 4, 66
Bennett, Tony, 26, 27, 186n13, 190n46
Benson, John, 182n13
Benson, Susan Porter, 187n21
Berenson, Bernhard, 135
Berenson, Mary (Costelloe), 135
Bermingham, Ann, 181n13
Bernstein, Susan David, 45, 196n64
Blacklock, Charlotte, 212n48
Blackwood, John, 80, 81, 198n4, 199n5
Blackwoods, 45, 80, 81, 83, 115, 198n4
Blaikie, Walter Biggar, 117
Bodley Head, 109, 110, 111, 112, 113, 114, 115, 116, 117, 119, 134, 135, 157, 172, 203n1
    belles lettres 111, 115, 116, 117, 119
body, female, 17, 26, 30, 89, 124, 132, 173–74
    and desire, 174
book-as-object, 111, 113, 114, 115, 119, 134
Botticelli, Sandro, 128, 130
boudoir, 47, 66, 67, 68, 69, 70, 71, 72, 73, 103
Bouvier, J. A., 156, 212n48
Bovary, Emma, 60
Bowlby, Rachel, 4, 22, 52, 181n12, 190n54, 216n2
Braddon, Mary Elizabeth, 44, 171
Bradley, Katharine, 111, 112, 113, 117, 122, 124, 130, 135
Breward, Christopher, 197n82
Brewer, John, 181n13
Bronner, Simon J., 187n21
Brontë, Charlotte, 22

231

Browning, Robert, 113
Bucknill, John, 56, 57
Burne-Jones, Edward, 16
Butler, Judith, 43, 182n20, 183n34

Camhi, Leslie, 58
Campbell, Elizabeth, 184–85n5
capitalism, 7, 8, 10, 11, 16, 18, 19, 28, 38, 40, 41, 42, 43, 46, 47, 58, 140, 189n45
Carpenter, Mary Wilson, 17, 29, 30
Carroll, David, 81
Cassell's Household Guide, 84
Chaudhuri, Nupur, 187n29
Chesham House, 23, 27
Christian Remembrancer, 44
circulating libraries, 44, 80, 81, 198n4
citizenship, 135, 141, 150, 157, 158, 168
clothing, 1, 15, 53, 63, 66, 82, 84, 86, 98, 99, 107. *See also* fashion
Cobbett, Anne, 84
Cole, Henry, 22
Colemore, Gertrude, 162, 214n69
commodity, 3, 7, 22, 27, 28, 30, 37, 38, 40, 42, 46, 47, 49, 50, 59, 61, 71, 79, 112, 122, 125, 134, 140, 165, 189n45
 book as, 81, 113, 116, 134, 135, 172 (*see also* book-as-object)
 as fetish, 19, 27, 33, 47, 189n45
 threat of, 8, 26, 75–76
 women as commodities, 2, 4, 5, 8, 12, 17, 107, 123, 124, 132, 134, 181n12
commodity aesthetics, 48, 112, 134
commodity culture, 98, 112, 179n5
Common Cause, 150
Complete Home, The (Wright), 46
connoisseurship, 12, 67, 109, 111, 116, 119, 123, 134, 135
Constable, T. A., 117
consumer, 3, 6, 8, 13
 male, 47, 48, 74–77
 See also shopper
consumer appetite, 2, 3, 4, 5, 8, 10, 11, 16, 26, 30, 59, 82
consumer choice, 8
consumer culture, 3, 4, 13, 17, 29, 42, 56, 57, 179n5
 and feminism, 139, 140, 141, 147, 148
consumerism, 2, 7, 17, 45, 59, 90. *See also* shopping
Consuming Subjects (Kowaleski-Wallace), 5

consumption, 2, 4, 6, 7, 8, 9, 10, 11, 14, 47, 56, 71, 77, 86, 122
 and production, 2, 7, 10, 111, 151, 152, 164, 172
 See also shopping
Cooper, Edith, 111, 112, 113, 117, 122, 124, 130, 135
Courtney, W. L., 137
credit, 87, 88, 89, 94, 97, 102, 104, 107
Crossick, Geoffrey, 187n21
Crystal Palace, 22
Cvetkovich, Ann, 46, 59, 198n83

Daily Mail, 138
Daily Telegraph, 34
Dale, Tim, 187n21
Dallas, Eneas Sweetland, 191n9
Daniel Deronda (Eliot), 108
 Gwendolen Harleth, 108
Davis, Dorothy, 182n13
Debenham and Freebody, 18
Debord, Guy, 140
debt, 83, 84, 88, 89, 90, 91, 94, 95, 97
de Certeau, Michel, 7, 11, 12, 40, 58, 111, 112, 141, 150, 152, 173
de Grazia, Victoria, 183n22
Deleuze, Gilles, 11, 173, 174, 216n6
department store, 3, 7, 10, 12, 15, 18, 19, 21, 22, 26, 28, 29, 42, 45, 46, 48, 49, 50, 53, 59, 68, 71, 87, 146, 147, 148
Derry and Toms, 146, 148, 149, 150
desire, consumer, 3, 7, 8, 10, 11, 12, 14, 16, 17, 18, 19, 27, 20, 22, 25, 26, 27, 28, 29, 30, 35, 39, 41, 42, 43, 52, 58, 60, 70, 71, 76, 173
desire, same-sex, 39–40, 75, 111, 123, 130
deterritorialization, 173, 176
D. H. Evans, 137
DiCenzo, Maria, 141
Discipline and Punish (Foucault), 7
display, 7, 19, 21, 22, 26, 27, 29, 47, 48, 49, 56, 69, 70, 72. *See also* shopwindows; spectacle
Doane, Mary Ann, 190n54
Dolin, Tim, 106
domestic economy, 82, 83, 84, 87, 89, 91, 94
 manuals, 52, 59, 84, 85, 86, 87, 93, 97, 105, 200–1n20, 201–2n38
 See also household management
domesticity, domestic sphere, 5, 8, 9, 10, 12, 19, 20, 21, 41, 46, 48, 59, 71, 77, 82, 84, 85, 86, 87, 89, 90, 91, 96, 97, 102, 107, 172, 175
domestic novel, 13, 107
domestic subject, 47, 69

Draper, 52
dress. *See* clothing

Early Closing Movement, 34
East India House, 15, 18, 19, 23, 25, 26, 31, 42
Eastlake, Charles, 68, 69, 75
Eates, Louise M., 159, 212n48
Ehnenn, Jill, 205–6n48, 206n52
ekphrasis, 111, 121, 122, 125, 131
Eliot, George, 80, 81, 82, 89, 97, 108, 115, 171, 199n5, 203n58
Elliot, Bridget, 203n3
Ellis, Sarah Stickney, 84, 86
Emma (Austen), 3
empire, 8, 17, 18, 19, 25, 26, 28, 30, 41, 42
English Housekeeper (Cobbett), 84
English Woman's Journal, 81
"Ethics of Shopping, The," 29, 49, 88
Etiquette for Ladies and Gentlemen, 99
Etiquette for the Ladies, 98
etiquette manuals, 52, 84, 97, 98
Eustance, Claire, 208n12
Everts, Orpheus, 194–95n40
everyday, the, 7, 11, 46, 58, 107, 141. *See also* practice
exhibitionary complex, 19, 26, 27, 30, 37, 41, 186n13
extravagance, 52, 68, 75, 83, 84, 85, 86, 87, 89, 90, 91, 95, 96, 97, 102, 107, 108. *See also* spending

Family Exchequer Book, 93
Farmer and Rogers Oriental Warehouse, 23
fashion, 2, 63
fashion periodicals, 13, 23–24, 52
Fawcett, Millicent, 207n6, 207n10
Felix Holt (Eliot), 81, 199n5
Felski, Rita, 209n22
Feltes, N. N., 198n1
femininity, 3, 4, 5, 6, 11, 12, 34, 46, 47, 56, 58, 61, 71, 72, 74, 84, 97, 134, 172, 173, 176
Ferry, John William, 187n21
Field, Michael, 109, 111, 112, 113, 114, 115, 119, 121, 122, 123, 128, 131, 132, 134, 171, 172
Finn, Margot, 87, 201n27
Fiske, John, 182n22
flaneur, 173
flaneuse, 215–16n2
Flaubert, Gustave, 89
Fortnightly Review, 29

Foucault, Michel, 7, 13, 26, 28, 186n13
Fox, Richard Wightman, 187n21
Frankel, Nicholas, 119, 123, 131
Franklin, J. Jeffrey, 202n53
Fraser, Hilary, 130
Fraser, W. Hamish, 182n13
Freedman, Jonathan, 112, 179n5, 206n49
Freud, Sigmund, 181n12
Friedberg, Anne, 190n54
Fulford, Roger, 208n10

Gagnier, Regenia, 10, 111
Gallienne, Richard, 115
gambling, 90, 96, 97
Gardner, Carl, 182n13, 183n22
Garvey, Ellen Gruber, 197n69
gaze
 male, 64, 65, 112, 121, 122, 123, 124, 125, 126, 127, 166, 173, 176
 shared female, 20, 111, 113, 119, 121, 123, 124
 shopper's, 12, 17, 25, 27, 28, 29, 35, 40, 41, 42, 64–65, 162, 190n54
gender, 5, 10, 48, 58, 71, 79, 145
 as performance, 58, 61, 74
 See also femininity; masculinity
Gilbert, Pamela K., 192n13
Gilbert, Sandra M., 184n4, 202n41
Giorgione, 129, 130
"Girl of the Period, The" (Linton), 9
Girl's Own Paper, 50
Goblin Market (C. Rossetti), 16, 17, 18, 19, 23, 29–43, 51, 111, 123, 133, 172, 175
 advertising, 30–32
 homoeroticism in, 40, 41
 as imperial marketplace, 29, 36–39, 41–43
 racialization of goblins, 31, 33, 38
 as shopping manual, 42
 significance of looking in, 29, 34–35, 40–42
 street-selling, 33–34, 40
Goddard, Henry, 194n36
Godwin, Edward, 26
Gozzoli, Benozza, 132
Grahame, Kenneth, 134, 135
Great Exhibition, 22, 180n12, 186n13
Great Masculine Renunciation, 76
Great Procession, 148, 149, 158
Green, Barbara, 140, 208n14
Griest, Guinivere L., 198n1
Grosz, Elizabeth, 11, 173, 174, 216n6

Index 233

Guattari, Félix, 11, 173, 174, 216n6
Gubar, Susan, 184n4, 202n41

Habermas, Jürgen, 165
Harris, Wendell, 213n54
Harrison, Antony H., 184n4
Harrods, 18, 21, 22, 29, 51, 87
Hartman, Kabi, 214n69
Haweis, Mrs., 66
Heimann, Amelia Barnard, 17
Helsinger, Elizabeth K., 185n5
Hints on Household Taste (Eastlake), 68
Holcombe, Lee, 200n12
Holt, Terrence, 185n5
Holton, Sandra Stanley, 208n10
homoeroticism, 30, 40, 41, 111, 113, 123, 124, 128, 130, 132
Honeycombe, Gordon, 187n21
household management, household manager, 52, 83, 85, 86, 87, 89, 90, 91, 93, 97, 172. *See also* domestic economy
household management guides. *See* domestic economy: manuals
How I Managed My House on Two Hundred Pounds a Year (Warren), 87
Hughes, Clair, 84, 99, 197n67, 202n50
Hughes, Winnifred, 191n9

identity, 6, 7, 8, 10, 11, 12, 16, 47, 48, 51, 53, 59, 61, 70, 71, 73, 74, 96, 107, 111, 157, 162, 163, 164, 172–77. *See also* subjectivity
ideology, 5
Image, Selwyn, 116
imperialism and the imperial marketplace, 3, 6, 16, 17, 18, 24, 26, 27, 28, 29, 35, 38, 39, 40, 43, 189n45
Ingram, Angela, 214n69
interior decorating, 46, 66, 68, 69, 76, 112, 113
Irigaray, Luce, 132

Jane Eyre (C. Brontë), 1, 2, 6, 13, 16, 99, 171
Jardine, Alice, 216n6
Jaumain, Serge, 187n21
Jay's, 137
Jeune, Lady M., 29, 49, 56, 88
Jewry, Mary, 85
Joannou, Maroula, 208n12
John, Angela V., 213n54
journalism, 13
Journal of Mental Science, 56

Kaplan, Joel H., 147, 150
Karl, Frederick R., 198n1
Keats, John, 119
Keepsake, 101
Kenney, Annie, 154, 209n22
Kipling, Rudyard, 18
kleptomania, 46, 47, 55, 56, 57, 60, 70, 78, 194n38, 194n40, 195n41, 195n42, 195–96n51. *See also* shopping: as compulsion; shopping: as disorderly behavior
Kooistra, Lorraine Janzen, 184n4
Kowaleski-Wallace, Elizabeth, 4, 194n36

Lacan, Jacques, 12, 184n36, 190n54
lack, 12, 58, 173, 196n51
"Ladies Don't Go Thieving," 53
Ladies Gazette of Fashion, 23–24
Ladies' Lavatory Company, 20
Lady Audley's Secret (Braddon), 44–48, 58–79, 172
  Lucy Audley: compulsive acquisition, 60, 67, 70, 72, 77–79, 82, 84; hyperfemininity, 61, 64–65; identity theft, 60, 61; portrait of, 64–65; rooms of, 60, 66, 69, 70, 71, 72, 78, 79; self-fashioning, 60, 62–63, 66
  Robert Audley: as consumer, 74–77; homoerotic attachment to George Talboys, 75, 77
  Phoebe Marks, 64, 69
Lady's World, 20
Laermans, Rudi, 61
Laird, Holly, 203n5
Lancaster, William, 187n21
Lane, John, 112, 115, 116, 117, 119, 134, 203n1
Langland, Elizabeth, 90, 200n13
Lears, T. J. Jackson, 187n21
Ledger, Sally, 111
Leighton, Angela, 203n5
leisure, 1, 6, 7, 11, 16, 75, 77, 112
Leisure Hour, 28
Leonardo da Vinci, 124
Lester, V. Markham, 199n10
Lewes, George Henry, 80, 81, 82, 108
Lewis, Reina, 179n2, 190n54
Liberty, Arthur Lasenby, 23, 137, 138
Liberty Lamp, 27
Liberty's, 15, 16, 18, 19, 22, 23, 24, 25, 26, 27, 28, 31, 32, 33, 34, 38, 41, 42, 116, 137
Liddington, Jill, 208n10
Lindner, Christoph, 4, 181n12

234 Index

Linton, Eliza Lynn, 9, 20, 49, 50, 63
Living Age, 29
Loeb, Lori Anne, 197n69
Logan, Thad, 69, 197n80
London, 6, 13, 15, 19, 20, 21, 29, 33, 45, 50, 113, 137, 163
London Labour and the London Poor (Mayhew), 33–34

Madame Bovary (Flaubert), 89
Mansel, Henry, 44, 45, 50, 68, 74, 79
Manual of Domestic Economy, A (Walsh), 85, 86, 87, 93, 94
Marcus, Jane, 209n22
Marcus, Laura, 216n2
marketplace, 6, 8, 12, 14, 16, 18, 19, 24, 29, 33, 43, 51, 111, 165
Marner, Silas, 102
marriage market, 90, 97
Marshall and Field, 21
Marshall and Snelgrove, 21, 137, 150
Martin, Carol A., 198n1
Marx, Karl, 4, 112, 125, 189n45
masculinity, 58, 71, 74–77, 79, 123. *See also* consumer, male
masquerade, 58, 71
Mathews, Elkin, 109, 112, 115, 116, 117, 119, 134, 203n1
Matus, Jill H., 60
Mayhall, Laura E. Nym, 208n10
Mayhew, Henry, 33–34, 40
McClintock, Anne, 33, 189n45
McCracken, Grant, 181n13
McKendrick, Neil, 181n13
Menke, Richard, 185n5, 185n6
Michie, Helena, 196n63
middle class, 3, 5, 6, 7, 9, 13, 17, 19, 20, 21, 34, 40, 46, 47, 48, 52, 53, 54, 55, 56, 57, 58, 61, 71, 79, 84, 85, 86, 87, 89, 93, 141, 144, 145, 165, 166, 175, 176, 183n29
Middlemarch (Eliot), 67, 80, 81, 82, 83, 84, 87, 89–108, 172
  Bulstrode, 83, 90, 96, 106
  Casaubon, 82, 101, 102, 103, 104, 105, 106
  Dorothea Brooke, 82, 84; deferral and risk, 97, 102, 104, 107, 108; as ethical spender, 105, 106, 107, 108; as manager, 106; reserve, 102, 104; sartorial restraint, 82, 94, 95, 98–102, 107, 108; self-expenditure, 107
  Farebrother, 90
  Fred Vincy, 83, 90 83, 90

  Lydgate, 82, 90, 91, 92, 93, 94, 95, 96, 101, 105
  Mrs. Garth, 91, 102
  publication of, 80–82, 108, 115
  Rosamond Vincy, 82, 84, 90, 94, 97, 99, 102, 106, 107; as economic agent, 95, 96, 107; as ineffective household manager, 90, 91, 92; as socially mobile, 96, 97, 107; clothing, 82, 90, 100, 101, 102; household spending, 82, 86
  Will Ladislaw, 90, 99, 100, 101, 102, 106
Miller, Andrew H., 4, 98, 180n12
Miller. D. A., 192n13
Miller, Jane Elridge, 214n69
Miller, Michael B., 187n21
Milligan, Barry, 188n41
Mitchell, S. Weir, 194–95n40
Mitchell, Timothy, 186n13
Moers, Ellen, 98
Montwieler, Katherine, 59, 191n9, 196n60
Morris, William, 16, 113
Mrs. Dalloway (Woolf), 172–77
  Clarissa Dalloway, 172, 175, 176, 215n1
  Elizabeth Dalloway, 171–77
Mudie's, 81, 198n4
Mui, Hoh-Cheung, 182n13
Mui, Lorna H., 182n13
Mulvey, Laura, 190n54
Murray, Simone, 141, 161

National Union of Women's Suffrage Societies (NUWSS), 137, 150, 207n6, 207n10, 210n24, 210n44
"Nature of Gothic, The" (Ruskin), 3
Nead, Lynda, 6, 51, 193n23
Nelson, Carolyn Christensen, 162
Nelson, James G., 115, 117
Nemesvari, Richard, 179n1, 198n83
Newman, Kenneth M., 192n14
New Woman, 109
nomad, 173
"Non Libri Sed Liberi" (Grahame), 134
Nord, Deborah Epstein, 216n2
Norris, Jill, 208n10
Nunokawa, Jeff, 102

O'Brien, Patricia, 195n41
"Observations on Credit," 88
Oliphant, Margaret, 45
Olivia's Shopping and How She Does It, 13, 24, 29, 176
oriental bazaar, 15, 18, 23, 26, 27, 28, 33, 34, 41, 42

orientalism, 3, 28, 37, 38, 42
Our Miss Gibbs (Ross and Greenbank), 51
"Out Walking" (Linton), 50

Pagan Papers (Grahame), 134
Pall Mall Gazette, 207n5
Pamphleteer, The, 88
Pank-A-Squith, 151
Pankhurst, Christabel, 138, 144, 209n19
Pankhurst, Emmeline, 137, 138, 139, 154, 209n19
Panko, 152, 153
Park, Sowon R., 213–14n69
parlor, 69
Parsons, Deborah L., 216n2
passante, 176, 215n2
Patai, Daphne, 214n69
Pater, Walter, 113, 121, 122, 124, 125, 126, 134, 206n53
Peter Robinson's, 146
Peterson, Shirley, 214n69
Pethick-Lawrence, Emmeline, 144, 150, 209n19
Pethick-Lawrence, Frederick W., 209n19
Phegley, Jennifer, 192n9
"Philosophy of Shopping, The" (Linton), 9–10
Picture of Dorian Gray, The (Wilde), 123
Pinch, Adela, 57, 194n36
pleasure, 8, 9, 10, 11, 13, 16, 17, 19, 21, 41, 42, 43, 46, 48, 49, 111, 112, 113, 121, 127, 132, 176, 177
Plumb, John H., 181n13
Poems (Wilde), 115, 119
Poovey, Mary, 5, 199n12
Porter, Roy, 181n13
practice, 6, 7, 10, 11, 12, 49, 52, 107, 112, 172, 174. *See also* everyday
Practice of Everyday Life, The (de Certeau), 7
Pre-Raphaelite, 13, 16, 47, 64, 65, 66
Prins, Yopie, 203n5
prostitution, 4, 36, 50
Psomiades, Kathy Alexis, 112, 124, 204n5
public sphere, 140, 141, 163, 165, 166, 169–70, 172
Publisher's Circle, 117
Punch, 142, 144
Purvis, June, 208n10, 209n22
Pykett, Lyn, 61, 191–92n9

Quarterly Review, 44
Queen, 52, 68

Rappaport, Erika, 6, 21, 87, 179n5
Rebel Women (Sharp), 162, 163, 214n73
Renaissance, The (Pater), 121, 122, 124

Richards, Thomas, 4, 22, 180n12
Ricketts, Charles, 113, 114, 115
Rivers, Bronwyn, 200n13
Rivière, Joan, 58
Robin Goodfellow, 45
Rolley, Katrina, 145
Rosen, Andrew, 208n10
Rossetti, Christina, 15, 16, 17, 18, 19, 29, 43, 51, 171
Rossetti, Dante Gabriel, 15, 16, 24, 121
Rothenstein, William, 113
Ruskin, John, 2
Ryan, Joan, 208n12

Said, Edward, 26, 186n13, 190n54
Sala, George, 23
Sanders, Lise Shapiro, 193n18
Saturday Review, 9
Saville, Julia F., 122, 206n52
Schaffer, Talia, 203–4n5
Scholz, Susanne, 193n16
self-regulation, 2, 4, 6, 8, 89
self-renunciation, 2, 11, 12, 16, 17, 98, 184n4
Selfridge's, 21, 22, 146, 147, 148, 150
sensation fiction, 13, 44, 45, 59, 79
  effects on readers, 44, 45, 46, 48, 50
  relationship to commercial sphere, 44–45, 74, 79
"Sensation Novels" (Mansel), 44
serial publication, 45, 68, 80
sexuality, 56, 123, 127
Shannon, Brent, 197n82, 198n85
Shannon, Charles, 113, 114
Sharp, Evelyn, 157–60, 162–65, 212–13n54
Sharpe, Becky, 88
Shaw, Gareth, 182n13
shawls, 23
Sheppard, Julie, 182n13, 183n22
Shields, Frederic James, 16
shop (origins as a verb), 5
shop assistant, 49
shopkeeping, 5, 87. *See also* Women's Social and Political Union
shoplifter, shoplifting, 8, 53, 44, 55, 57, 58, 70, 78, 194n36, 194n40, 195n42, 196n51
shopper, 1, 2, 3, 5, 6, 7, 10, 11, 12, 13
  agency of, 7, 8, 12, 28
  cultural anxieties over, 2, 3, 4, 5, 36, 46, 54
  as disorderly, 48, 51, 52, 53, 59, 60, 74, 77, 79, 109, 111, 135
  "prowler," 53 (*see also* shoplifter)

236   Index

as target for harassment, 50, 51
  See also consumer
shopping, 1, 2, 3, 4, 5, 6, 7, 8, 9, 10, 12
  browsing, 22, 29, 45, 46, 49, 109, 164, 171
  as compulsion, 2, 4, 8, 10, 27, 46, 50, 57, 58
  dangers of, 2, 3, 16
  as disorderly behavior, 25–26, 46, 46, 47, 51, 52, 56, 57, 58, 71, 111
  as idleness, 2, 50, 52
  as leisure, 20–21
  pathologies related to, 46, 47, 55, 56, 57
  as seduction or temptation, 1, 2, 5, 8, 13, 16, 49, 50, 51, 52, 56, 89
  as urban strolling, 172–77
  window-shopping, 50, 51. *See also* consumption
shopping guide, 13, 24, 42, 176
"Shopping without Money," 28–29
shops (n), 3, 5, 6, 13, 14, 20, 21, 29, 68
shopwindows, 6, 10, 20, 135, 136, 137, 154, 155, 160, 161, 169, 171
"Shrieking Sister, The," 142, 143
Shuttleworth, Sally, 192n13
Sight and Song (Field), 109, 111, 112, 113, 114, 121–35, 206n53
  autoeroticism, 129, 130, 131
  "Birth of Venus, The," 128–29
  commercial publication of, 115, 117, 118
  design, 114, 115, 117, 118, 119, 120
  economy of pleasure, 121, 123, 127, 128, 130, 131, 132, 133, 134
  female gaze, 123, 134
  homoeroticism, 128, 132
  "La Gioconda," 123–26, 134
  "L'Embarquement pour Cythère," 133–34
  "Pen-Drawing of Lena, A," 131–33
  "Portrait, A," 126–27
  "Sleeping Venus, The," 123, 129–31, 134
  "Treading the Press," 132
Silhouettes (Symons), 117
Sixpenny Magazine, 45
Smiles, Samuel, 84, 85, 88, 89, 90, 108
Smith, Angela K., 209n19
Smith, Logan Pearsall, 114, 135, 206n53
Sonnets for Pictures (D. G. Rossetti), 121
"Soul of a Suffragette, The" (Courtney), 137
spectacle, 6, 10, 19, 22, 24, 27, 28, 35, 41, 42, 49, 69, 140, 169. *See also* display
Spectator, 116
spending, 12, 14, 47, 82, 84, 85, 86, 87, 88, 89, 92, 93, 94, 97, 106, 107

as ethical, 83, 105, 107, 108
as futurity, 82, 97, 102, 105, 107, 108
See also extravagance
Standard, 138
Stern, Rebecca F., 185n5
Stetson, Dorothy M., 199–200n12
Stetz, Margaret D., 116, 119, 134
Stowell, Sheila, 147, 150
Strange, Martina, 193n16
street-sellers, 33–34, 40
Sturgeon, Mary, 114
subjectivity, 5, 8, 10, 11, 12, 30, 47, 48, 51, 59, 66, 67, 74, 75, 107, 111, 172–77. *See also* identity
suffrage, women's, 8, 139
suffragettes, 13, 135, 175
  as fashionable, 142, 144, 145
  as shoppers, 138, 139, 141, 145 (see also *Votes for Women*)
  stereotypes of, 142, 144, 152
suffragists, nonmilitant, 137
street pageantry and processions, 140, 144, 147, 167, 168
Summer Night, A (Tomson), 117
Swan, Annie S., 162, 214n69
Swan and Edgar, 17, 18, 21, 137
Symons, Arthur, 112, 117

tactics, 7, 8, 11, 58, 136, 141, 151–52, 157, 169
Tennyson, Alfred, 108
Thackeray, William Makepeace, 88
Thousand Plateaus, A (Deleuze and Guattari), 173
three-decker, 81
thrift, 83, 84, 85, 88, 89, 97, 98, 102, 108
Thrift (Smiles), 85, 88, 90
Tickner, Lisa, 140, 208n14
Times, 83, 207n5
Tomson, Graham R., 117
Tucker, Herbert F., 30

Ugolini, Laura, 208n12
Unto This Last (Ruskin), 2

Vadillo, Ana Parejo, 114, 122
Valverde, Marianna, 193n25
Veneto, Bartolommeo, 126
Volumes in Folio (Le Gallienne), 115
Vote, 150
Votes for Women, 136, 138, 140–70, 172, 209n19
  advertising, 142, 145, 147, 148, 150, 151
  colors and costume code, 144, 145, 150, 151

Index   237

Votes for Women (cont.)
    fashion columns, 142, 145, 147, 150
    "Painting Kensington Purple, White, and Green," 159–60, 162
    photographs in, 165–68
    "Popularising the Colours," 150
    shopping directories, 142, 145, 147, 148, 150
    "Suffragette and the Dress Problem, The," 144
    "Under the Clock," 157–58, 166
    "Whet Your Weapon!" 148
    WSPU games, 151–53, 169
    WSPU merchandise, 142, 150–54, 158, 168, 169
    WSPU shops and shopkeeping, 141, 142, 150, 154–70, 211n44, 211–12n48, 213n59
    "Xmas Gifts at the W.S.P.U. Shops," 154
    "Votes for Women—Forward!" 162–68

Walkowitz, Judith, 50, 52
Walsh, J. H., 85, 87, 93
Warehouseman and Draper's Trade Journal, 29
Warne's Model Cookery and Housekeeping Book (Jewry), 85
Warren, Eliza, 87
Weiss, Barbara, 199n10
West End, 6, 15, 16, 19, 20, 23, 26, 28, 29, 42, 45, 51, 70, 111, 135, 137, 139, 171, 172, 173, 176
White, Chris, 127, 203n5
Whiteley's, 18, 21, 87
Whitlock, Tammy C., 194n36
W. H. Smith, 81, 198n4

Wilde, Oscar, 112, 115, 119, 123
William Owen, 146, 148
"Window Breaking: To One Who Has Suffered," 139
Wolff, Janet, 216n2
woman, 4, 5, 12, 65, 107, 124, 134
"Woman in a Shoe Shop, A" (Fisk), 29
"Womanliness as Masquerade" (Rivière), 58
Women of England, The (Ellis), 84, 86
Women's Freedom League, 150, 207n10, 210n24, 210–11n44
Women's Property Acts, 84, 199–200n12
Women's Social and Political Union (WSPU), 136–70, 207n10, 211n46, 211n47
    colors, 144, 150
    founding, 138, 142
    militant tactics, 137, 138, 139, 140, 148, 158, 162, 169, 170
    shops and shopkeeping (see *Votes for Women*)
    shopwindow vandalism, 137, 138, 139, 140, 152, 171
Wood, Jane, 192n13
Woolf, Virginia, 172, 177, 214n69, 216n6
Works and Days (Field), 113, 130
World War I, 13, 168, 172
Wright, Julia McNair, 46
Wynn, Deborah, 192n9

Yeats, William Butler, 114
Yellow Book, The, 109, 110, 203n1, 212n54

Zonana, Joyce, 179n2

www.ingramcontent.com/pod-product-compliance
Lightning Source LLC
Chambersburg PA
CBHW031241290426
44109CB00012B/389